"This is a monumental work for our times. It reminds us of the radical spirituality of Wesleyan ontological formation—ecclesiological, eschatological: 'grace-drenched, cross-shaped, and incarnational'; and, at a time of geopolitical agonism, reminds us of the 'expansive, liberating love of Christ,' pointing the way to re-enter the rhythm of grace."

—C. J. C. Pickstock, Norris-Hulse Professor of Divinity, Cambridge University

"Henry and Hank Spaulding, father and son theologians, present a compelling, wise challenge to the idolatry of fundamentalism rooted in fear and resistance to change. They intricately weave a profound connection between the beauty of holiness and 'apocalyptic forgiveness,' disrupting false moral codes and perpetual patterns of violence within church and empire. Writing from retirement and exile, their insights invite us into a transformative rhythm of grace, revealing a communal witness to God's Peaceable Kingdom. Nothing embodies the beauty of holiness more than a community practicing inclusive forgiveness without exception."

—K. Steve McCormick, Faculty Emeritus, Nazarene Theological Seminary

"*The Rhythm of Grace* is for anyone interested in plumbing the depths and breadth of philosophical thought to debate Wesleyan-Holiness theological tenets. The Spauldings write with sincere concern and love for the church and careful scholarship in equal measure."

—Tammie Grimm, Associate Professor of Christian Discipleship and Practical Theology, Wesley Seminary

"This superb collection of essays from the Spauldings, father and son—and each a gifted theologian in their own right—provides both rich introduction and critical insight into the serious and important debates in Wesleyan theology over the last four decades. This rich compilation, centered in the loci of ecclesiology, ethics, and political and public theology, makes an important contribution to the Wesleyan understanding of Christian perfection, fundamentalism, human sexuality, atonement, and, most importantly, the doctrine of Grace. Their treatment of the subjects chosen teems with quotes both ancient and modern, extending from Augustine and Aquinas to Paul Bassett and Billy Abraham. The footnotes and extensive bibliography are a rich mine of the necessary sources for providing a robust Wesleyan theology today. This is a 'must read' for any serious Wesleyan-Holiness thinker."

—Steven Hoskins, Professor of Church History, Trevecca Nazarene University

"A profound and timely look into Wesleyan understandings of grace and holiness that reminds us that God's heavenly vision—though 'already/not yet'—is strange and radical. What a gift to observe the wisdom of father and son expanding the vision of Wesleyan theology, ecclesiology, education, and ethics."

—Nell M. Becker Sweeden, CEO, Nazarene Compassionate Ministries

"This collection of scholarly essays is shaped by a pastoral concern and question: Can Wesleyanism 'go on' without a serious re-examination of what it means to be holy? An invitation and challenge await those willing to enter the conversation proposed by the authors. I can only hope those following in Wesley's footsteps will find the courage to read this book and consider what is at stake in leaving the question unanswered."

—Carole Taylor, Director of College Counseling, St. Cecilia Academy, Tennessee

"In this wide-ranging and insightful set of essays, father and son theologians point a way forward for Wesleyan theology, especially as understood in the tradition of the Church of the Nazarene. They rightly point to problems in the tradition's landscape today, most of which stem from a fundamentalist leavening. As an alternative, the two offer a Christ-centered, love-oriented, and ecclesial-grounded commitment to sanctified life today. I agree with the authors that reclaiming Wesleyan theology for the twenty-first century requires a turn away from theological legalism and toward a renewed imagination of grace. May the goals of this book be realized!"

—Thomas Jay Oord, author of *A Systematic Theology of Love*

"Could old-fashioned 'holiness' possibly have any relevance for today? In this creative, learned, and engaging work, the Spauldings unfold a fruitful model of how to do Wesleyan theology, one rooted in our tradition while engaging crucial issues in our world. They make bold to embrace insights from many different contemporary theologians—something not always found in older holiness theologies. Their proposal takes 'the beauty of holiness' seriously as a way of life for the church in greater communion with the Holy Trinity: a community which opposes injustice and oppression by the grace of God and in the power of the Living Christ. The result is a fresh, lively theology of holiness for the church today."

—Alan G. Padgett, Northwestern Lutheran Theological Seminary Chair of Theology, Luther Seminary, St. Paul

"John Wesley's heirs have too often forgotten that he was a serious intellectual, albeit one on horseback. Not so Henry Spaulding, in this lively serious of essays. They show us why the Wesleyan Holiness tradition belongs to the Christian and Catholic mainstream, by bringing together the spiritual quest for deification of the East with the ethical quest for personal and social improvement of the West. Its message is uniquely relevant for today when we are realizing how the mere pursuit of compromise engenders global chaos and conflict. We need instead to listen once more to Wesley's view that aiming for perfection is curiously the most realistic, pragmatic, and 'methodical' option."

—John Milbank, Professor Emeritus, Department of Philosophy, University of Nottingham

The Rhythm of Grace

The Rhythm of Grace

A Broad Vision for Wesleyan-Holiness Theology

Henry Walter Spaulding III
Henry Walter Spaulding II

CASCADE *Books* · Eugene, Oregon

THE RHYTHM OF GRACE
A Broad Vision for Wesleyan-Holiness Theology

Cascade Books
An Imprint of Wipf and Stock Publishers
199 W. 8th Ave., Suite 3
Eugene, OR 97401

www.wipfandstock.com

PAPERBACK ISBN: 979-8-3852-4201-6
HARDCOVER ISBN: 979-8-3852-4202-3
EBOOK ISBN: 979-8-3852-4203-0

Cataloguing-in-Publication data:

Names: Spaulding, Henry Walter, III, author. | Spaulding, Henry Walter, author.

Title: The rhythm of grace : a broad vision for Wesleyan-holiness theology / Henry Walter Spaulding III and Henry Walter Spaulding II.

Description: Eugene, OR : Cascade Books, 2026 | Includes bibliographical references and index.

Identifiers: ISBN 979-8-3852-4201-6 (paperback) | ISBN 979-8-3852-4202-3 (hardcover) | ISBN 979-8-3852-4203-0 (ebook)

Subjects: LCSH: Church of the Nazarene—Doctrines. | Theology, Doctrinal. | Sanctification.

Classification: BT75.2 .S63 2026 (print) | BT75.2 (ebook)

This book is dedicated to our family:
Sharon, Shelly, Matt, Megan, Kyle, Michaela, Hunter, Bella, Aiden, Jax
We love you and hope you find churches with a broad vision

Contents

Article Sources

Chapter 1 originally published: Spaulding, Hank. "'Be Ye Holy as I Am Holy': The Implications of Wesleyan Theological Aesthetics for Entire Sanctification Language." *Didache: Faithful Teaching* 10 (2011) 1–15.

Chapter 4 originally published: Spaulding, Henry W., II. "The Path of Peaceful Flight: Milbank's Trinitarian Ontology and a Re-Narration of Wesleyan-Holiness Theology." *Wesleyan Theological Journal* 38 (2003) 134–59.

Chapter 5 originally published: Spaulding, Henry W., II. "'To Shew the Fly the Way out of the Fly-Bottle': A Reconstruction of the Wesleyan Understanding of Christian Perfection." *Wesleyan Theological Journal* 34 (1999) 145–71.

Chapter 7 originally published: Spaulding, Henry W., II. "Good Conscience or Good Confidence: A Postmodern Re-Thinking of Ethical Reflection in the Wesleyan-Holiness Tradition." *Wesleyan Theological Journal* 35 (2000) 41–66.

Chapter 8 originally published: Spaulding, Henry W., II. "Practicing Holiness: A Consideration of Action in the Thought of John Wesley." *Wesleyan Theological Journal* 38 (2003) 110–37.

Chapter 9 originally published: Spaulding, Hank. "Sanctifying Atonement: Womanist Theology, Wesleyan Ethics, and the Future of Nazarene Atonement Theology." *Wesleyan Theological Journal* 49 (2014) 162–86.

Chapter 10 originally published: Spaulding, Hank. "Loophole of Retreat: Charles Wesley's Political Worship." *Wesleyan Theological Journal* 58 (2023) 72–104.

Chapter 11 originally published: Spaulding, Hank. "Empire, Evil, Eschaton, and Location of Forgiveness as a Political/Apocalyptic Act." *Wesleyan Theological Journal* 48 (2013) 90–106.

Acknowledgments

MY EARLIEST ACADEMIC DESIRES were not shaped in the lecture halls of graduate school, but in the quiet observation of a man who modeled theology as a way of life. Before I ever wrote a paper or delivered a presentation, I wanted to do theology with and like my father. This book is, in every sense, a thank you. To my father, Dr. Henry Spaulding II—my co-author, mentor, and theological companion—this project is an expression of deep gratitude. Your way of doing theology has always been marked by generosity: you taught me to consider all perspectives, to listen before responding, and to remain open without ever abandoning the classic form of the faith. In your classroom and in our home, theology was not merely a system of thought but a practice of grace, creativity, and hospitality.

I have long dreamed of giving the world greater access to your thought. Your students have longed for it, and so has your family. We have watched the impact of your teaching over the years and yearned for a broader audience to encounter what we have known all along—that your theology carries both intellectual depth and spiritual wisdom, always tethered to the real lives of people. My hope is that this book becomes a platform for your voice, bringing your theological vision to a wider world. It has been my joy and honor to write alongside you. The chapters that bear my name are deeply shaped by your presence and example. What I offer here is my Wesleyan theology, placed beside yours not as a counterpoint, but as a continuation of the witness you began.

To our family—thank you. Your patience, encouragement, and love have sustained this work. This project was born not only from academic interest but from the rhythms of our life together. Thank you for letting us disappear into stacks of books and drafts of chapters, and for believing that this work matters.

Finally, I want to extend heartfelt thanks to the team at Wipf and Stock/Cascade, especially Rodney Clapp, Charlie Collier, and Michael Thomson. Your belief in this project—and in me—has meant the world. Your support has been more than professional; it has felt personal. You saw value in this book from the start, and your encouragement helped bring it to life. This book is more than a publication. It is a son's thank you, a family's celebration, and a shared theological offering to the church we still love.

—Henry (Hank) Spaulding III

It has been the joy of my life to watch and participate in the theological development of my son, Hank Spaulding. I remember Sunday night as we gathered for a post-evening service meal at our home in Hendersonville, Tennessee, he announced to the family that he intended to enter the family business. By this, he meant the ministry, but I felt like he meant University teaching. While I had pastored, my primary identity was that of a college teacher. I recall the first time we read a book together, when he was in high school. We did not make it far before he lost interest, but he formed a relationship with the author of the book while doing his doctorate. The author was D. Stephen Long. I have had the privilege of teaching many students over the years. Some of these individuals have gone on to serve the church and university as distinguished pastors and faculty members. The work I have cherished most is being a parent to my son. I never dared think that we would write a book together one day. He has taught me a great deal. I admire his character and scholarship. I thank God for the opportunity to think with my son about these matters that mean so much to us.

—Henry W. Spaulding II

Introduction

A Wesleyan Theology at the Crossroads

Henry Walter Spaulding II and Henry Walter Spaulding III

INTRODUCTION

Wesleyan theology stands at a critical juncture. Once marked by a vibrant commitment to grace, sanctification, and social holiness, Wesleyan traditions—especially within the Church of the Nazarene—face a growing crisis. At the heart of this crisis is the leavening influence of fundamentalism and a theological narrowing that threatens the broad, generous, grace-infused vision of John Wesley. The symptoms are manifold: confessional rigidity, moral legalism, an elevation of propositional inerrancy over spiritual encounter, and the displacement of the Living Christ by the Bible as a quasi-divine authority. The renewal of Wesleyan theology today must begin with a recovery of its theological soul—one shaped by a Christ-centered, grace-oriented, and ecclesially grounded commitment to sanctified life in the world.

This book emerges as both a critique and a constructive vision. It critiques the historical and theological drift that has seen Wesleyan-Holiness traditions, particularly the Church of the Nazarene, capitulate to the polemical frames of early twentieth-century fundamentalism. As Paul Merritt Bassett has documented, the Nazarene movement's theological formation was slowly but decisively marked by fundamentalist assumptions about Scripture and authority, despite early efforts by theologians like H. Orton Wiley to chart a distinctively Wesleyan path—a path that refused the false binary between liberalism and fundamentalism and instead pointed toward a theology rooted in the inward witness of the Holy Spirit and the living.[1]

More recently, the late William J. Abraham has pronounced the death of Wesleyan theology in its historic form, noting how the proliferation of competing interpretations of Wesley—and the ideological appropriation of his legacy—has resulted in theological incoherence. For Abraham, the very attempt to recover Wesley became a way of avoiding the deeper ecclesial and epistemological crises confronting Protestant theology writ large.[2]

While Abraham's conclusion is sobering, it is also clarifying: if Wesleyan theology is to have a future, it must be reborn not as a nostalgic retrieval of the past but as a theological renewal that engages the world with the breadth of Wesley's original vision in conversation with other theological voices and traditions.

This book argues that such a renewal is possible, but only if we take seriously the fractures within Wesleyanism today. The rise of fundamentalist theology within the Church of the Nazarene, for example, has led to a form of holiness preaching more concerned with rule enforcement than with cultivating holy curiosity and love. The Wesleyan vision of sanctification as participation in divine grace—marked by joy, beauty, justice, and freedom—has too often been reduced to conformity, suspicion, and moralism. We contend that reclaiming Wesleyan theology for the twenty-first century requires a turn away from theological legalism and toward a renewed imagination of grace.

The essays and reflections in this book offer such a vision. Drawing on post-colonial theory, theological aesthetics, virtue ethics, and Wesleyan tradition, we propose that the future of Wesleyan theology lies not in retrenchment but in expansive renewal. Each chapter is a theological act of resistance against narrow visions and a call to recenter Wesleyan thought on the living Christ, on grace rather than law, and on the communal, embodied practices of holiness that respond to real suffering in the world.

Wesleyan theology, we believe, is not dead. But if it is to live—truly live—it must be reborn again and again as a theology of grace that rises from the ruins of fundamentalism and moralism. It must shed the brittle shell of legalism and reclaim its center in the radical, unmerited love of

1. Bassett, *Fundamentalist Leavening*, 65–85.

2. Abraham, *End of Wesleyan Theology*, 101–18.

God that empowers transformation without coercion and invites holiness without fear. This rebirth will not be a return to sentimentality or a softening of doctrine, but a deepening—an opening to the Spirit's movement in contexts old and new, local and global. In a world marked by exclusion, anxiety, and theological gatekeeping, a renewed Wesleyanism must become a living witness to a grace that sanctifies without domination, restores without shame, and invites the whole human family into the expansive, liberating love of Christ. This is not merely theological recovery; it is a resurrection.

PART I

Beginnings—Reclaiming the Church Through a Sanctified Imagination

THE FOLLOWING FOUR CHAPTERS expand the theological imagination of the church through the distinct but interwoven lens of Wesleyan theology. Together, they form a rich tapestry of ecclesiological reflection that is both playful and profound, retrieving John Wesley not as a figure of static tradition but as a live theological interlocutor capable of guiding the church's imagination in a time of crisis.

Chapters 1 through 4 establish the theological foundation for holiness by rooting it not in moral striving but in the invitation to participate in the life and beauty of God. Drawing from Scripture and liturgical tradition, chapter 1 frames holiness as a gift received through worship, where God reshapes our affections through word, sacrament, and doxology. Chapter 2 builds on this by showing how the Church of the Nazarene's revivalist and countercultural DNA offers resources for resisting the consumerist captivity of contemporary ecclesial life. Chapter 3 furthers this critique by calling for a sanctified imagination grounded in eschatological hope, rather than market logic, urging the church to resist neoliberal patterns and embody the future reign of God. Chapter 4 creatively reinterprets Wesley through an apocalyptic lens, drawing on Barth, Bulgakov, and Pauline theology to present Christian perfection as a vision of divine disruption and glory. Together, these chapters contend that ecclesiology is not about structure alone but about the Spirit's imaginative and visible work of sanctification in and through the church.

CHAPTER 1

"Be Ye Holy as I Am Holy"

The Implications of Theological Aesthetics for Wesleyan-Holiness Theology and Entire Sanctification

Henry Walter Spaulding III

INTRODUCTION

What does it mean to be holy? It is hard to digest the weight of glory that such a call represents. If the individual seeking holiness tries to abide in their own strength, they surely will not meet the demands of holiness. The call is not impossible. The language of Entire Sanctification is in quite a precarious position. The current state of the Wesleyan-Holiness movement allows a wonderful opportunity to adopt a new language that allows for room and vitality. The last few decades have produced a plethora of Holiness material to deepen one's understanding of holiness in ways never thought before. However, a common misconception is present in the language of Entire Sanctification, namely that Entire Sanctification is reducible to a moral imperative. There has arisen some good scholarship that suggests it is not a question of morality.[1] When reduced to a moral imperative, the language of Entire Sanctification runs the risk of being lost or impossible. The understanding of Entire Sanctification can be expressed as the Old Testament commandment in Lev 11:44 when the

1. See Part II of this work for more on this theme, specifically the work of Henry Walter Spaulding II who pioneers the appropriate connection between holiness and ethics.

Lord says to Moses, " . . . be holy, for I am holy" (Lev 11:44 NRSV). This view, coupled with the Deuteronomic imperative, "Choose life so that you and your descendants may live" (Deut 30:19b NRSV), would suggest that it is a question of the will/morality. However, I believe that to be a misreading of this passage. Correctly read, these passages, coupled with our task in the Wesleyan-Holiness tradition, reveal that the call to be holy needs context in order to be intelligible. The question before us, then, is, what context?

The problem can be visualized philosophically. Wesleyan–Holiness tradition can begin with the question, "what is the Good?" Once that answer is settled, the goal of holiness becomes merely achieving the defined good. The situation this question finds its origin in is the Greek philosophical system. It is in this system that we find the Good, but we do not find the good alone. I believe that one must shift from the question of the Good to the Beautiful in order to appreciate the full measure of God's call to holiness. The Good and the Beautiful cannot be found independently. The whole of the history of philosophy knows this to be true. The Good is the ultimate reality for which Plato and Aristotle long, but the Beautiful is where the Good finds concrete expression. Goodness is expressed as the beautiful. Yet, it is the beautiful that ultimately attracts our actions. The Beautiful presents a transcendent logic, which is its appeal. Ethics, then (meaning understanding how to do the good) lies in an understanding of proper aesthetics (i.e., beautiful living). Beauty allows life to transcend duty as a primary category. Beauty provides the context for which the ethical person knows that they live rightly. The question here is not merely to discard the moral category in appropriating Entire Sanctification as an aesthetic act. Rather, it is my task to represent Entire Sanctification as an act, which transcends mere act, and allows the subject to envision themselves as a part of the divine life of the Trinity. Again, we do not discard the ethical dimension but rather opt to give fuller expression to the ethical dimension by locating Entire Sanctification as an aesthetic practice.

Likewise, with Christianity, the beauty of God provides context. Also, with Christianity, the Wesleyan-Holiness tradition benefits from an aesthetic to provide a context in which we can see the life of Entire Sanctification. The context of beauty is not the philosophical concept of beauty, but the beauty of God. Theologian Karl Barth presents this best when he writes, "it is as He is God that He is also beautiful, so that He is the basis and standard of everything that is beautiful and of all ideas of the beautiful."[2] Thus it is that God provides God's own context for the command to holiness.

Thus, I argue that to begin to discuss Entire Sanctification for our Wesleyan-Holiness tradition is to develop a Wesleyan Theological Aesthetic. When this happens, we might properly interpret the command to holiness as a call to beauty. A Wesleyan Theological Aesthetic lays bare the limits of morality alone for expressing holiness and Christian Perfection. Therefore, holiness when understood in this way refuses to reduce Entire Sanctification to an act of the will. This is a notion that is developed in our Wesleyan tradition because it was John Wesley who understood holiness and sanctification in light of the fullness of grace when he writes, "If any doubt of this privilege (Christian Holiness) of the sons of God, the question is not to be decided by abstract reasonings, which may be drawn out into an endless length, and leave the point just as it was before . . . By his Word will we abide, and that alone. Hereby we ought to be judged."[3] Entire Sanctification is the opening up of the fullness of the possibility of action in light of the revelation of Christ. Swiss theologian Hans Urs von Balthasar writes,

> This seeing, which by God's grace brings no blinding of the human spirit through an immoderate light, but gives the capacity to stand firm in the presence of the infinite simplicity, has as its first effect on man a sinking down in adoration before the glory; but at the same time, it is the strongest impulse for the subsequent thinking that converts what is seen into action, for the unity of the form offers a fullness of approaches, doors and possibilities for entry.[4]

The two quotes seem to suggest that we abide in the simplicity of the word of God and the breaking in of God's revelation, which is understood aesthetically, to live holy lives. The statement from Balthasar, "converts what is seen into action," represents the central aspect of an aesthetic reading of Entire Sanctification.[5] For the revelation of beauty in the Glory of the Lord, the action is not merely an act of the will. Instead, as Balthasar suggests, the will is transformed in the encounter with the beautiful, opening to the fullness of Entire Sanctification. It is a truth that Wesley saw at the

2. Barth, *Church Dogmatics*, 2:318.
3. Wesley, "Plain Account of Christian Perfection," 74.
4. von Balthasar, *Glory of the Lord*, 7:15.
5. von Balthasar, *Glory of the Lord*, 7:15.

heart of the Scripture, namely, an aesthetic that develops a theology of holiness.

My project will begin by demonstrating the significance of aesthetics in the history of philosophy, with a particular focus on the thought of Plotinus, Augustine, Hegel, and Kant, and how aesthetic reflection shapes one's understanding of the good life. Building on this foundation, I will then explore how a theological aesthetic differs from a philosophical one precisely in the way it binds the Good and Beautiful together. Finally, I will propose a Wesleyan theological aesthetic that articulates the holy life and offers a renewed framework for understanding the doctrine of "Entire Sanctification" within the Wesleyan-Holiness tradition.

HISTORY OF THE ROLE OF AESTHETICS

Before turning to the distinct features of a theological aesthetic, it is essential to consider the broader philosophical tradition from which such a conversation emerges. Aesthetics, far from being a peripheral concern, has played a central role in shaping conceptions of truth, beauty, and the good life throughout the history of philosophy. By examining key figures such as Plotinus, Augustine, Kant, and Hegel, we can trace how aesthetic experience has been understood not merely as a matter of taste or perception but as a vital mode of human flourishing and moral formation.

Plotinus

I start with Plotinus because of his particular emphasis on the beautiful. Plotinus makes a separate distinction, which was not uncommon for his era, between what we perceive as the beautiful in material reality (pretty) and what is formal (truly beautiful). Ludwig Wittgenstein can best summarize this: "What is pretty cannot be beautiful."[6] The distinction between material and formal shows a vestige of Platonic dialectic in which there exists a perfect form and an imperfect representation. This is the distinction that I draw from Plotinus.

There is no need here to provide an exhaustive account of Plotinus. Instead, I desire to demonstrate how a particular thread of logic in the beautiful fulfills and enhances human life. Plotinus offers a profound and metaphysical account of beauty in his *Enneads*, particularly in Treatises

6. Wittgenstein, *Culture and Value*, 43e.

"On Beauty" and "On the Intellectual Beauty." For Plotinus, beauty is not merely a matter of sensory delight or aesthetic appreciation; it is a metaphysical reality that reveals the soul's origin and destination. He distinguishes between physical and intelligible beauty, arguing that material objects are beautiful not in themselves but because they participate in higher forms. A statue, for instance, is beautiful insofar as it reflects an ideal form that transcends it: "The beauty, therefore, exists in a far higher state in the art; for it does not come over integrally into the work; that original beauty is not transferred; what comes over is a derivative and a minor."[7] This participation is not passive: the soul recognizes beauty because it originates from the same realm of forms, and in doing so, it begins a journey of return. Plotinus describes this as an ascent: from the appreciation of sensible beauty to the contemplation of moral virtues, then to the soul itself, and finally to the One, the source of all beauty and unity.

Beauty, in this sense, serves as a guide or catalyst, leading the soul from multiplicity to unity. Since the One is the purest form of unity, it is also the highest form of beauty. To encounter beauty is to discover the trace of the divine, and thus the experience of beauty has ethical consequences. It purifies, orders, and elevates the soul, turning it away from the distractions of the material world and orienting it toward the Good. In Plotinus's vision, then, beauty is not a decorative aspect of reality but the very structure of the soul's return to its source—a transformative participation in the divine unity that grounds all being. Plotinus achieves, in his work, my first claim about the beautiful, namely union with and importance to the good. For Plotinus, the good is found in the ultimate foundational reality he calls the One. The One emanates out of his own fullness into material reality, thus giving it depth. Plotinus maintains that beauty constitutes this reality that pours into the material. Furthermore, as commentator Emile Brehier writes, "The aesthetics of Plotinus is impregnated with the idea that beauty is not added to things as an external accident but constitutes their very essence."[8] For Plotinus, beauty is not merely aesthetic—it is a radiant manifestation of the Good itself. Beauty reveals, or illumines, the presence of what is supremely good, drawing the soul toward its divine origin. In this light, the experience of beauty is not passive or ornamental; it is transformative. When beauty "breaks in"

7. Plotinus, *Enneads* V.8.1, trans. MacKenna, 403.

8. Bréhier, *Philosophy of Plotinus*, 87.

upon us, it is not an interruption but a disclosure—an unveiling of the Good that beckons the soul to ascend.

This dynamic is central to Plotinus's doctrine of emanation, the process by which all things flow from the One in ordered gradations of being. Emanation is not a movement away from the divine, but the expression of divine generosity—each level of reality bearing traces of the beauty of its source. To participate in beauty, then, is to live in harmony with this divine order, to follow the soul's longing upward toward the Good. In this sense, beauty becomes the shape of the good life—what it means to live beautifully is to live in alignment with the divine.

The task of living beautifully for the human being is difficult, for the journey back to the "One" must be accomplished by the soul. It might be good to point out that this journey of the soul retains the Platonic dualism of soul and body.[9] In the passage above, it becomes clear that for Plotinus, the soul's need to be freed from the body is not framed as a moral imperative in the typical ethical sense. Instead, it is presented as a process of transformation—a reorientation of the soul's desire. For Plotinus, the soul's uncomeliness is not the result of moral failure or poor behaviour, but a failure of love. The soul does not properly love what is *truly* beautiful. This failure is not overcome through effort alone, but through illumination: when the soul encounters true beauty, it becomes conscious of its disordered state in contrast. This awareness compels the soul to cast off its "ugliness" and turn toward the light of the beautiful. This movement is not merely moral; it is metaphysical and affective—a celebration of the possibility of fullness that beauty discloses. As Plotinus writes, "It is sound, I think, to find the primal source of Love in a tendency of the Soul towards pure beauty."[10] In this sense, love is the soul's response to the call of beauty—a desire for union, transformation, and return. This movement toward beauty cannot be separated from the Good, for to behold and love the beautiful is to move toward what is ultimately Good.

The strength of Plotinus's account lies not merely in its grounding in Greek metaphysics but in its invitation to consider the possibility of human transcendence. As philosophy enters modernity, it largely abandons the language of the soul—a vocabulary once central to articulating depth, desire, and transformation. This is not to argue that we should re-center the soul as a metaphysical category in contemporary thought. Instead,

9. Plotinus, *Enneads*, trans. MacKenna, 51.

10. Plotinus, *Enneads*, trans. MacKenna, 175. Emphasis mine.

the language of the soul offers us a conceptual space for reimagining our encounter with beauty, not as a detached aesthetic experience, but as an inner awakening that calls us toward fullness.

Plotinus's significance for aesthetics, then, is not simply in his mystical or poetic descriptions of beauty. His enduring power stems from the way he associates beauty with the Good, understood in his system as the One. Through the emanation of the One, which is simultaneously the source of the True, the Good, and the Beautiful, human beings are drawn into a relationship with ultimate reality. Our response to beauty, then, is a response to the fullness of the Good itself. For Plotinus, beauty marks the soul's opening toward this divine source, and in doing so, reveals what it means to live beautifully. Such living is not reductive or moralistic, but expressive of a deep and joyful participation in being itself. This is the beauty of living—the unity of the True, the Good, and the Beautiful made manifest in the life rightly ordered toward its source.

Kant

Immanuel Kant casts light on the difficulty of the relationship between aesthetics and moral consequence. One challenge that Kant shows is the embeddedness of duty in his ethics. The problem lies in Kant's need to contend an ethical imperative for genuine human existence. He argues that all experience can be understood through the categorical imperative, thus making reason a universal phenomenon, but to say that Kant has no use for the beauty would be a misunderstanding. The third volume of his *Critique* is devoted entirely to aesthetic discourse. Yet, Kant stands with Plato and Aristotle as a cornerstone of aesthetic theory, even moving beyond them by writing the first integrated aesthetic theory with a philosophical system, *The Critique of Judgment*. I believe that the key contribution of Kant lies in his understanding of the role of the beautiful. For it is Kant who specifies, as does Plotinus, beauty (or any of the other transcendentals) as a something that cannot be fully comprehended. This is fundamental for Kant who argues that beauty (along with other realities) lies beyond the veil of the Sublime, which is not to be equated with the beautiful. Rather, the Sublime is a limitation imposed by Kant on reason. The Sublime reveals that, for Kant, a lacuna exists between aesthetic judgements and moral ones. Nonetheless, Kant presents a unique account of the beautiful.

Kant's *Critique of Judgment* offers a revolutionary account of aesthetics by detaching beauty from metaphysical or theological origins and rooting it instead in the structure of human judgment. For Kant, beauty is not a property of the object itself nor a reflection of divine order, but rather a *subjective* judgment that carries a *claim to universality*. That is, when we say something is beautiful, we do not mean merely that we like it—we assert that others *ought* to agree, even though the judgment is not based on concepts.[11]

Kant famously describes aesthetic judgment as involving a *disinterested pleasure*—a pleasure that arises not from the object's usefulness or moral value but from the "free play" of the imagination and understanding in contemplating its form (§9). This pleasure is purposiveness without purpose (§10)—the form appears as if it were designed for our faculties, but it serves no end. It is this harmony between faculties that gives rise to the aesthetic experience.

The significance of Kant's account of aesthetic judgment is twofold: first, it offers a distinctive account of how beauty functions with human cognition; and second, it affirms that the experience of beauty, while subjective, can nonetheless carry a claim to universal validity. Within the *Critique of Judgment*, Kant explores not only the beautiful but also the sublime—a category that reveals the limits of human reason. While beauty arises from the harmonious "free play" between imagination and understanding, the sublime confronts the mind with magnitude or power that exceeds our capacity to comprehend. The sublime thus becomes a kind of boundary marker: it discloses the inadequacy of our sensibility when faced with the infinite, yet simultaneously affirms the supremacy of reason, which can conceive the idea of infinity even if it cannot intuit it. In this way, the sublime produces a complex experience: a displeasure at the failure of the imagination, followed by a pleasure in the moral and rational vocation of the human subject. Kant's broader project—to "make room for faith" by delimiting the bounds of reason—is evident here, for in both beauty and sublimity, aesthetic judgment gestures toward freedom and moral feeling, not through metaphysical speculation but through reflective experience. Thus, the sublime, like the beautiful, points beyond the empirical without violating Kant's critical limits. As Kant writes, "The sublime is the name given to what is *absolutely great*."[12]

11. See §1–5 of Kant, *Critique of Judgment*.

12. Kant, *Critique of Judgment*, 78, trans. Meredith.

The sublime functions as an intuitive awareness within our mind that makes us aware of our limitations and thus prompts us to a deeper understanding of reality. As Kant writes about the sublime, it is "a faculty of the mind that surpasses every standard of sense."[13] The sublime poses within its truth the fundamental ability to order reality. For example, we can never experience/know the beauty in its fullness, but its contemplation leads to a more complete understanding and opens up a greater totality of knowledge. This leads us into how it affects humans more particularly.

Kant argues for a universality of recognition of the beautiful in objects. An example of this recognition would be the recognition of a flower or building as beautiful. To universalize the beautiful is not the Kantian position. Rather, as stated by Kant, "The beautiful is that which, apart from concepts, is represented as the object of a universal delight."[14] Beauty is a judgment rather than the innate universal claim of an object. This makes room for the particularity of regular appearances of beauty and validity for personal experience for the self. Thus, Kant here makes room for the self to perceive the beautiful not as a universal principle but according to a practice and habit of the transcendental unity of reason and experience.

This brings us to a central feature of Kant's aesthetic theory: the concept of disinterestedness. While the sublime draws us toward the limits of our faculties and points to a deeper totality of reason, the appreciation of beauty itself depends on a particular kind of stance—one that is free from desire or utility. As Kant writes, "Taste is the faculty of judging an object or a mode of representation employing a delight or aversion apart from any interest. The object of such a delight is called beautiful" (*Critique of Judgment*, §5). For Kant, only the disinterested observer—one who is not motivated by personal gain, moral imperative, or practical use—can make a proper judgment of beauty. This claim has not gone unchallenged. Friedrich Nietzsche, one of Kant's most forceful critics, argues that all judgments of value are inextricably bound up with the will to power—there is no such thing as a "pure" or "disinterested" judgment. Martin Heidegger, reflecting on this debate, suggests that Nietzsche's rejection of disinterestedness may stem from a misreading of Kant. Heidegger views Kant's aesthetic disinterest not as a negation of human engagement but as a means of preserving a space where the object is allowed to reveal itself

13. Kant, *Critique of Judgement*, trans. Bernard, 63.

14. Kant, *Critique of Judgment*, trans. Meredith, 42.

as it is, free from domination by concept, desire, or utility. In this light, disinterestedness is not indifference but disciplined openness, a condition for allowing the beautiful to disclose itself on its terms.[15]

Heidegger draws out a concealed insight within Kant's aesthetic theory: namely, that beauty is to be apprehended through *disinterestedness*. For Kant, to be "disinterested" does not imply apathy or detachment, but rather a kind of disciplined receptivity—a mode of judgment in which the object is allowed to present itself freely, without being subsumed by personal desire or conceptual utility. Beauty, in this sense, arrives as a gift: it comes to us without coercion, without demand, and precisely in this freedom, it interrupts us. Beauty, then, is not merely observed; it *trespasses* upon our constructed realities, opening new possibilities of perception and action. It disorients and reorients, not by force, but by delight. This suggests that beauty does not simply evoke pleasure—it compels a kind of attentiveness. It moves us beyond ourselves, toward a higher regard for being itself.

This movement—this moral stirring in response to beauty—shares a dynamic with the experience of the sublime, which overwhelms our faculties and makes us aware of reason's vocation beyond the limits of sensibility. While the sublime reveals our finitude, beauty quietly persuades us of the possibility of harmony. And yet, in both cases, we are faced with a kind of frustration: we cannot comprehend the beautiful in its fullness. But this very frustration becomes generative—it awakens in us the desire to act following something greater than ourselves. Kant argues that such aesthetic judgments are universal not because they are objectively true, but because they arise from the a priori structures shared by all rational beings: the harmonious interplay of imagination and understanding.

From this, two theological insights emerge that bear directly on the possibility of entire sanctification. First, beauty points to an ordering principle that exceeds complete comprehension—a transcendent reality that can only be postulated through the unity of experience and reason. Second, the apprehension of beauty requires disinterestedness: a form of attention that is freed from ego and open to transformation. It is in this openness that the aesthetic becomes moral, and the beautiful becomes sanctifying.

Kant diverges significantly from the Platonic tradition. Plotinus understands beauty as an *ontological reality*. Beauty is not judged or a

15. Heidegger, "Kant's Doctrine of the Beautiful," 105–6.

faculty of the mind; it is *beheld* and *participated in*. Plotinus teaches that beauty originates in the One and descends through the intelligible realm into the sensible world via emanation. Material beauty reflects higher beauty, which in turn reflects the One. The soul, by recognizing beauty in the world, is stirred to ascend through contemplation to the realm of the Forms, ultimately seeking unity with the divine source. Kant, by contrast, refuses to conflate beauty with truth or goodness (though he does call it a *symbol* of morality in §59). Plotinus binds beauty, truth, and goodness inextricably together. For Plotinus, beauty is a metaphysical ladder, a sign of divine origin; for Kant, beauty is a reflective mode of judgment that discloses not the nature of reality but the harmony of our cognitive faculties.

Hegel

As noted at the beginning of this section—and again here, as we approach the final philosopher under consideration—this chapter does not aim to offer a comprehensive history of aesthetics in Western philosophy. Rather, the focus has been to trace a particular thread running through the thought of three philosophers, each building upon the last, in a way that illuminates the theological implications of aesthetic theory, particularly as they pertain to the doctrine of entire sanctification. This section serves to clarify what is meant by "aesthetic" about the good and the true. I suggest this approach because we must first grasp the nature of the aesthetic before we can appreciate how distinctively theological aesthetics differ. Moreover, we must recognize that morality—that is, the performance or enactment of the good—can only be fully understood and realized when situated within the horizon of the beautiful. With that in view, we now turn to the thought of Georg Wilhelm Friedrich Hegel.

The purpose of including Hegel in this discussion of the history of aesthetic theory is brief but significant. Hegel's contribution provides the dialectical culmination of the thread I have been tracing—a culmination that reveals how aesthetics not only reflects but shapes the unfolding of human self-understanding and *Geist*. Central to Hegel's philosophy is his dialectical method, through which reality develops in a triadic structure: thesis, antithesis, and synthesis. This same structure governs his philosophy of art. Hegel views the development of art as a historical and philosophical process that culminates in absolute spirit. In his *Lectures on Aesthetics*, Hegel divides the history of art into three stages: the symbolic, the classical, and the romantic. Each stage represents a moment in the unfolding of *Geist*, from the obscure and indeterminate forms of early symbolic art, through the harmonious and balanced expressions of classical art, to the inward, spiritual depth of romantic art. As Hegel puts it near the conclusion of his *Introductory Lectures on Aesthetics*, these distinctions reveal how art becomes increasingly adequate to the expression of freedom and truth, culminating not in aesthetic experience alone, but in its integration with religion and philosophy.[16]

Hegel outlines the historical and philosophical unfolding of the *Idea of beauty* through three distinct artistic forms: symbolic, classical, and romantic. Each represents a stage in the dialectical development of *Geist's* effort to express itself in material form. Symbolic art, which finds its fullest expression in architecture, attempts to signify the divine or the infinite but does so through external, often disproportionate forms. Architecture, working with inorganic material, gestures toward meaning without fully embodying it, making it a powerful yet incomplete medium. Classical art, on the other hand, achieves a more harmonious balance between form and content, realized most purely in sculpture. In sculpture, the human form becomes a fitting vehicle for spiritual expression, uniting inner meaning and external beauty in an ideal synthesis. While classical art uses architecture as a backdrop, it does not rely on it for its content. Romantic art marks a decisive shift: the spiritual becomes too inward and boundless to be captured by physical form alone. Instead, it turns to more subjective and emotionally resonant media like painting, music, and especially poetry—forms that evoke the infinite rather than embody it. Among these, poetry holds a unique place. Because it operates through imagination and language—the very faculties essential to artistic production itself—poetry transcends and participates in all three types of art. For Hegel, this triadic progression of symbolic, classical, and romantic forms mirrors the larger movement of Geist toward self-realization. Art, then, is not merely decorative or expressive; it is a spiritual vocation through which humanity's evolving self-understanding is disclosed in sensuous, historical form.

The movement toward philosophical comprehension reaches its apex in one of Hegel's most profound and controversial claims about the destiny of art. While art plays a vital role in the unfolding of spirit, it

16. Hegel, *Introductory Lectures on Aesthetics*, 96–97.

ultimately gives way to higher forms of self-understanding—namely, religion and philosophy. Hegel writes: "The form of art has ceased to be the supreme need of the spirit. No matter how excellent we find the statues of the Greek gods, no matter how we see God the Father, Christ, and Mary so estimably and perfectly portrayed, it is no help; we bow the knee no longer."[17] This statement is not a dismissal of art, but a recognition of its historical and spiritual limitations. For Hegel, art once held the power to manifest the divine sensibly—it was, in the classical and romantic periods, a medium through which *Geist* disclosed itself to human beings. But in modernity, *Geist's* "supreme need" is no longer satisfied through aesthetic form. The visible image—no matter how sublime—can no longer bear the full weight of divine truth. We no longer *worship* through images; instead, *Geist* now demands inwardness, conceptual clarity, and self-conscious freedom. Religion and philosophy, according to Hegel, provide these in more adequate ways.

Theologically, this has a dual resonance. On one hand, it signals the insufficiency of beauty alone to secure transformation or sanctification—it must be taken up into a broader vision of truth and ethical life. On the other hand, it opens a space for a properly theological aesthetic—one not confined to sensory delight or artistic form, but one that speaks to the transformation of the self. This transformation, which the Wesleyan tradition names as *entire sanctification*, may still begin in the aesthetic encounter, but it reaches its fulfillment only when beauty yields to the inward life of grace and the moral vocation of the person. Hegel, then, brings us to the edge of a theological aesthetic: one that begins with form, but must pass through inward spirit to reach completion.

Yet this inward turn comes with a surprising consequence—what Hegel famously describes as the "end of art." This claim is especially striking given the cultural context in which he was writing, during the flourishing of some of the greatest artists in Western history—figures such as Goethe, Mozart, Haydn, Schubert, and Beethoven. The brilliance of their work makes Hegel's claim appear almost paradoxical, if not dismissive. Indeed, this aspect of Hegel's aesthetic theory has often been met with resistance by artists and critics alike. But the point of engaging Hegel in this discussion is not to rehearse the controversies surrounding his supposed dismissal of art's future vitality. Instead, the actual value of Hegel's

17. Hegel, *Aesthetics*, quoted in Inwood, "Hegel," 76.

aesthetics for our purposes lies in his emphasis on the formative and developmental role that art plays in the life of the mind.

For Hegel, art is not only a representation of truth but also a site of human becoming. It draws the subject into more profound reflection, participation, and transformation. Nowhere is this more evident than in his treatment of poetry. Hegel writes, "Poetry, however, is conformable to all types of the beautiful, and extends over them all, because the artistic imagination is its proper medium, and imagination is essential to every product that belongs to the beautiful, whatever its type may be."[18] Poetry, for Hegel, is unique among the arts because it most fully engages the imaginative faculties—not only of the creator but also of the one who receives it. Unlike architecture or sculpture, which may be contemplated from a distance, poetry invites participation. Its rhythm, form, and inner logic draw the reader or listener into its world. This is no accident: the very word "poetry" comes from the Greek *poiesis*, meaning "to make" or "to bring forth." Art, in this sense, is not a passive object of aesthetic delight—it is an invitation to create, to respond, to make beauty in our own way.

This brings us to a final synthesis of the trajectory traced through Plotinus, Kant, and Hegel. First, aesthetic experience reminds us that there is a deeper reality beyond what is merely material or measurable—a reality that gestures toward fullness, transcendence, and the unity of truth, goodness, and beauty. This deeper reality, while never fully grasped, calls us into a broader way of thinking, doing, and being. Second, this transcendent reality reveals an ordering structure that gives shape to our moral and spiritual lives. Though we cannot know it completely, we can discern its outlines through the correspondence of reason, experience, and aesthetic perception. Third, beauty comes to us as an interruption—an unexpected event that breaks into our constructed reality and opens space for reflection. It is precisely this surprise that creates the possibility for transformation. Lastly, aesthetics is not fulfilled until it becomes participatory. The observer must be drawn into the work of making—of forming beauty in response to what she has encountered. This act of *poiesis* completes the aesthetic movement and prepares the way for a theological aesthetic, where the beautiful becomes not only that which is beheld but that which is lived and given.

18. Hegel, *Introductory Lectures on Aesthetics*, 97.

A Philosophical Aesthetic for Entire Sanctification

Plotinus, Kant, and Hegel each offer influential, yet distinct, visions of aesthetic experience, rooted in their broader metaphysical, epistemological, and even spiritual commitments. Each thinker locates beauty within a larger account of reality—whether as a metaphysical principle, a structure of human judgment, or a historical expression of freedom. While they all affirm that beauty plays a critical role in shaping human understanding, desire, and moral formation, they differ profoundly on what beauty ultimately reveals: for some, it gestures toward the divine; for others, it reflects the autonomy of reason or the unfolding of spirit through history. These differences are not merely theoretical—they speak to deeper assumptions about the nature of the soul, the purpose of art, and the possibility of transcendence. By examining these thinkers together, we can discern a trajectory that leads us to the threshold of a theological aesthetic—one in which beauty is not just contemplated but lived, not just seen but participated in, as part of the soul's sanctifying journey toward the good.

Plotinus: Beauty as Ontological Ascent

For Plotinus, beauty is metaphysical. It is not a category of taste or judgment, but a sign of participation in the divine order. All beautiful things are beautiful insofar as they reflect the eternal Forms and ultimately emanate from the One. Thus, beauty is a transcendent reality that draws the soul upward through contemplation. The aesthetic experience is an *ascent*—an awakening of the soul to its divine origin. The observer of beauty is not a detached judge but a participant in a spiritual return. Beauty wounds the soul in a holy way, exposing its distance from perfection and igniting its longing for union with the Good. In Plotinus, the beautiful is not merely pleasing—it is salvific.

Kant: Beauty as Reflective Judgment and Moral Preparation

Kant, by contrast, offers a radical reconfiguration of aesthetics grounded in subjectivity and epistemological limits. In the *Critique of Judgment*, beauty is not a property of the object but a mode of judgment. The beautiful arises from the harmonious "free play" of imagination and understanding, producing a disinterested pleasure that is subjectively felt but universally communicable. Beauty prepares us, Kant argues, for moral feeling—not by commanding action, but by awakening the soul's capacity for autonomy and respect. It is not transcendent in a metaphysical sense, but symbolic of moral vocation. While Plotinus sees beauty as revealing divine order, Kant sees it as evoking rational freedom. Importantly, Kant's sublime pushes beyond beauty to underscore the limits of sensibility and the dignity of the moral law, yet even here, it is human reason—not divine reality—that stands at the center.

Hegel: Beauty as Historical Expression of Spirit

Hegel mediates between these positions by interpreting beauty in a historical and dialectical manner. Beauty, for Hegel, is neither an otherworldly transcendence (as in Plotinus) nor a merely subjective feeling (as in Kant), but a moment in the self-unfolding of Geist—absolute spirit—through history. Art reveals truth by sensuously expressing the freedom of spirit in concrete form. In his *Lectures on Aesthetics*, Hegel outlines three stages of art: symbolic (where form struggles to express content), classical (where form and content are in harmony), and romantic (where inwardness supersedes external form). Beauty thus develops over time, revealing the spirit's increasing self-consciousness. But this historical development also leads Hegel to assert the controversial "end of art": in modernity, spirit can no longer find adequate expression in aesthetic form alone. Art yields to religion and philosophy, which more fully express freedom and truth.

Theological Implications

These contrasting accounts matter deeply for theology. Plotinus offers a vision of beauty as *a soteriological* means of salvation through contemplation. Kant provides a vision of beauty as *preparation*—a tuning of the soul toward freedom and duty. Hegel offers a vision of beauty as *historical fulfillment*—a chapter in the story of spirit's self-realization. Each contains insight for a theological aesthetic, yet none is sufficient on its own.

A theological aesthetic, particularly within a Wesleyan-Holiness tradition, might synthesize these by affirming with Plotinus that beauty is more than sensation—it reveals the depth of reality. With Kant, it would recognize that beauty must move us beyond self-interest, awakening our moral response. And with Hegel, beauty is seen not as timeless but as unfolding historically, requiring participation and transformation. In this way, beauty becomes not merely what we see, but how we are sanctified by what we behold. This, then, brings us to the next and final movement of this project: a theological aesthetic—one that is attuned not simply to the presence of beauty, but to its sanctifying power.

THEOLOGICAL AESTHETIC

The purpose of engaging the history of philosophy in relation to aesthetics is not to suggest that metaphysical systems can fully account for, or define, the mystery of Entire Sanctification. On the contrary, it is precisely by tracing these philosophical trajectories—Plotinus's ontological ascent, Kant's moral preparation, Hegel's dialectical unfolding—that we begin to see the limits of philosophical aesthetics. The goal is not to subsume theology under metaphysics, but to reveal how a theological aesthetic exceeds and out-narrates its philosophical counterparts. Only through the paradox of Christ crucified and risen—the event that disorients every category of beauty, power, and wisdom—can we perceive the radical distinctiveness of Christian holiness. This is the strange beauty at the heart of the Wesleyan-Holiness tradition: a beauty that shatters our illusions, judges our failed aesthetic projects, and reveals the truth of sanctification as participation in divine love.

The history of theological reflection on beauty is comparatively sparse, with only a few figures offering sustained attention to its importance. Among these, Hans Urs von Balthasar stands out. The Swiss theologian's multi-volume *The Glory of the Lord* remains one of the most ambitious and compelling efforts to reclaim beauty as a theological category. For Balthasar, theology must not begin with abstract concepts or ethical demands but with the radiant splendor of divine self-disclosure. "The fundamental principle of theology," he insists, "is not truth or goodness, but beauty." It is beauty that first arrests us, draws us in, and prepares us to see and love the truth. In this way, Balthasar's project aligns with and intensifies the claim this essay seeks to make: that a theological aesthetic is not peripheral to sanctification—it is its starting point.[19] The main point in such a claim is that, to begin with an accurate view of God

19. Balthasar, *Glory of the Lord*, 1:17.

or theology, you cannot start with logic, but with beauty. This is because beauty breaks into our reality with the revelation of God and naming that reality is an aesthetic one for Balthasar. The revelation of God, as Balthasar writes, in the "form of Christ," calls for deep contemplation as we continually seek to understand that level of beauty. It is truly a paradox to understand, because it is an offense to our reason to see something as grotesque as the crucifixion that can only appear beautiful through revelation.[20]

Such a revelation is the hinge upon which Wesleyan-Holiness accounts for Entire Sanctification: the form of beauty in philosophical aesthetics is overcome at the cross. Philosophically, beauty is understood as a form that compels the observer to yearn for it—to aspire toward its ideal. Yet no such form, defined on purely philosophical terms, can fulfill or name that longing. Only the Christ-form—disfigured in the incarnation and crucifixion—meets and transcends the very standard philosophical aesthetics sets. In the realm of philosophical aesthetics, beauty remains an unattainable form: palpable, desirable, but ultimately unsatisfying to the human thirst for transcendence. There, beauty generates endless striving, a competition born at the intersection between the transcendent nature of the beautiful and the human desire to possess it. The logical end of such striving is futility—the form can never be grasped, only pursued. Each momentary realization of beauty is eclipsed by another, in an endless cycle of achievement and loss. This restless pursuit, driven by lack, ultimately exposes the insufficiency of philosophical aesthetics to fulfill its own longing. In response to this deficiency, theological aesthetics begins from a different premise. Where philosophical aesthetics yearns, theological aesthetics receives.

The form of beauty is not achieved—it is given. It is a gift, and this gift is veiled, even to the point of appearing ugly. To behold it requires the eyes of faith. Here, we do not reason our way to the gift; rather, we reason from and participate in the gift. In this way, theological aesthetics fulfills what philosophical aesthetics can only promise. The cross becomes the moment where true beauty is revealed—not in its perfection of form, but in the disfigured gift that calls forth worship.

Philosophical aesthetics, as traced through Plotinus, Kant, and Hegel, presents beauty as something that orients the soul toward transcendence, moral autonomy, or historical self-realization. In Plotinus,

20. Balthasar, *Glory of the Lord*, 2:135.

beauty participates in the divine order and draws the soul upward toward the One; in Kant, beauty arises from the harmony of cognitive faculties and prepares the subject for moral judgment; in Hegel, beauty is the sensuous appearance of the Idea, a moment within the dialectical unfolding of Spirit. Each of these systems identifies beauty as meaningful and formative, yet within each, beauty ultimately remains contingent upon the structures of human striving—whether contemplative, rational, or historical. Beauty functions as an ideal to be approached, a form to be discerned, a truth to be interpreted.

But the theological aesthetic, particularly as illuminated by Hans Urs von Balthasar, begins from a radically different starting point. The goal is not to subsume theology under philosophy, but to demonstrate how theology—in the paradox of the crucified Christ—exceeds and transfigures all philosophical accounts of beauty. As Balthasar insists, theology must begin not with logical clarity or ethical rigor, but with the *form of beauty* revealed in the incarnation. This is not the idealized beauty of symmetry, proportion, or harmony, but a beauty that breaks into reality—veiled, disfigured, and yet radiant. Beauty, for the theologian, is not an abstraction or aspiration—it is the form of divine self-revelation. And that form is cruciform.

The scandal of the cross marks the decisive break with philosophical aesthetics. Philosophical beauty invites the observer to ascend toward the ideal; theological beauty descends into suffering flesh. Where Plotinus's Forms dazzle the mind and Kant's disinterested pleasure refines moral taste, the cross wounds the aesthetic sensibility and offends the intellect. It is, paradoxically, only through this offense—only through the grotesque form of the crucified—that true beauty is revealed. As Balthasar observes, Christ veils his beauty not simply to share in our disfigurement, but to make the disfigured beautiful by love.

This is the hinge upon which theological aesthetics turns. In philosophical aesthetics, beauty generates longing—a striving toward the unattainable. It remains an object always deferred, a form glimpsed but never grasped, leading to a restless cycle of desire and disappointment. In theological aesthetics, beauty is *given*. It is not the reward of contemplative ascent or dialectical resolution; it is the gratuitous self-giving of God in Christ. And because it is gift, it must be received—not by the clarity of reason, but by the eyes of faith.

Thus, theological aesthetics is not simply a parallel system to its philosophical predecessors. It is their judgment and their fulfillment.

It names the longing that philosophy reveals, and it offers the gift that philosophy cannot secure. The beauty of Christ crucified is not one we arrive at; it is one that arrives for us. In this, the cross becomes the true form of beauty—not by conforming to our aesthetic expectations, but by transfiguring them from within. Here, beauty no longer compels by form alone, but by love—a love that does not demand comprehension, only participation.

THEOLOGICAL AESTHETICS AND WESLEYAN-HOLINESS THEOLOGY

Such an understanding of beauty and gift is precisely how John Wesley, albeit implicitly, envisioned holiness and Christian perfection. Holiness, in this light, can be rightly described as a theological aesthetic. This is not to suggest that Wesley himself worked within the formal language of aesthetic theory—he did not. In fact, Wesleyan theology has often been explored in moral, ethical, and ecclesial categories without recourse to aesthetics. However, what I propose is not a replacement of those frameworks, but a reframing of them: to read Wesley through the lens of theological aesthetics is to recognize that his vision of Christian perfection is not merely an ethical achievement but a divine *poiesis*—a work of beauty wrought by grace. Holiness, for Wesley, is not moralism refined; it is the form of divine love made visible in the life of the believer.

Wesley's account of Christian perfection is steeped in the language of love, not law. It is not a state of flawlessness or moral rigidity, but a life transfigured by love of God and neighbor. This love is the substance of sanctification, and like all beauty in the theological register, it is both gift and task. The Christian, in Wesley's view, does not *climb* toward holiness by ethical effort alone, but is *drawn* into it through the continual shaping power of grace. This shaping is not unlike the poetic labor of making: it is imaginative, participatory, and deeply relational. Wesley's emphasis on inward transformation, heart religion, and the communal practices of the means of grace all point to a vision of the Christian life as one in which divine beauty takes form—slowly, vulnerably, but truly—in and among the faithful.

To say that holiness is a theological aesthetic, then, is not to abstract it into artful language, but to recover its formative power. Holiness is the beauty of love made real in flesh and time. It is the gift of divine likeness received through the cruciform love of Christ. And like all true beauty, it must be *received* before it can be *performed*. Wesley's theology allows us to see this clearly: Christian perfection is not perfectionism; it is the harmony of the soul with the will of God. And this harmony is not static—it is musical, poetic, aesthetic. It is the song of grace echoed back in the life of the believer.

In this sense, my aim is not to introduce a wholly new reading of Wesley, but to draw attention to a feature often overlooked: that his theology gestures toward an aesthetic of holiness, where the perfection of love is not an abstract ideal, but a lived participation in divine beauty. In fact, as Wesley points out in "The Character of a Methodist,"

> Nor do we desire to be distinguished by actions, customs, or usages, of an indifferent nature. Our religion does not lie in doing what God has not enjoined, or abstaining from what he hath not forbidden. It does not lie in the form of our apparel, in the posture of our body, or in the covering of our heads; nor yet in abstaining from marriage, or from meats and drinks, which are all good if received with thanksgiving. Therefore, neither will any man, who knows whereof he affirms, fix the mark of a Methodist here,—in any actions or customs purely indifferent, undetermined by the word of God.[21]

The point for Wesley is the same point that has animated this entire theological-aesthetic reflection: holiness is not reducible to external actions or pious behaviors, but the cultivation or Chrisian maturity and holy tempers. It is not enough to perform holy actions but rather to gain the capacity for holiness shaped through participation in a holy God. As Wesley makes clear, the "marks" of holiness do not lie in actions, customs, or usages, of an indifferent nature. What we wear, how we posture ourselves, or even what we abstain from—these are not in themselves the signs of sanctification. They may have significance, but they do not constitute the beauty of holiness. Furthermore, it is not external conformity but internal transformation. It is the response to a divine interruption—the encounter with the revealed Christ—that reorders the soul. As Wesley writes elsewhere, the sanctified Christian "giveth thanks from the ground of his heart to Him who orders it for good."[22] Here lies the aesthetic and theological core of Wesleyan sanctification: it is not wrought by the disciplined might of the individual, but by the shaping grace of

21. Wesley, "Character of a Methodist," 341.

22. Wesley, "Character of a Methodist," 342.

the one who orders it for *good*. Correct orientation in the truly beautiful, paradoxically revealed in the cross, illustrates that only through the gain of a "taste" for the divine does one gain morally praiseworthy appetites.

This aesthetic grammar of sanctification resounds with the philosophical insights we have explored. The philosophical tradition, from Plotinus to Hegel, offers us a language for how beauty shapes the self. In Plotinus, the soul is drawn upward by the radiance of beauty—it turns toward the Good in contemplative desire. In Kant, beauty interrupts with moral force—it disorients the ego and beckons a response that transcends self-interest. In Hegel, beauty unfolds historically and dialectically—it enlists us in a poetic labor, drawing us into the imaginative creation of a world suffused with spirit. The aesthetically formed person, in each of these visions, is one who has been arrested, transformed, and redirected by an encounter with the beautiful. That person thinks differently, acts differently, and lives differently—not to impress or conform, but because beauty has restructured their being.

The sanctified life is not a life of spiritual performance; it is a life reordered by love. Beauty, in the theological sense, is not something one achieves—it is something one receives. It interrupts. It wounds. It transforms. It draws us into a new mode of life, one no longer centered on the self, but on the gracious beauty of God in Christ. In this way, the sanctified Christian does not simply imitate beauty—they become, by grace, a bearer of it. The very being of the person is reshaped by the love to which they have surrendered. This transformation is not arbitrary or ornamental; it is ordered toward the Good. It is the fulfillment of desire, the healing of the will, the harmony of life with divine love. Thus, the aesthetic enhances our understanding of Entire Sanctification not by replacing Wesley's theological grammar, but by illuminating its form. Holiness is beautiful not because it conforms to a code, but because it reflects the divine. The life of sanctification is the life ordered by grace, shaped by beauty, and lived in love.

These conclusions bring us to the heart of what we seek to say about Entire Sanctification. Each philosophical vision we have engaged—Plotinus, Kant, and Hegel—offers compelling insights into the formative power of beauty. Yet each remains, in the end, incomplete. Plotinus offers a poignant vision of the soul's ascent toward the Good through beauty, yet the soul can never fully arrive. Beauty remains something one strives for, but never possesses. By contrast, the beauty of Christ is not a goal to be achieved but a gift to be received. As John 3:16 declares, He is given.

Or, as Rowan Williams says of Wesley's conversion: "The new convert [is] touched at last by the good news that God gives what we shall never earn."[23] Christian perfection, in Wesley's theology, is never an accomplishment—it is grace. It is beauty, bestowed.

Moreover, while philosophical aesthetics often unfolds within the bounds of reason, particularly in Kant, the beauty of Christ resists such logic. Christ is not merely an interruption in the moral order; he is an interruption in the very logic of what we call beautiful. The cross is not a rational aesthetic object; it is grotesque, offensive, and illogical. And yet, through the eyes of faith, it becomes beautiful—not because of its form, but because of its love. As David Bentley Hart writes, "Theology must, because of what its particular story is, have the form of martyrdom, witness—a peaceful offer that has already suffered rejection and must be prepared for rejection as a consequence."[24] The cross cannot be understood through Kantian judgment; it can only be received as gift through the broken grammar of agape.

Wesley understood holiness as participation in this Christ-shaped love. Holiness is not conformity to moral law, but conformity to Christ. It is a poetics of incarnation, where the believer is drawn into the aesthetic form of Jesus's life—his mercy, meekness, forgiveness, and longsuffering. As Wesley writes, "[The sanctified person] hath now put on bowels of mercies, kindness, humbleness of mind, meekness, longsuffering . . . even as God in Christ hath forgiven him."[25] The call to holiness is not a demand for perfectionist rigor—it is a summons to embody the beauty that has first been shown to us. It is, in this sense, a christological aesthetic: the reenactment of divine beauty in the form of human life.

No philosophical system can re-create this beauty. Philosophy may illuminate aspects of holiness—it may give us language to explore the dynamics of transformation, desire, and selfhood—but it cannot incarnate love. Only Christ can do that. And only those drawn into his life by grace can reflect it. This is the theological aesthetic Wesley assumes when he writes, "And having the mind that was in Christ, he so walks as Christ also walked."[26] That, finally, is Entire Sanctification: not an abstract ideal, but a lived beauty—given, received, and embodied in love.

23. Williams, *Ray of Darkness,* 176.

24. Hart, *Beauty of the Infinite,* 441.

25. Wesley, "Character of a Methodist," 343–44.

26. Wesley, "Character of a Methodist," 346.

CONCLUSION: THE BEAUTY GIVEN, THE BEAUTY LIVED

This exploration has not sought to dismiss philosophy, but to honor it—and to move through it toward the horizon where theology begins. Plotinus taught us that beauty awakens longing, and that the soul, upon seeing the Beautiful, cannot help but rise. Kant taught us that beauty calls forth judgment—disinterested, universal, and ethical. Hegel taught us that beauty unfolds in time, drawing the human spirit toward ever greater expressions of freedom and inwardness. Each has offered profound tools with which to trace the outlines of beauty. But none could name the cross as beautiful. None could see in a scarred body, mocked and bleeding, the radiant glory of divine love. None could declare that holiness is not only beautiful, but cruciform. This is where theology must speak, and where the Wesleyan-Holiness tradition bears its unique witness. Entire Sanctification is not the triumph of the will, nor the perfection of form—it is the beauty of a life reordered by grace. It is not aestheticism. It is not moralism. It is the slow, aching, radiant shaping of a soul into the likeness of Christ, not through force, but through love. As Wesley insists, the holy life is not marked by customs or outward acts alone, but by a heart remade. It is gratitude, flowing "from the ground of the heart to Him who orders it for good."

In this, we find the true nature of a theological aesthetic: it begins not in ideal forms, nor in human striving, but in divine interruption. Christ is not the culmination of aesthetic logic—He is its undoing and fulfillment. His beauty cannot be possessed, only received. It comes to us veiled, wounded, and yet, by grace, more beautiful than we could have imagined. It does not flatter our sensibilities. It calls us to die. And in dying, to live again.

Holiness, in this vision, is not a posture of the pious but the poetry of the crucified. It is not behavior to be admired but beauty to be embodied. It is the echo of a divine music that catches the soul unaware and teaches it to dance in rhythm with love. To be holy, then, is to become beautiful—not by force or form, but by grace. Not by achievement, but by surrender. Not by climbing to the heights, but by being drawn to the one who descended into our depths.

CHAPTER 2

The Path of Peaceful Flight

Milbank's Trinitarian Ontology and a Re-Narration of Wesleyan-Holiness Theology

Henry Walter Spaulding II

INTRODUCTION

The horizon of Wesleyan-Holiness theology must include a serious engagement with the work of John Milbank. One clear area where Milbank might point the way forward for Wesleyan-Holiness theology is his gesture toward Trinitarian ontology. This is a thoroughly Wesleyan move as these words of John Wesley indicate: "The knowledge of the Three-One God is interwoven with all true Christian faith; with all vital religion."[1] While Wesley seems to have been uninterested in metaphysical speculation regarding the Trinity, he saw its importance. Those who followed Wesley, while undoubtedly recognizing the importance of the Trinity, have not given sustained attention to the doctrine. Therefore, a disciplined reflection on this point will enrich the capacity of Wesleyan-holiness theology to address its most fundamental theological commitments. It is precisely at this point that Milbank might be of great importance for Wesleyan-holiness theology.

I begin by examining Milbank's Trinitarian ontology. First, consideration is given to his philosophical account of Trinitarian ontology,

1. Wesley, "On the Trinity," 205.

then to his more doctrinal approach, and finally to how all of this might help those of us within the ranks of the Wesleyan-Holiness tradition to re-narrate the nature of redemption, which is the "peaceful flight" that I promise in the title of this chapter. It is a concept that requires considerable effort to appreciate fully. While it will take some time to get there, the path of peaceful flight is the ultimate goal of my reflections.

MILBANK'S TRINITARIAN ONTOLOGY: THE PATH OF PEACEFUL FLIGHT

Milbank's theology is a radical attempt to "reclaim the world by situating its concerns and activities within a theological framework."[2] The depth and breadth of his theological analysis, as well as his constructive proposals, testify to the seriousness of his project. The fundamental theological commitment that stands at the center of his work is evident in his two major books, *Theology and Social Theory* and *The Word Made Strange*. What emerges is called "Radical Orthodoxy" and is dependent on an underlying attempt to define "Trinitarian ontology." He begins the last chapter of *Theology and Social Theory* by suggesting that "theology itself . . . will have to provide its account of the final causes at work in human history, based on its particular, and historically specific faith."[3] In light of this conviction, it is significant that he sketches a counter-history (telling the whole of history from an ecclesial origin) and a counter-ethic (the distinction between premodern and postmodern ethics). Yet, the crucial part of this re-narration is counter-ontology, for it is here "where theology articulates the framework of reference implicit in Christian story and action, that this 'total' difference is fully clarified, along with its ineradicable ties to non-provable belief."[4] It is with his clear linking of Christian belief and practice that he begins to lean toward a Trinitarian ontology as counter-ontology.

One preliminary indication of this counter-ontology can be inferred from the last words of *Theology and Social Theory*: "Amid the self-torturing circle of secular reason, there can open to view again a series with which it is in no continuity: the emanation of harmonious difference, the

2. Milbank et al., "Suspending the Material," 1.
3. Milbank, *Theology and Social Theory*, 380.
4. Milbank, *Theology and Social Theory*, 381.

exodus of new generations, the path of peaceful flight."[5] I will attempt to trace "the path of peaceful flight" to suggest its importance for Wesleyan-Holiness theology. This path requires very specific moves on Milbank's part. The first is his critical move or his attempt to provide the parameters of a "theo-metaphysic." Peaceful flight is metaphysics in such a way that all of life is situated through theology. The second move in Milbank is more doctrinal, as he examines the "Second Difference."[6] In other words, the path of peaceful flight encompasses both ontology and cosmology, as well as theology. The first part of this section will be toward Creation and difference, which is the cosmological/ontological move of Milbank. This is the ontological dimension of Milbank's Trinitarian ontology.

1. Creation and Difference

One of the more interesting concerns for Milbank is Creation. He suggests that one of the ways philosophers, sociologists, and others have attempted to underwrite secular reason is with an idea of Creation that includes order from chaos. Modernity denies the Christian doctrine of Creation. Secularity and modernity depend upon a "reversion to an antique mythology of rational action as the 'inhibitor of chaos.'"[7] Milbank begins to gesture toward a Trinitarian ontology by suggesting that "the absolute is no longer just 'limit,' no longer finite, as it was for antique philosophy. What was chaos, *Apeiron,* the unlimited and finite, is now God himself."[8] There is something more fundamental for Milbank than chaos or even difference. God is not a bare, undifferentiated Being who is beyond difference and, for that matter, Creation. Milbank's basic starting point for metaphysics is neither an unapproachable unity nor a yet-to-be-realized nature. Accordingly, "Infinite realized act and infinite unrealized power mysteriously coincide in God, and it must be this that supports the circular 'life,' that is more than *stasis,* of the Trinity."[9] Understanding creation and difference, therefore, is not about finding the hints of the

5. Milbank, *Theology and Social Theory,* 434.

6. The "Second Difference" is pneumatology and, while Milbank does not express it this way, the "First Difference" is Christology or as he does express it, "Christological Poetics."

7. Milbank, *Theology and Social Theory,* 148.

8. Milbank, *Theology and Social Theory,* 423.

9. Milbank, *Theology and Social Theory,* 423.

Triune God in Creation; it is rather about understanding Creation as the outflow of a still more fundamental harmony.

The harmony, which is the plentitude of God in Creation, begins with a sense of the relationality of a Triune God.[10] Unity is understood through the difference, and difference is comprehended in unity. Yet, it is more than a preliminary or temporary triumph of unity in the face of difference. The relations, which are the Trinitarian life of God, are "not the harmony of a finished totality but a 'musical' harmony of infinity."[11] Understanding how difference and Creation are related is essential for getting at Milbank's counter-ontology. It requires that we look at time itself as relational.

Time is the way God relates to Creation. I have already discussed participation as crucial for understanding Milbank, but it is essential to understand that such participation depends on his Trinitarian ontology. He says, "Creation is therefore not a finished product in space, but is continuously generated *ex nihilo* in time. To sustain this process, the monads, seeds, or ratios also self-generate. Still, in this, they do not 'assist' God, who supplies all power and all-being, but rather participate in God."[12] Understanding time through the "external relationality" of the Triune life of God is to begin to see everything through counter-ontology. Milbank says, "The great failure of modern Christian ontology is not to see that secular reason makes the essentially Platonic assumption that 'the made' lies beneath the portals of the sacred, such that a humanly made world is regarded as arbitrary and as cutting us off from eternity."[13] This radical understanding of participation is framed at the human level by charity. Such an understanding underscores the fact that all human initiative is a response as a signal of our dependence. Therefore, Trinitarian ontology helps us to understand more fully the anti-Christian dimensions of asserting a separate reality from God. It suggests, at an even more fundamental level, that any sense in which theology is treated as just another field of inquiry is not only wrongheaded but also tragic. This means that time is not a matter of linking tenuously, however, finitude with infinitude, nor is it even a matter of finding a correspondence between an idea and God, but a participation in the very God who is triune. This ontology is characterized by a difference in unity and unity in difference.

10. Milbank, *Theology and Social Theory*, 423.

11. Milbank, *Theology and Social Theory*, 424.

12. Milbank, *Theology and Social Theory*, 425.

13. Milbank, *Theology and Social Theory*, 425.

It is not only time and Creation but also language that accounts for externality and points toward a Trinitarian ontology. Milbank says, "A Christian ontology that takes account of language and culture will then be, more fully than before, a *Trinitarian* ontology."[14] I will explore this idea more fully when we examine the "Second Difference." Still, it is essential to note here that language is tied to externality and, as such, to Trinitarian ontology in Milbank's project. According to Bauerschmidt, "Milbank's point . . . is that there is a Christian metaphysics that sees reality as fundamentally linguistic."[15] When looking at Creation, this Christian metaphysic posits *ex nihilo,* and regarding language, it posits its primordial character.[16] Therefore, Milbank is after a Christian ontology "which does justice to culture and history as an *integral* element of Christian being alongside contemplation and ethical behavior rather than as a 'problem,' external to faith."[17] This desire is entirely consistent with the theological situation of life and thought, which is so central to Milbank's project. Language is not the human construction of reality; rather, it is participation in the Triune life of God.

While we must admit at this point that Milbank is merely leaning toward a doctrine of the Trinity, it is a significant gesture. Further, it is one that we must acknowledge and look for in future reflections on Milbank's developing work. Milbank's direction is unmistakable: "When *Verbum* is included as a transcendental, all the transcendentals are transformed into personal, intersubjective, Trinitarian categories: but this leaves us with more than a 'social God' which might be open to appropriation by an ahistorical theology, it leaves us also with a *cultural* God."[18] Therefore, a Trinitarian ontology will avoid the kind of sharp distinctions which tend to complicate participation.

The trajectory of Trinitarian ontology avoids positing violence as having any ontological ground. It avoids the chaos, which figures so importantly in antique metaphysics, but it also avoids the underlying nihilism of postmodernism. Either of these options begins with a difference in the fundamental reality. Milbank wants to start elsewhere: "The God who is, who includes difference, and yet is unified, is not a God sifted out

14. Milbank, *Word Made Strange,* 80.

15. Bauerschmidt, "Word Made Speculative?" 418.

16. Bauerschmidt, "Word Made Speculative?" 418–19.

17. Milbank, *Word Made Strange,* 79.

18. Milbank, *Word Made Strange,* 80.

as 'truth,' but a God who speaks in the harmonious happening of being."[19] Therefore, Christian theology, when it is true to its ontology, posits not conflict but peace as logically prior, albeit a Trinitarian logic.

Evil is accounted for as that unrelated flight from the infinite peace, which is the Triune life of God. It is, perhaps, due to complicity with secular reason and the inevitable positing of violence that leads Christian theologians to emphasize evil. The tendency toward dualism is a consistent threat to genuine Christian reflection. Yet, such a threat is only real to the extent that the Trinitarian life of God recedes in favor of an ontology that posits chaos as its starting point. While it may not be possible to convincingly demonstrate the priority of peace, at least a gesturing toward a Trinitarian ontology can point toward the possibility, even hope, of a liturgical consummation of philosophy and life. Perhaps in such a movement, we can better understand that all Creation will join in worshiping the God who is One in Three.

2. The Second Difference

The previous section attempted to provide a philosophical account of Milbank's Trinitarian ontology. Toward that end, the emphasis on act/event, relation, time, harmony, culture, and language served to indicate the conviction with which he attempts to define an alternative. The power of this alternative involves two moments, one critical and the other constructive. The necessary movement is dependent on the persuasiveness with which he can name the implications of those theologies that have wrapped themselves around secular reason. At one level, this becomes evident in the emergence of liberalism; however, the larger picture encompasses the notion of theology. Wayne Hankey defines onto-theology in the following way: "Philosophical theology confuses Being with beings and turns God into a super being. God becomes comprehensible within a particular conception of being . . . . This relation reduces being so understood to manipulable things."[20] Milbank, with remarkable breadth, defines this alien conception concerning liberalism, positivism, dialectics, and difference. He does this critically by pointing to the presence of secular reason and constructively by pointing to counter-ontology, that is, Trinitarian ontology. Milbank develops his more doctrinal reflection

19. Milbank, *Theology and Social Theory*, 430.

20. Hankey, "Theoria Versus Poesis," 388.

on the Trinity in an essay entitled "The Second Difference."[21] Essentially, he argues, the problem with Trinitarian reflection has most often been an account of the Spirit, which is more than a bond between Father and Son or an echo of the Son. Milbank looks for "A latent Trinitarian logic, perhaps, in which the sequence of substantial relations can be stated in such a way that threefoldness becomes inescapable."[22] He justifiably feels that such logic is necessary to avoid either arbitrariness or positivity regarding pneumatology or a doctrine of the Trinity. It is with the articulation of a theology of the Spirit that Trinitarian thinking begins.

Milbank looks at two solutions to the problem he is addressing. The first is Catholic transcendentalism. He is specifically examining the work of three Roman Catholic theologians: Louis Bouyer, Yves Congar, and Walter Kasper. Milbank tends to see the Trinitarianism that arises from these theologians as "an uneasy amalgam of personalist and Kantian perspectives."[23] Fundamentally, his problem is that they "turn primary discourse and practice into *a foundational* point of reference."[24] It is in this light that Milbank first indicates his point of view: "Neither theological concepts, *nor* 'original' narratives and images are foundational, but a constant movement between the two ensures a mutual enrichment."[25] He sees, by contrast, that Catholic transcendentalism turns on "mythic foundationalism" and "epistemological foundationalism." Here, the Father becomes a self-positing subject, and the Spirit "the categorical possibility of freedom which allows the first paternal instantiation of freedom to evoke a commensurate response."[26] The foundational tendencies of this view, along with its alternative positivism, suggest the need for an alternative.

Milbank also examines what he calls Protestant Hegelism, which is characterized by "the Trinity is seen in terms of God's involvement in historical becoming, and the Spirit as God's eschatological arrival in the Kingdom, already anticipated in the Church."[27] He feels that Jürgen Moltmann, Wolfhart Pannenberg, and Eberhard Jüngel all present variations on this understanding. According to Milbank, Moltmann's Trinity incorporates a necessary alienation, which is problematic for Trinitarian

21. Milbank, *Word Made Strange*, 171.

22. Milbank, *Word Made Strange*, 173.

23. Milbank, *Word Made Strange*, 175.

24. Milbank, *Word Made Strange*, 179.

25. Milbank, *Word Made Strange*, 180.

26. Milbank, *Word Made Strange*, 180.

27. Milbank, *Word Made Strange*, 180.

reflection. He suggests that Pannenberg's approach is more sophisticated in that "he retains the logic of substantial relations concerning historical becoming, such that the Son and the Spirit are 'always already' present as an anticipation of the future, which alone finally defines their subsistent content."[28] Yet, this analysis, according to Milbank, weakens Moltmann's emphasis on suffering in favor of "a developmental immanence of the final, peaceful outcome."[29] Milbank observes that Jüngel is still Hegelian and modalist, "the transcendent paternal subject freely identifies himself with the man Jesus Christ in his death on the Cross."[30] The problem here is that "necessary estrangement is justified by outcome."[31] This locates the problem not only in comprehending the Trinitarian relations in non-modalist and non-tritheistic terms but also in linking the Trinity to Creation and the Fall. This is problematic in that it unduly separates the immanent Trinity from the economic Trinity. Yet, it is the dependence on Hegel that saves Protestant reflection on the Trinity from fully incorporating the separation. Milbank's critique locates the problem in two very distinct places. First, it posits a necessary estrangement in the conception of the economic Trinity. This leads to a second difficulty, which can be stated as some posited interval between Creator and Creation. This problem amounts to an inadequate Trinitarian theology.

Since Hegel is, according to Milbank, "the most profound modern mediator upon the identity of the Holy Spirit,"[32] he offers a pathway for considering "the pathos of Christ's absence, of the Spirit's atoning work, and the connection between Spirit and community."[33] This suggests that, while Hegel will ultimately be inadequate for understanding either a Trinitarian ontology or a fully developed doctrine of the Trinity, his philosophy might help link salvation and the Trinitarian life of God. What is important for my current investigation is a fuller account of the Second Difference in Milbank's theology. He goes on to call this a case "of the philosophical tail wagging the theological dog."[34] Whether this is the case or not is a matter of dispute, but it accurately reflects the fundamental

28. Milbank, *Word Made Strange*, 181.
29. Milbank, *Word Made Strange*, 181.
30. Milbank, *Word Made Strange*, 181.
31. Milbank, *Word Made Strange*, 182.
32. Milbank, *Word Made Strange*, 183.
33. Milbank, *Word Made Strange*, 183.
34. Bauerschmidt, "Word Made Speculative?" 429.

direction of Milbank's understanding, as it draws attention to his linguistic ontology.

Milbank has already observed that the Second Difference is the decisive movement of Trinitarian theology. While this is hardly a surprising observation, it does hit at the core of Trinitarian reflection by insisting that an adequate pneumatology be defined. The critique of Bauerschmidt notwithstanding, Milbank is drawing attention to an issue that anyone who has ever taught systematic theology has faced: how to account for the person of the Spirit. As Milbank observes, "time and again the Spirit is falsely seen as more immanent, more economical, than the other two persons: a 'go-between God' whose redundant mediation only obscures the immediacy of the divine presence."[35] This leads Milbank to argue "that if one conceives of God as 'interpersonal,' then one must also conceive him as 'linguistic.'"[36] He believes that this will enable a clearer understanding of the relationship between the Spirit and the Trinity.[37]

All of this leads Milbank to suggest an "aesthetics of reception"[38] for providing a more adequate Trinitarian logic.[39] According to Milbank, this is the only way the Second Difference can be understood adequately. He is after an understanding of the Trinity that "takes absence as the occasion for rhetorical community, and not dialectical unity, nor infinite concealment and betrayal."[40] This means that the "important thing for the future of Trinitarian doctrine is at once to reclaim the themes developed in all kinds of Gnosticism in all their profundity, and yet to show that orthodoxy exhibits a wisdom which is beyond even that of the Gnostics."[41] Thus, it is possible to see in Milbank a linking of Trinitarian ontology, ecclesiology, liturgy, and atonement. This is the precise place where his reflections might enable Wesleyan-holiness theology to "go on."

The importance of Milbank's Trinitarian reflection is so nuanced, so broad, and so original that a full accounting of it is not possible here. Yet, I have attempted to locate the parameters of his reflection by calling attention to his Trinitarian ontology. First, it is crucial to understand

35. Milbank, *Word Made Strange*, 174.

36. Milbank, *Word Made Strange*, 177.

37. Cf. Taylor, *Go Between God*. This book is an example of the danger that Milbank is addressing here.

38. Milbank, *Word Made Strange*, 188.

39. Milbank, *Word Made Strange*, 188.

40. Milbank, *Word Made Strange*, 188.

41. Milbank, *Word Made Strange*, 189.

the importance of harmonic peace, musicality, and external relationality in Milbank. It is precisely with these ideas that he begins to flesh out counter-kingdom, defined by peaceful flight. It appears that the church is the field on which the Second Difference receives the *logos* and extends the sphere of musical harmony. Indeed, this is played out amid the contingencies of history. Second, it is also important to begin to see the possibilities of linguistic ontology for defining the Trinity in such a way that liturgy and ecclesiology become more than an appendix for theology.[42] Although some questions remain unanswered, Milbank's proposal is worth considering. His critical engagement with onto-theology is his major contribution to contemporary theology. His clear diagnosis regarding the nihilism inherent in most postmodern theology is helpful. Yet, it would be unwise to pass over "too quickly" his constructive proposals. Even if Milbank only gestures toward pneumatology or a doctrine of the Trinity, his work is worthy of serious consideration. The next section should be understood as a basic attempt to recover Trinitarian reflection for Wesleyan-holiness theology, which is the path of peaceful flight.

A PRELIMINARY RE-NARRATION OF A WESLEYAN-HOLINESS UNDERSTANDING OF SALVATION

The absence of sustained Trinitarian reflection among Wesley and those who have consciously sought to work within the Wesleyan-holiness tradition has been noted. This fact should not, however, be interpreted as meaning that Wesley was not interested in the Trinity, just that the kind of reflection that could be defined as metaphysical, ontological, and/or speculative was of little interest to him. Even so, the significance of Trinitarian reflection is evident at the core of Wesleyan theology. Randy Maddox explains this apparent contradiction by describing Wesley's theology as a "practical-theological activity."[43] It is, perhaps, the task of the present generation of theologians to develop a Trinitarian ontology, which will enrich not only the practice of Christian holiness but also the speculative capacities of the tradition. This section should be understood as a preliminary gesture in that direction.

Wesleyan-holiness theology must become more explicitly Trinitarian. Such a move can have far-reaching effects on our tradition. For

42. Milbank, "Intensities," 486.

43. Maddox, *Responsible Grace*, 139.

example, we must lift the horizon of theological reflection in the Wesleyan-Holiness tradition beyond an exclusive consideration of the moral imperative. While such considerations are important, there is much more that demands our sustained attention. It will be important to relate doctrines such as ecclesiology and Christology in a material way.[44] Trinitarian reflection may also help us define the relationship between liturgy and the self or the theological orientation of Christian practice.[45] Perhaps Trinitarian reflection could help the Wesleyan-Holiness tradition come to terms with the doctrine of the Spirit in ways other than purely experiential and expressive. A fair reading of the themes that have given shape to Wesleyan-Holiness theology might suggest that articulation of a Second Difference, that is, a Trinitarian ontology, will be necessary for our tradition to "go on." Perhaps our legitimate concern to call attention to the work of Christ has run the risk of turning Christ into a hero who defeats our enemy and pleads our case to the Divine Judge. There is little need for a Second Difference in such a scheme. One might even wonder if the Trinity could be anything other than an afterthought within such a scheme. Trinitarian reflection within the Wesleyan-Holiness tradition could provide a means to re-examine our most fundamental theological commitments.

1. The Problem Stated

The Satisfaction Theory of the Atonement enjoys a long history in the Christian tradition, including the Wesleyan-Holiness tradition. H. Ray Dunning discusses "Satisfaction Theories," under which he categorizes Anselm, Calvin, and even Grotius. It is, of course, true that variations on this view are nearly universal among Christians. Essentially, this family of theories assumes the "necessity of an 'antecedent satisfaction' as the condition for the remission of sins."[46] This is all the more problematic because Wesley held to a Satisfaction Theory, which, according to Dunning, is "antithetical to his central soteriological claims."[47] This is a problem that many have noted or otherwise struggled with in the Wesleyan-Holiness tradition. It is both a theological and a practical problem.

44. Cf. Bassett, "Interplay of Christology and Ecclesiology."

45. Cf. Anderson, "Trinitarian Grammar of the Liturgy."

46. Dunning, *Grace, Faith, and Holiness*, 337.

47. Dunning, *Grace, Faith, and Holiness*, 362.

H. Orton Wiley, in his *Christian Theology*, points to several limitations of the Satisfaction Theory. First, "It is in [the] attempt to impute our sin to Christ as His own that the weakness of this type of substitution appears."[48] Sin is not punished, or it is punished without demerit in the one being punished. Second, there is a tendency to conceive of substitution in a too narrow fashion; that is, only the penal substitution theory is appropriate. Wiley argues that the Governmental theory offers an alternative and better understanding. Third, the "theory leads of necessity, either to universalism on the one hand or unconditional election on the other."[49] Fourth, Wiley sees that this "theory is associated with the Calvinistic ideas of predestination and limited atonement."[50] This observation is related to how grace is to be understood. Finally, Wiley thinks that it leads "logically to antinomianism."[51] It inevitably separates faith and sanctity. This alone raises significant issues for a Wesleyan-holiness theology. All of this can be summed up in the words of Dunning: "The real problem for a sound theology is making provision for sanctification without losing the biblical emphasis on justification by faith alone."[52] While both Wiley and Dunning highlight important issues, an underlying concern ties everything together. It is toward this reality that I think our attention should be turned.

For Wesleyan-Holiness theology, the fundamental problem with maintaining a satisfaction theory of atonement is the radically different understanding of God that each assumes. The satisfaction theory posits that the primary issue in the atonement lies with God. Either God's honor or his holiness must be addressed before atonement can be consummated. Leaving aside the substantial notions that such a view of sin and, for that matter, grace/holiness implies, the real problem is the assumption that God has constructed a barrier separating himself from humankind. Inevitably, this pits Jesus against the Father; it is Jesus who, as our redeemer, pleads for mercy to the Father, who is our Judge. Such a construction seems, at the most fundamental level, to be tritheistic, and as such, it is sub-Trinitarian and perhaps anti-Trinitarian.

Examining the issue from a more consistent Trinitarian perspective, we see a God who, in the fullness of his grace, has extended his reach

48. Wiley, *Christian Theology*, 2:245.

49. Wiley, *Christian Theology*, 2:246.

50. Wiley, *Christian Theology*, 2:247.

51. Wiley, *Christian Theology*, 2:248–49.

52. Dunning, *Grace, Faith, and Holiness*, 364.

to us. This view is unapologetically relational, yet it is also Trinitarian in nature. I am aware of two interrelated attempts to address the problem within the ranks of Wesleyan-Holiness theology. H. Ray Dunning makes the first attempt in *Grace, Faith, and Holiness,* where he argues that Wesley's uses of the threefold office of Christ lend itself to "an Atonement motif."[53] He argues his case persuasively, drawing on both biblical and Wesleyan grounds. R. Larry Shelton offers a second approach: "The central paradigm of this saving relationship in Scripture is the covenant in both its cultic and its interpersonal elements as understood and expressed in the life of the community."[54] He argues that this paradigm has the advantage of being both biblical and personal, as well as communal. He says further: "The covenant relationship between God and His people is thus central to the entire biblical message of salvation."[55] In this light, it is intriguing that Shelton observes: "Anselm's emphasis on the importance of maintaining God's honor and on the atoning significance of Christ's obedience are important elements to be maintained in a theory of Atonement."[56] Both attempts use relational categories regarding sin and holiness. Both Dunning and Shelton believe that such a description is more biblical and truer to Wesley. In other words, approaching salvation either through the threefold office of Christ or the Covenant frees those within the Wesleyan-Holiness tradition to avoid the weaknesses named by Wiley. Both are serious attempts to deal with the incongruity described above. Yet, Trinitarian concerns are not central to either view.

After briefly examining the problem, as noted by many, including Wiley and Dunning, it seems to me that Milbank's perspective might be of service. I argue that the "Satisfaction/Holiness" problem can be best addressed through a more sustained reflection on the Trinity. Wesley himself seems to pull all of this together in a comment on 1 John 5:7–8:

> The testimony of the Spirit, the water, and the blood is by an eminent gradation corroborated by three who give still greater testimony. The Father—Who testified of the Son, both at His baptism and at His transfiguration. The Word—Who testified of Himself on many occasions, while He was on earth; and again with still greater solemnity, after His ascension into heaven. And the Spirit—Whose testimony was added chiefly after His

53. Dunning, *Grace, Faith, and Holiness,* 366. Cf. Deschner, *Wesley's Christology.*

54. Shelton, "Redemptive Grace of God in Christ," 1:473.

55. Shelton, "Redemptive Grace of God in Christ," 1:473.

56. Shelton, "Redemptive Grace of God in Christ," 1:505.

> glorification. And these three are one—Even as those two, the Father and the Son, are one. Nothing can separate the Spirit from the Father and the Son.[57]

It is essential to recall the comprehensive saturation of redemption and salvation that informs the text Wesley is addressing. This fact, when linked to Wesley's reflection on the Trinity in his notes, gives me a warrant call for the same. Specifically, I intend to outline briefly the need to more fully comprehend the concept of sanctity through Milbank's Trinitarian ontology. I believe that such a gesture is not only Milbankian but also Wesleyan and ultimately biblical. It is in every way the path of peaceful flight.

2. Can a Gift Be Given?

The path of peaceful flight unfolds the beauty of God as it opens all reality to the gift of God in Christ and envisions the eschatological presence of the church in the power of the Spirit. Such a re-narration of salvation must include three movements: beauty, poesis, and vision. First, understanding salvation requires a reemphasis on beauty and harmonic peace. The Christian faith, and particularly Wesleyan-Holiness theology, seems to be positioned to recover beauty as a theological conviction. Beauty begins with an understanding of God as beautiful, whole, musical, and holy. It also means that God invites all of Creation to join in the music of his harmonic peace. Perhaps theology is akin to aesthetics when viewed through the lens of the Trinity. Music is an apt metaphor for beginning to appreciate beauty. David Cunningham says, "Christianity proclaims a polyphonic understanding of God—one in which *difference* provides an alternative to a monolithic homogeneity, yet without becoming a source of exclusion."[58] Such an understanding cannot be the product of formal logic or a preoccupation with some completed substance; rather, it points to a more fundamental beauty of Creation out of nothing, the unceasing love of God. Therefore, beauty as a theological conviction finds warrant in a Triune God. The unceasing love of God weaves a musical harmony that invites everything to participate in it. It has long been recognized that part of what Trinitarian theology attempted involved a clear linking of God, salvation, and Creation.

57. Wesley, *Explanatory Notes*, 917.

58. Cunningham, *These Three are One*, 129.

Wesleyan-Holiness theology has discussed the renewal of the image of God but often stopped short of understanding the cosmological implications of salvation. Beauty is the conviction that within the Triune life of God, there is the capacity to fashion a musical harmony for the cosmos. Can the gift be given? Yes, the gift is the beauty of the Triune life of God, which envisions wholeness instead of alienation and peace instead of violence.

The second movement in a re-narration of salvation is *poesis*. Milbank describes this as "the idea that human making is not a merely instrumental and arbitrary matter, but itself a route which opens towards the transcendent."[59] Such an understanding prevents the temptation to view salvation in purely personal terms. At the very least, it seems shortsighted to conceive of salvation "purely" in terms of a decision or a response. Salvation is not what God and the individual accomplish together; it is what God preveniently brings about in the life of the believer. To the extent that salvation is construed through a "possessive individualism," it becomes a transaction between God and humankind, one that all too often is as much a personal achievement as it is a divine gift. *Poiesis* can enhance the capacity of Wesleyan-holiness theology to more fully comprehend the meaning of putting our salvation to work. Perhaps this emphasis can help us to see salvation/holiness as participation. It resists the tendency to reduce holiness to morality because it reminds us at every point that putting our salvation to work is engendered by a transcendent God. Too often, salvation is reduced to "my" moment, a time when "I" made the "choice." *Poesis* is construed through the triune life of God, the One who offers a gift, the One who opens the self to its poetic possibilities. Can the gift be given? Yes, if we understand that in the Triune life of God, the gift flows from a plentitude of graciousness. It is not withheld until some satisfaction is accomplished or a punishment is accepted. Salvation has always been given, even from the foundation of the world.

The third movement in the re-narration of salvation is vision. This final movement is eschatological to the core. It is the working out of the counter-ontology into another city, or counter-kingdom, one that looks toward its completion as it practices the stubborn hope of redemption. Vision serves as a reminder that there is a "not-yet" aspect to salvation. It admits that evil still exists. Sometimes, it even appears to reign.[60] Above

59. Milbank, *Theology and Social Theory*, 148.

60. There are several implications for theodicy that will be need to be fleshed out.

all, it highlights the centrality of the church, the "Body of Christ," and the "Temple of the Holy Spirit" in the eschatological vision of redemption. If salvation is not "just" a personal thing, we must see the importance of the church for continuing to incarnate Christ in the world. Cunningham puts it this way: "It can thus help us to recognize the contours of a specifically *Trinitarian* polyphony; it should also begin to *form* us poly-phonically, urging us to understand ourselves and others as the various melody-lines that contribute to the symphony of the Church."[61] Milbank makes it clear that the Counter-Kingdom or the Other City is about salvation. He is equally clear that the Triune life of God constitutes it. Yet, he is neither blind to the violence that appears to reign still nor to the church's complicity with such violence.[62] The cross makes such violence absurd, even as it points to the path of peaceful flight. Milbank observes: "An abstract attachment to non-violence is therefore not enough—we need to practice this as a skill and learn its idiom. The idiom is built up in the Bible. It reaches its consummation in Jesus, and the emergence of the Church."[63] What is really at stake for the church is its faithfulness to situate all of life within the "emanation of harmonious difference."[64] The obvious sense in which this is consistent with the Wesleyan-Holiness tradition is striking. There are two reasons for this. First, Wesleyan-Holiness theology views salvation more comprehensively within the context of the Wesleyan understanding of the Spirit's holiness. Salvation is not only forensic; it is also therapeutic. Second, Wesleyan Holiness is presented as an eschatological hope that suggests human beings can indeed become holy, not just appear to be so, but be so.

It remains the task of this generation of Wesleyan-holiness theologians to flesh this out more fully. I contend that such work requires Trinitarian ontology to serve as the prolegomena for a fuller re-narration of Wesleyan-Holiness theology. Can a gift be given? Yes, a gift is given in the continuing and unceasing love of the Triune God in the community of the incarnation. It should be understood from the start that the One who sends the Son gives the Spirit without reserve to reclaim Creation. If giving is a matter of sacrifice, either to Satan, who holds the rights to humankind, or the justice of a holy God, then it is not a gift. Any attempt to reduce the economy of salvation to a mere contract diminishes the

61. Cunningham, *These Three Are One*, 135.

62. Milbank, *Theology and Social Theory*, 433.

63. Milbank, *Theology and Social Theory*, 398.

64. Milbank, *Theology and Social Theory*, 434.

capacity for a Trinitarian theology to inform our speculation and practice. Catherine Pickstock attempts to define one such practice (medieval Roman Rite) and, as such, points to its Trinitarian implications.[65] Liturgy, then, is one dimension of the externality of salvation. It is one way in which the church seeks to extend the sphere of aesthetic harmony first envisioned in the Trinity but eschatologically completed as all nature joins in the chorus.

These three movements—beauty, *poesis,* and vision—gesture toward a more genuine Trinitarian understanding of salvation. They suggest something of the power and possibility of the gift being given. To comprehend this preliminary reflection, it may be helpful to examine the demands of soteriology. First, sin must be accounted for, not just dismissed. This Trinitarian ontology begins with an even greater conviction, the harmonic peace of God, but it does not ignore sin. Yet, it tends to see that evil is never more fundamental. Rather, evil is always and actually overcome in the fullness of the Triune God and eschatologically overcome in the extension of the sphere of harmonic peace through ecclesial doxology. Second, any understanding of soteriology must be careful to define the place of Jesus Christ. The kingdom of God, that is, the counter-kingdom, has appeared in Christ. Jesus has walked into the face of sin, evil, and death for us to subvert the power of darkness.

Graham Ward attempts to deal with this: "From the moment of the incarnation, this body then is physically human and subject to all the infirmities of being and yet is also a body looking backward to the perfect Adamic corporeality and forward to the corporeality of resurrection. The materiality of this human body is eschatologically informed."[66] In other words, the incarnation and the resurrection must be accounted for and are in the eschatological community, the church. Jesus Christ has "already" subverted evil through his obedience, even unto death. Jesus Christ has eschatologically delivered all of Creation through the resurrection to life as the first fruits of the resurrection to come. This is the "not-yet," which is progressively called into being through the practice of faith in this new community called into being by word and Spirit. This suggests the adequacy of a new understanding of salvation, viewed through the lens of Trinitarian ontology.

65. Pickstock, *After Writing,* 219.

66. Ward, "Bodies," 164.

Trinitarian ontology engenders the practice of charity, first in the life of God and then in the paradisal community of peace.[67] Charity, when envisioned through the Trinitarian life of God, resists being reduced to a gift exchange. It means that we are to understand salvation as the free offer to participate in the Trinitarian life of God. It also means that the gracious God of everlasting relation is neither appeased nor fooled. Instead, God "forgives."

I have attempted to argue that a Trinitarian ontology alone is adequate to re-narrate salvation in such a way that the metaphor of punishment/satisfaction is subverted and Christian holiness envisioned. While the covenant is a more acceptable approach than satisfaction, it is still possible to miss the gift and reduce salvation to the calculus of a contract. Likewise, the attempt to resolve the dilemma through an insertion of the threefold office of Christ may miss the Trinitarian horizon of salvation by overlooking the unfolding work of the Spirit in the church. Milbank's Trinitarian ontology is a preliminary gesture toward a richer understanding. It is just such reflection that enables us to understand Jesus as more than a "moral" person or a "mask" of divinity.[68] Christ lives as the "body of Christ" in and through the telling of and the practice of the story. As Milbank says, "The doctrine of the atonement must be drastically reconceived from an ecclesiological vantage point."[69] It is in this way that atonement, forgiveness, salvation, and even holiness are construed eschatologically. It is in this way that atonement can be "already" and "not yet." It is in this way that "transposing Chalcedonian orthodoxy into a new idiom" makes it possible to be orthodox. The christological question is always a Trinitarian question.

In this way, we begin to understand Trinitarian ontology as a gesture of holiness. As often as you do this, remember, that is, as usually as you do this, re-narrate the gift of the Trinitarian God. Ultimately, remembering is a practice, not an abstract commitment or a transcendentally secured idea. Understanding the link between the Trinity and vital religion is the pathway to a deeper, more profound music. It is understanding salvation as something more than a transaction between a feudal lord and a serf. Neither is it an Almighty God who conquers an inferior challenger. Salvation is the everlasting musical harmony that we begin to hear in the

67. Milbank, "Can a Gift Be Given?," 154.

68. Milbank, *Word Made Strange*, 149–150.

69. Milbank, *Word Made Strange*, 162.

echo of the eschatological community. It is heard in the path of peaceful flight.

CHAPTER 3

"To Shew the Fly the Way Out of the Fly-Bottle"

A Reconstruction of the Wesleyan Understanding of Christian Perfection

Henry Walter Spaulding II

INTRODUCTION

THIS PAPER IS ABOUT finding a way about. It arises from my questions about Christian perfection after years of pastoral service, both in the parish and classroom. It is guided by the conviction that each new generation must find its own way about. Ludwig Wittgenstein makes a perceptive comment, "A philosophical problem has the form: I don't know my way about" (PI 123).[1] The context of this statement suggests that our problem is with language, "A picture held us captive. And we could not get outside it, for it lay in our language and language seemed to repeat itself to us inexorably" (PI 115). Language frames a "picture" from which we find it difficult to escape, a prison of sorts. This is our problem and challenge, "To shew the fly the way out of the fly bottle" (PI 309). What I hope to do

1. Due to the frequent references to several of Wittgenstein's works in this chapter, I will use the following abbreviations: TLP (*Tractatus Logico-Philosophicus*), PI (*Philosophical Investigations*), PG (*Philosophical Grammar*), BB (*Blue and Brown Book*), C (*Lectures and Conversations on Aesthetics, Psychology, and Religious Belief*).

on the following pages is, at least, uncork the bottle, and if not, shew the fly the way out.

First, I intend to outline what things mean for Wittgenstein, especially the "Later Wittgenstein." Second, I will attempt a limited grammatical investigation of the *Plain Account*. Third, I intend to reconstruct Christian perfection in basic terms using Wittgenstein's philosophy. This is an ambitious undertaking, yet as a theology professor and preacher of the gospel, I find myself discontent to be caught in a bottle.

WITTGENSTEIN AND PULLING UP THE LADDER

The turn toward language in our century is one way philosophy attempts to find a way about. Dan Stivers refers to this as the linguistic turn in philosophy, "The major philosophical movement in the English-speaking world in the first half of this century, logical positivism, was a reappropriation of David Hume in light of the new logical tools and, not least, a new concern for the philosophical significance of language."[2] In other words, meaning requires a careful scrutiny of our language because it is a way to get at thought. Ludwig Wittgenstein looks toward language to get at meaning. He published only one book during his lifetime, *Tractatus Logico-Philosophicus*, which provoked philosophical discussion nearly eighty years after its publication. His more mature views are to be found in a series of edited books, the most influential being *Philosophical Investigations*, which is composed of notes that Wittgenstein hoped would become a book. He says in the Preface of the *Investigations*, "I have been forced to recognize grave mistakes in what I wrote in that first book to a degree which I myself am hardly able to estimate" (PI vi). In fact, Wittgenstein reportedly wrote in a copy of the *Tractatus* given to Moritz Schlick that it is "the symptom of a disease."[3] Even so, it is a mistake to assume that there is no connection between the *Tractatus* and the *Investigations*. The continuity and the discontinuity of these two philosophical works (or the early Wittgenstein and the later Wittgenstein) reveal a theory of meaning that will serve our theological project.

Wittgenstein's interest in language is the thread that runs throughout his philosophy, although it is treated somewhat differently in the *Tractatus* and *Investigations*. In another book, he says, "It is in language that

2. Stiver, *Philosophy of Religious Language*, 4.

3. Glock, *Wittgenstein Dictionary*, 23.

it's all done."[4] This is evident from the earliest portions of the *Tractatus*, where questions of meaning are raised in a new way. Glock observes: "it marks the point at which the nineteenth-century debate about the nature of logic, between empiricism, psychologism, and Platonism merges with the Post-Kantian debate about representation and the nature of philosophy. The point of contact is thought."[5] Wittgenstein says in the Preface of the *Tractatus*, "The truth of the thoughts that are here communicated seems to me unassailable and definitive. I believe myself to have found, on all essential points, the final solution to the problems. Yet, the following sentence illustrates the tension that lies at the center of Wittgenstein's early philosophy: "Little is achieved when these problems are solved."[6] This is the first expression of a fault line in the *Tractatus*, and it opens the door to what will become the *Philosophical Investigations*. I will first look at the Tractatus, where Wittgenstein develops several key ideas: logical constants, general propositional form, tautology, and picture theory.

Wittgenstein calls his most fundamental idea (in the *Tractatus*) as the idea that "logical constants are not representatives; that there can be no representatives of the logic of facts."[7] Logical constants refer to propositional connectives and quantifiers, which Bertrand Russell, Gottlob Frege, and others describe as the most general aspects of reality. As Russell suggests, Wittgenstein criticized this view by suggesting that propositions are truth functions, not names. The point of the discussion in the *Tractatus* is to see that "Propositions represent the existence or non-existence of states of affairs."[8] Thus, logical constants are not truth functions because they do not represent/name anything: "Propositions cannot represent logical form: it is mirrored in them . . . Propositions show the logical form of reality. They display it."[9] Wittgenstein's "most fundamental idea" assumes that propositions are constructed logically but aim to depict things as they are. The meaningfulness of language depends upon the clarity with which it depicts/presents states of affairs.

The general propositional form is crucial to the argument of the *Tractatus*: "This is how things stand."[10] Glock calls this the "essence of

4. Wittgenstein, *PG*, 143.
5. Glock, *Wittgenstein Dictionary*, 16.
6. Wittgenstein, *TLP*, 4.
7. Wittgenstein, *TLP*, 4.0312.
8. Wittgenstein, *TLP*, 4.1.
9. Wittgenstein, *TLP*, 4.121.
10. Wittgenstein, *TLP*, 4.5.

the proposition."[11] Wittgenstein indicates that the "general propositional form is variable."[12] Therefore, a proposition presents a possibility. In this way, "A proposition is a truth function of elementary propositions."[13] This goes back to the fundamental argument that Wittgenstein is making. Namely, that meaning is attached to the state of affairs. This reveals Wittgenstein's early assumption regarding logical atomism. He felt that the sure path of clarity, thus meaning, is to break the proposition up into its irreducible parts. Then, it was hoped that logic could help, not as Russell had proposed by providing names, but by clarifying the truth-functional nature of the proposition. This avoids the tendency to confuse the formal with the ontological.

The issue is the relationship between representation and meaning. Wittgenstein seems to be assessing the sense that meaning is a function of the clarity with which a thought corresponds to the reality it depicts. He says, "A proposition must restrict reality to two alternatives: yes or no. To do that, it must describe reality completely. A proposition is a description of a state of affairs."[14] This leads us to the well-known picture theory: A picture is a model of reality. Wittgenstein adds, "A picture is a fact."[15] If we go back to the beginning lines of the *Tractatus*, we will see that Wittgenstein links facts with "states of affairs" and "the world." Therefore, the picture theory attempts to depict, that is, model the world. The meaningfulness of propositions is the clarity with which they model the world. He says, "A picture agrees with reality or fails to agree; it is correct or incorrect, true or false."[16] This is important because, "A proposition is a picture of reality. A proposition is a model of reality as we imagine it."[17] In other words, "We picture facts to ourselves."[18] Looking at all these indications in Wittgenstein reveals two characteristics of a meaningful proposition: it represents a state of affairs and is determinate.

Essentially, Wittgenstein is calling into question the "old logic" as it is represented in Russell and Frege. His unhappiness with this way of doing logic is too complex for the shape and scope of this chapter to address

11. Glock, *Wittgenstein Dictionary*, 140.
12. Wittgenstein, *TLP*, 4.53.
13. Wittgenstein, *TLP*, 5.
14. Wittgenstein, *TLP*, 4.023.
15. Wittgenstein, *TLP*, 2.141.
16. Wittgenstein, *TLP*, 2.21.
17. Wittgenstein, *TLP*, 4.01.
18. Wittgenstein, *TLP*, 2.1.

fully, but we need to call attention to Wittgenstein's fundamental critique. Wittgenstein tended to concentrate on a theory of symbolism instead of a theory of judgment, as is evident in the analysis of the general propositional form and the picture theory. Wittgenstein attempts to clarify this by holding philosophy and language accountable for reality. He talks about the pictorial form: "It is laid against reality like a measure."[19] Thomas Ricketts suggests that Wittgenstein "employs two intertwined notions of representation distinguished in German by the verbs 'vertreten' and 'darstellen.'"[20] The first indicates that names go proxy for the objects. The second indicates a representation of logical space. This distinction is outlined in the following way: "The essence of a propositional sign is very clearly seen if we imagine one composed of spatial objects (such as tables, chairs, and books) instead of written signs. Then the special arrangement of these things will express the sense of the propositions."[21] This means that while Wittgenstein doubts the adequacy of the old logic, he still shares a significant commitment, the correspondence theory of truth. The fundamental difference is the way that the name or object functions. For Russell, the name has a kind of independence that Wittgenstein rejects. The issue for Wittgenstein is that clarity in propositions is achieved by understanding the situation, and the importance of the signs is found in their ability to aid in this process of understanding. Wittgenstein believed that one must be rigorous in this process to avoid overlap between the simple and the complex.

Wittgenstein gives a clear indication of his intentions in the *Tractatus*: "The whole sense of the book might be summed up in the following words: what can be said at all can be said clearly, and what we cannot talk about we must pass over in silence."[22] He closes with these words, "My propositions serve as elucidations in the following way: anyone who understands me eventually recognizes them as nonsensical, when he has used them as steps to climb up beyond them. (He must, so to speak throw away the ladder after he has climbed up on it)."[23] According to Ricketts:

> When we throw away the ladder, we give up the attempts to state what this conception of representation and truth demands of

19. Wittgenstein, *TLP*, 2.1512.
20. Ricketts, "Pictures, Logic, and the Limits of Sense," 75.
21. Wittgenstein, *TLP*, 3.1431.
22. Wittgenstein, *TLP*, 3.
23. Wittgenstein, *TLP*, 6.54.

> language and the world, give up trying to operate at an illusory level of generality, without however rejecting the conception of truth as agreement with reality. Rather we understand what this conception comes to, when we appreciate how what can be said clearly, when we appreciate the standard of clarity set by the general form of sentences.[24]

Therefore, Wittgenstein has taken us up the ladder and has kicked it out from under us. He has offered this advice, "What we cannot speak about, we must pass over in silence."[25] A problem arises, however, when such silence confronts the complexity of life. What happens when the ladder is pulled up in the face of the complexity of life is the occasion for what is usually called the "Later Wittgenstein."

Wittgenstein begins *Philosophical Investigations* with a critique of Augustine's understanding of language. He quotes Augustine and then says, "In this picture of language, we find the roots of the following idea: Every word has meaning. This meaning is correlated with the word. It is the object for which the word stands. Augustine does not speak of any difference between kinds of words" (PI 1). The view that Wittgenstein is looking at here is similar to the general propositional form, which he espouses in the *Tractatus*. Here, it becomes an example of the general way in which language is oversimplified and meaning obscured. This, in turn, leads to idealized and, finally, false pictures. As Marie McGinn says, "The tendency to take a narrow, over-simplified view of the phenomenon of language is thereby combined with a tendency to idealize or mythologize it, which arises in connection with our desire to provide a clear model that explains how it functions."[26] Wittgenstein suggests that "Augustine . . . does describe a system of communication, only not everything that we call language is this system."[27] The basic problem that Wittgenstein sees is that language is not about communicating "thoughts and wishes" which come from within, it is more like "a tool within a particular activity . . . where the point of using language is not to convey our state of mind, but to bring about a certain sort of response."[28] It is this critique of Augustine's *primitive* language that leads Wittgenstein to the *whole* language. He says, "We can also think of the whole process of using words . . . as

24. Ricketts, "Pictures, Logic, and the Limits of Sense," 94.

25. Wittgenstein, *TLP*, 7

26. McGinn, *Wittgenstein and the Philosophical Investigations*, 39.

27. Wittgenstein, *PI*, 3.

28. McGinn, *Wittgenstein and the Philosophical Investigations*, 40.

one of those games utilizing which children learn their native language. I will call these games 'language-games.'"[29] This suggests a new turn in Wittgenstein's conception of meaning, which we need to investigate.

Four interlaced ideas converge in Wittgenstein's mature philosophy in response to the problem he addressed in Augustine's understanding of language: language games, forms of life, family resemblance, and grammar. The sheer quantity that has been written on these ideas makes it clear that they are crucial to understanding Wittgenstein; it also suggests that it is not possible within the constraints of this chapter to fully address their nuances. There is, however, a thread that goes through all the discussion—activity. Wittgenstein comments on the meaning of language games, which is a term "meant to bring into prominence the fact that the speaking of language is part of an activity or a form of life."[30] Language is part of what we do, how we act, and the life which defines us. The idea of a language game is linked with "forms of life" and "family resemblance." These ideas remind us of the multiplicity of language games, which must keep clarity in view (PI 24). Wittgenstein says, "to imagine a language is to imagine a form of life" (PI 19). He also says, "What belongs to a language game is a whole culture" (C 26). Glock says, "A form of life is a culture or social formation, the totality of communal activities into which language-games are embedded."[31] This represents a significant shift in Wittgenstein's thought from seeing language in terms of "object" and "logical space" to "shifting patterns of communal activity."[32] According to McGinn "the structure and function of language are inextricably linked with the structure and function of the complex activities in which its use is embedded."[33]

The idea of forms of life is linked to a very interesting comment in the *Investigations*, "If a lion could talk, we could not understand him."[34] Wittgenstein is suggesting that thinking of language as an abstract enterprise associated with learning words in a dictionary is a hollow version of language and meaning. Using his example, a lion who could learn our words would still not be able to communicate with us, because we would not share a culture. It is not the dictionary, it is the culture that is crucial.

29. Wittgenstein, *PI*, 7.
30. Wittgenstein, *PI*, 23.
31. Glock, *Wittgenstein Dictionary*, 125.
32. Glock, *Wittgenstein Dictionary*, 125.
33. McGinn, *Wittgenstein and the Philosophical Investigations*, 59.
34. Wittgenstein, *PI*, 223.

Wittgenstein says, "Our mistake is to look for an explanation where we ought to look at what happens as a 'proto-phenomenon.' That is, where we ought to have said: this language is played."[35]

The other thread that runs through the idea of language games is family resemblance. This begins to address the question of how language games are connected. The concept of family resemblance is the path consciously chosen to stress how particularity is preserved, even when some likeness is evident. He suggests that language arises from a complex set of games/forms of life.[36] Once again Wittgenstein is determined to avoid a "paper" universal by suggesting that meaning emerges out of the way we are in the world.

Language games, life forms, and family resemblance suggest that meaning is not about the clarity with which the world is depicted or the rigor of its formal characteristics. Instead, meaning is an expression of the activities that comprise it. In other words, meaning is the visible expression of life, the intertwining of culture and language. All these ideas form the fabric from which the notion of grammar emerges. He says, "Essence is expressed by grammar" (PI 371). Further, "Grammar tells us what kind of object anything is" (PI 373). According to Newton Garver, "It is nonetheless the case that for the last twenty years of his life, the years of his greatest productivity and his most profound work, Wittgenstein identified what he was doing and should be doing, with grammar."[37]

Wittgenstein says, "Every sign by itself seems dead. What gives it life?—In use it is alive. Is life breathed into it there?—Or is the use its life?" (PI 432). Therefore, "One cannot guess how a word functions. One has to look at its use and learn from that" (PI 340). Wittgenstein uses grammar to express the conviction that meaning is use. The general concept of meaning is embedded in the forms of life, the activities which comprise life. Wittgenstein also talks about grammar as rule-following or obeying a rule. He says, "To understand a sentence means to understand a language. To understand a language means to master a technique" (PI 199). This suggests that life is learning in struggle. Hauerwas discusses this, and his comments are suggestive of the meaning of mastering a technique. He says, "To be a person of virtue involves acquiring the linguistic, emotional, and rational skills that give us the strength to make

35. Wittgenstein, *PI*, 654.

36. Wittgenstein, *PI*, 67.

37. Garver, "Philosophy as Grammar," 139.

decisions and our life our own."[38] It seems clear from this analysis that mastering a technique is about living amid things. Wittgenstein adds, "And hence also 'obeying a rule' is a practice. And to think one obeys a rule is not to obey one. Hence, it is impossible to obey a rule privately; otherwise, thinking one was obeying a rule would be the same thing as obeying it."[39] Rule following is about the practices that comprise life; it suggests a public dimension.

Since Wittgenstein is engaged in a general investigation of meaning through an examination of language, his interest in grammar is understandable. Glock sees this emphasis upon a rule-guided activity as crucial to "the link between language, meaning, and rules."[40] This also makes the point that meaning as it is linked to an activity helps us to go on. He says, "He finds the series 4, 6, 8, 10 and says: Now I can go on."[41] This means that understanding arises out of the forms of life, that it is about an activity. Wittgenstein says, "The grammar of a language isn't recorded and doesn't come into existence until the language has already been spoken by human beings for a long time . . . primitive games are played without their rules being codified, and even without a single rule being formulated."[42] We tend to think of language as hanging out there, as something we find and learn. According to Wittgenstein, this is too simple and does not correspond to how we learn. Before we ever say a word, we are a part of a culture that forms our life and from which we speak. We are first a part of a form of life, that is to say, grammar, then we "go on." This concept links all the central ideas together. And it is a total fabric that begins to express a theory of how things are meaningful.

Wittgenstein says, "I want to say the place of a word in grammar is its meaning . . . The explanation of the meaning explains the use of the word. Grammar describes the use of words in the language."[43] Especially toward the end of his life, he looked for grammatical differences, such as differences in how language is used. This allowed him to see that different activities comprise life, and so do different grammars. In understanding these different grammars, we will know what things mean. A grammatical investigation examines how the activities, forms of life, and language

38. Hauerwas, *Community of Character*, 115.

39. Wittgenstein, *PI*, 202.

40. Glock, *Wittgenstein Dictionary*, 151.

41. Wittgenstein, *PI*, 151.

42. Wittgenstein, *PG*, 25.

43. Wittgenstein, *PG*, 59–60.

games clue us into meaning. We will apply this to the *Plain Account* in the next section.

A PLAIN ACCOUNT OF CHRISTIAN PERFECTION: A GRAMMATICAL INVESTIGATION

Christian perfection lies at the heart of the identity of Wesleyanism. It was Wesley's conviction that God had raised up the Methodists to proclaim this grand biblical truth. Its centrality is evident in the volume and fervor of theological reflection within the Methodist family related to Christian perfection. Yet, it is clear, both in Wesley's writings and in those that have followed, that a fully satisfying explanation of this doctrine has been elusive. It is possible to point to some changes or adjustments in Wesley's understanding through the years.[44] William Greathouse says, "Wesley's fully developed doctrine is outlined in his *A Plain Account of Christian Perfection*, which appeared in 1766. Its fourth edition, in 1777, remained Wesley's definitive statement of his position."[45] It is here that Wesley describes his attempt to set forth "a plain and distinct account of the steps by which I was led, during many years, to embrace the doctrine of Christian Perfection."[46] The purpose of this section is to attempt a grammatical investigation of the *Plain Account* as part of reconstructing it.

A grammatical investigation, in the sense that Wittgenstein used it, will require that we look for how Christian perfection is used—that is, what forms of life give it energy. When we do this, two things will happen: first, we will understand, and second, we will be able to go on. Wittgenstein says, "But there is also this use of the word 'to know': we say, 'Now I know it!'—and similarly 'Now I can do it!' and 'Now I understand'" (PI 151)! Understanding is the result of a "grammatical investigation." The point that he wants to make is that understanding is more than getting hold of a formula. He says, "Try not to think of understanding as a 'mental process' at all. For that is the expression which confuses you. But ask yourself: in what sort of case, in what kind of circumstances, do you say, 'Now I know how to go on,' when, that is, the formula has occurred to me."[47] I hope that a grammatical investigation of Christian perfection will

44. These shifts or adjustments are reviewed by Maddox, *Responsible Grace*, 180–87.

45. Bassett and Greathouse, *Historical Development*, 205.

46. Wesley, "Plain Account of Christian Perfection," 366.

47. Wittgenstein, *PI*, 154.

help us to understand so we can go on. This means that understanding Christian perfection is not purely a matter of thinking but of life; it is embedded in the forms of life. Therefore, the following paragraphs will not be to reconsider the theological development of the doctrine of Christian perfection. I will look at what Wesley said in the *Plain Account* through the lens of a grammatical investigation as conceived of by Wittgenstein and then to ask what theological importance this analysis suggests.

John Wesley offers a straightforward answer to the question: What is Christian perfection? He says, "The loving of God with all our heart, mind, soul, and strength. This implies, that no wrong temper, non-contrary to love, remains in the soul; and that all the thoughts, words, and actions are governed by pure love."[48] The clarity of this answer is dependent on the connection one makes between "loving God with all our heart" and "no wrong temper." John Cobb illustrates the usual path taken in our attempt to understand what Wesley means. He interprets this to mean "love has its way . . . There is no competing motive."[49] Yet, this merely says something similar; it says it again. We could add to this any number of other attempts to restate this definition. Wesley himself offers his clarification when he explains that when people love God, they have "one desire . . . one delight, and they are continually happy in him."[50] Much of the *Plain Account* attempts to clarify the meaning of the basic understanding of Christian perfection. We are left to ponder what Wesley means by "all the thoughts, words, and actions are governed by pure love?" Does this adequately describe the way people experience God's perfecting grace? Is this how people "go on"? Does such a consideration even matter once we have established a scriptural explanation? Maddox offers a clarification by referring to Wesley's understanding of affection. He suggests that Wesley identifies "will" and "affections."[51] Getting at precisely what this love is all about is complicated by how it is usually approached. The most available way is to go to the Scripture, as a "sort of" dictionary of faith, and determine what love means.[52] How is love to be defined? Once we have chosen this, we present it as the "ideal of holiness." The point seems

48. Wesley, "Plain Account of Christian Perfection," 394.

49. Cobb, *Grace and Responsibility*, 108.

50. Wesley, "Plain Account of Christian Perfection," 418.

51. Maddox, *Responsible Grace*, 184.

52. Frank Carver suggests what he calls a "holiness hermeneutic," which he thinks is more "theologically wholistic rather than psychologically analytic" (Carver, "Biblical Foundations," 12).

to be that theological understanding is a matter of linking our words with transcendental references. Then, holiness is "love having its way," "heart purity," or other terms.[53] Understanding holiness is a matter of finding a definitive metaphor. Those who search for such a metaphor are left to the process of linking Scripture with the Christian tradition in a persuasive manner. The problem is that we can never entirely agree on which term to use.

A grammatical investigation may open another pathway to understanding. If we have difficulty locating a metaphor, we might look instead at how the term is used in Christian practice. We look to the dynamic of the lives of the saints and the community touched by the preaching of the gospel and the power of the Spirit to determine the meaning of Christian perfection. How are Christians made perfect? Using Wittgenstein's method, we understand when we see circumstances. In other words, understanding is not merging the picture of the Scripture with the image of the person who is seeking. Christian perfection is defined by understanding what happens in the lives of the redeemed, as those who have accepted the gracious offer of the gospel. Christian perfection is discovered in the community dynamic shaped by the gospel story. In this story, we hear of a God seeking a personal relationship with all humans. Christian perfection is engendered not by carefully delineating a place that secures its meaningfulness and truthfulness but by establishing practices and habits that help us to go on. When we understand, we know how to go on because we have been found in the gospel, we are encouraged by the saints and made accountable by the habits and practices of the church. All of this is dependent upon a God who continually offers himself to us. It is to the extent that our habits and practices are reflective of this dynamic that they help to establish Christian perfection.

Doing a grammatical investigation of Wesley's basic definition of Christian perfection requires that we look at how the activities of the Christian life define love. It seems that Wesley does this very thing in the *Plain Account* because just as he talks about love, he describes it in the context of a form of life (a way of being) that is characterized by "no wrong temper." He also says that Christian perfection is "love filling the heart, expelling pride, anger, desire, self-will; rejoicing evermore, praying without ceasing, and in everything giving thanks."[54] Therefore, we can

53. Grider, *Wesleyan-Holiness Theology*, 367–78.

54. Wesley, "Plain Account of Christian Perfection,"418.

conclude that, as Wesley understands it, love is defined as a form of life characterized by a reorientation of affection. Wesley clarifies that he does not see any reason in Christian life, as it is lived by the faithful, to believe that this love makes one flawlessly perfect. When we look at Christian perfection the way Wesley does, it becomes clear that flawlessness is the wrong standard to define the doctrine. In fact, "the most perfect do, on this very account, need the blood of atonement, and may properly for themselves and their brethren, say, 'Forgive us our trespasses.'"[55] This is how Wesley qualifies what he means by perfection, not some flawless standard, but a reorientation of life by a holy love. What is essential for our purposes is that we see him looking at the form of life that arises out of the gospel to understand the meaning of perfection. Wesley says:

> If I were convinced that none in England had attained what has been so clearly and powerfully preached by such a number of Preachers, in so many places, and for so long a time, I should be clearly convinced that we had all mistaken the meaning of those scriptures.[56]

The insight of this comment must not be passed over. Wesley is courageously interpreting the Scripture through the forms of life which emerge from it. Wesley "understands" or interprets the Scripture and shapes doctrine by pressing the issue of how people "go on." A grammatical investigation frees us to see the extent to which Christian perfection is understood by the way it is evident in the lives of those who are shaped by the preaching of the Scripture, which is God's call to healthy relationships.

One way to understand Christian perfection is "expelling love." This way of expressing the doctrine reminds us that it is an affection that begins to exclude other less worthy interests. It also suggests that we should look at the full texture of a life being redeemed through the grace of God. Yet, it is easy to reduce the fullness of this doctrine to one or two concerns, such as perfection or intentions. Wesley faced this in four distinct ways in the *Plain Account*. These four fronts are indicated by the types of questions that Wesley raised. The first of these we have already addressed is, what does perfection mean? The other fronts are: "What does it mean to talk about purity of intention?" "What does it mean to say we are delivered from sin?" And "How can Christian perfection be understood

55. Wesley, "Plain Account of Christian Perfection,"419.

56. Wesley, "Plain Account of Christian Perfection," 406.

as instantaneous?" These questions can become temptations to qualify the meaning of Christian perfection, thereby losing its significance in the process. Yet, if we do a grammatical investigation of these questions, we will be able to more adequately respond and, at the same time, preserve the meaning of Christian perfection. I will illustrate my thesis by looking at one of these fronts—instantaneousness.

When we look at how Wesley treated the issue of instantaneousness in the *Plain Account*, it becomes clear that the point of time is not the real issue. The only way to make sense of his discussion is to understand that Christian perfection arises in the context of the call of God through scriptural preaching in the Christian community.[57] There are many ways in which an understanding of Christian perfection can be clouded. One of those ways is to become lost in a discussion regarding the "instant" one receives it. For example, this happens when we study the tenses in the New Testament or search for metaphors like circumcision and baptism to prove that "it" happens in an instant. When this happens, the meaning of Christian perfection, at least as Wesley taught it, is lost. Another mistaken course is the attempt to locate the psychological conditions and effects of the experience of Christian perfection. When this is done, the idea of attitude or our attitude about our attitude becomes the focus. A grammatical investigation of Christian perfection is a much better approach because it allows us to see it in its native form. After all, who would deny that when the Scripture is preached in a faith community, that character is shaped toward the love of God and neighbor? Who would deny that a reorientation occasioned by faith would be a gift offered by God to his children and not the product of reasonable discipline? Understood in this way, one misses the point when the discussion hinges upon "when" because the plain account of things is how all of this arises in the forms of life associated with scriptural preaching and the Christian community. In other words, if one is inclined to argue for Christian perfection as instantaneous, the best way to do this is to focus on the story which engenders it.

57. Wesley, "Plain Account of Christian Perfection," 444–45.

CHRISTIAN POLITY: "ANOTHER" ACCOUNT OF CHRISTIAN PERFECTION

This paper began by indicating that there is a problem, a philosophical problem, that has to do with how our words and language can capture us. This problem is intertwined with every informed discussion of Christian perfection throughout the Methodist family.[58] One symptom of this problem can be found in the language that embodies our holiness theology. Wittgenstein's theory of meaning, the way he understands language, may help to free us for a more productive understanding of Christian perfection. Such an understanding will avoid the doctrine of parochialism or lazy generality. A careful examination of his later philosophy might help us see how our language is embedded in life forms. These activities comprise the community being renewed by the Holy Spirit. Further, we suggested that a grammatical investigation of the doctrine of Christian perfection avoids the pitfalls that often cloud the appropriate understanding of the doctrine. Our final step is to set out the parameters for a comprehensive understanding of Christian perfection.

A fully adequate, or at least a more complete, statement of Christian perfection is a task of systematic theology. The reconstruction of Christian perfection will begin with a name change to Christian polity. This change will help to keep the idea that we are talking about—a mutually engendered grace—clearly in view. Such a change will remind us that Christians appropriate this grace or reach maturity in the community as God intended. Polity is a better word than perfection because it is a word that reminds us of our need for one another in the process of coming to maturity. A word of clarification here is essential. The talk about maturity is always understood in terms of process. There is no time when our growth in grace ends, but there is a time when a new and qualitatively different relationality becomes evident.

Aristotle developed the idea of polity in *Politics*, where he talks about the fundamental political nature of humankind. He says further that we form associations to achieve certain goods that are not possible apart from these associations. Aristotle talks about three associations: family, village, and state. Each association is improved and, simultaneously, dependent upon the one above it because the next association achieves a good that is impossible for the one below it. The next level is more mature, that is, more complex or adequate in facing life's challenges. Maddox reminds

58. Outler, *Evangelism and Theology*, 118.

us that Wesley's most characteristic description of Christian perfection is "adult-mature Christians."[59] I am suggesting that a name change will serve as a vehicle to continually remind us that as mature (and maturing) Christians, we are more aware of our mutuality (both with others and God) and as such are better able to live in light of this grace. Hauerwas says, "Any community and polity is known and should be judged by the kind of people it develops. The truest politics, therefore, is that concerned with the development of virtue."[60] He sees this, as we should, in the fabric of a story-formed people.

Christian polity is characterized by a healthy relationship with God that opens us up toward others, world, and self. H. Ray Dunning calls attention to this by referring to shalom, which is "harmony of an individual with himself."[61] He goes on to talk about the "complete openness" that characterizes the "restored relationship to God."[62] This healthy relationship reorients our lives. The opposite of this is ill-health or sin, which subverts our life by alienation and bondage. Therefore, we have two images: one characterized by freedom, mutuality, and health; the other by bondage, alienation, and ill health. This relationship described above is shaped by a grace that opens the world to us through God's love, guiding our lives together. This is the sense in which we are swallowed by a grand story that, through the power of the Spirit, transforms our lives. This happens personally, but it is never distinct from a larger picture engendered by the community of incarnation, the church. We will discuss this further later, but it is essential to recognize that this "restored relationship" is indeed a relationship. As such, it must be understood in consideration of the community that engenders it. The church embodies Christian polity, a community that continues to tell the story of grace, as the very story constitutes it. This illustrates how Scripture operates within the community of incarnation. This leads to the following characteristic of Christian polity: interdependence. We have already suggested that Christian polity is characterized by health and grace, which reminds us of the mature Christianity described by Wesley.

This leads us to see that we are created in the image of God and, as such, are created as being with a God who is Father, Son, and Holy Spirit. Therefore, Christian polity is described as that grace of God which comes

59. Maddox, *Responsible Grace*, 187.

60. Hauerwas, *Community of Character*, 2.

61. Dunning, *Grace, Faith, and Holiness*, 486.

62. Dunning, *Grace, Faith, and Holiness*, 490.

to rest upon our life in communion with God and others in the world and, as such, brings us to ourselves a situation of health.

The final characteristic that I want to discuss is happiness. Here, I mean to suggest that Christian polity is evident in the happiness or congruence that it produces in one's life. Outler suggests that Wesley was an "eudaemonist . . . all his emphasis upon duty and discipline are auxiliary to his main concern from human happiness."[63] Christian polity creates a happy life that is healthy in its relationships, empowered and envisioned by grace, and aware of its deep interdependence. Christian polity in its reconstructed form is the Wesleyan idea that expresses the Christian hope for life that it will mature by the grace of God through an appreciation of our mutual relationships in the church and be characterized by happiness.

Unsurprisingly, Christian polity assumes that the church will play an essential role in the Christian life. Wesley advises the "greatest professors in the Methodist societies"[64] in the *Plain Account*. These are intended to suggest ways in which the style of life engendered by the grace of God can be more surely maintained. The sixth piece of advice of the seven offered in the *Plain Account* links our idea of Christian polity to the church, "Beware of schism, of making rent in the Church of Christ. That inward disunion, the members ceasing to have a reciprocal love, one for another (1 Cor. xii. 25), is the root of all contention and every outward separation. Beware of everything tending thereto."[65] From this point, he gives warnings and admonitions toward which one can more effectively profit from the church. How does the church become a part of the process of Christian polity? Seeing Christian polity considering the church's practices will be necessary. First, it teaches the virtues of the Christian life. This is not easy, and it is not always greeted with joy, but it is the business of the church to set these virtues forth. This requires that the story of God's grace be told repeatedly to each new generation. Hauerwas observes, "Rather I will try to show how an analysis of virtue turns on an understanding of human nature as historical and why, therefore, any account of virtue involves the particular traditions and history of a society."[66] And it is hoped that long before the words are fully understood that the young and the "young-again" will see them in the lives of the

63. Outler, *Evangelism and Theology*, 127.

64. Wesley, "Plain Account of Christian Perfection," 427.

65. Wesley, "Plain Account of Christian Perfection," 433.

66. Hauerwas, *Community of Character*, 112.

mature Christians. In this way, virtues will be taught as they are lived. James McClendon says, "The character we investigate in a biographical study is always character-in-community."[67] The teaching that the church is called to do will come in many ways, not just the formal teaching in the classroom, but in the lives of those who are "going on" toward maturity as it is empowered and envisioned by the Holy Spirit. This suggests the crucial role of understanding our tradition. In fact, ignorance of our tradition diminishes our self-awareness and reduces our capacity for maturity.

A second way the church becomes vital in the process of Christian polity is to engender social grace. Maddox develops this idea: "The point that I want to make . . . is that Wesley's ecclesiological interconnection of intentional small groups (*ecclesiolea*) and the worship of the larger church (*ecclesia*) is a central aspect of his dynamic conception of the means of grace."[68]

Maddox also talks about this social grace in four dimensions: corporate liturgical worship, mutual encouragement and support, mutual accountability, and presence in the society at large.[69] This is precisely the point that the paper has been attempting to make regarding Christian polity; it is not something we do alone. Instead, it is what we do in that community called into being by the Spirit through preaching the word. Because of this social grace, we need to listen to Wittgenstein's plea that we give attention to natural history, which I take to mean something like Wesley envisioned by urging that we allow Christian perfection to appear in its native form. The tendency of modern understanding of the self makes perfection purely a personal matter. This same movement makes the community so tricky to achieve, a fact that has been analyzed often. Likewise, we in the Methodist family have usually found it irresistible to talk about grace as if it were unrelated to life in the church. A serious reading of Wesley and, for that matter, the Scripture reveals grace as a relational term, first with God and then with all else. As we understand this, we will see that social grace, or Christian polity, is an apt description of how the Holy Spirit completes salvation in us. It suggests that as we are conversing about what matters, God's grace characterizes the maturing process. Therefore, our language becomes the house of our being-in-relation. Understanding this will enhance how we understand the grace of God and, thus, Christian polity.

67. McClendon, *Biography as Theology*, 202.

68. Maddox, "Social Grace." 133.

69. Maddox, "Social Grace," 133–34.

This comes down to the importance of our life together as the body of Christ. We must understand precisely the way the individual and the communal interact. Central to this clarification is the fact that holiness is personal. We each reach that place on our way to "Damascus" as pilgrims. Yet, this is only part of the story, and we are always affected, even shaped, by a culture or increasing cultures. Enlightenment taught us to think individually and to take charge of our lives, but that project has crashed and is burning on the mountainside of history. Therefore, any attempt to construct a holiness theology must include an understanding of the "socially constructed self," a self that is nonetheless a self but a very different self than what the Enlightenment depicted. Christian polity is dependent upon the socially constructed self and it is engendered in community through worship. Such an understanding includes the way we name God and call a world into existence by our habits and practices in worship, a world not of our creation but of the symbiosis of a community of intentionality in response to the gracious movement of God toward humankind.

Here, we see the importance of ritual, a practice that can be understood both in a sacred and a secular sense. After all, many rituals characterize and form our life. For example, handshakes, verbal greetings, meals, ordering of time and space, etc. These are important for a meaningful life. What is true of our life in general is our spiritual existence. It is as we pray that we first learn to think about God. Early in our lives, we are taught to pray, which is how we begin to think about God. Sometimes, these images will follow us through years of formal theological study, a testimony to the power of ritual and prayer. An Old Testament scholar, Paul Hanson, discusses the triadic pattern in his excellent book, *The People Called.*[70] In this book, he suggests that Israel maintained a healthy balance between righteousness and compassion in worship. He extends this thesis to the church. I feel that attention to worship is a key to engendering the Christian polity at the heart of Wesleyanism.

I am attempting to consider the strength of Christian polity in light of the role the church plays in the life of holiness. When the church preaches the virtues of the Christian life, or more appropriately, when it hears the call in its own story, it begins to embody Christian polity. It is the church's business to be that place in the world where social grace characterizes our life together. This brings us to the third aspect

70. Hanson, *People Called.*

of Christian polity, which relates to the church and commends it to us—happiness. Christian polity is consciously chosen for what Wesley discusses as Christian perfection because it suggests a different context for joy. It is generally acknowledged within the Wesleyan tradition that Wesley's theology is teleological. The problem is that such teleology has usually been conceived in a purely personal sense. The very term Christian perfection may be easily interpreted in exclusively personal terms. Christian polity may serve as a reminder that personal perfection cannot be separated from a social context. Indeed, Wesley's understanding is teleological, but our reconstruction needs to see more fully the importance of a community that lives toward the goal. Polity also reminds us that the truth of something can be justified by the kind of person it shapes. Applying this idea to Christian polity suggests its validity is determined by the type of people who emerge from it. The crucial question becomes, what is the character of the people called Methodist, Nazarene, Wesleyan, and all who follow the wisdom of the Wesleys? We could contend forever over what text is most critical to the meaning of Christian polity. There is sufficient evidence to suggest that we often spend time spinning our wheels at whatever "dictionary of faith" is available to us. We could spend time defending a particular tradition within the Methodist family as inherently more biblical or more adequate. But the real question seems to relate to the character of the life that emerges from the gospel call to be holy. This is the final question that must be answered if Christian polity is to survive in a postmodern world. It is my conviction that Christian polity does suggest a happy life, one that is guided continually by the vision of health, grace, and interdependence. Such a life grows out of the narrative of God's grace as it swallows our life.

Outler talks about three central pillars of Wesleyan theology: original sin, justification by faith alone, and holiness of heart and life.[71] These ideas are grounded in soteriology and the practices of the church, which give rise to them. This suggests that Wesleyanism is, through and through, a theological perspective grounded in the saving grace of God. It is because of this that a highly speculative theology edges away from the spirit of Wesleyanism. The gift of Wesley to the church is a theology that intends to engender a redeemed humanity. Therefore, its native home is not epistemological propositions nor continual appeals to make sense to the world. The meaning of Wesleyanism is wrapped up in the Christian

71. Outler, *Evangelism and Theology*, 89.

hope for life, which is nurtured by the grace of God through an appreciation of our mutual relationships in the church, including the graces of the church characterized by happiness. Just as for Wesley, it is true for those who have chosen the Methodist family as home, we have been raised up to live our lives in the vision of the story of Christian polity.

Antony Flew develops a story told by John Wisdom. It tells the story of two explorers, one a skeptic and the other a believer, who stumble upon a well-kept garden in the middle of a jungle. The believer thinks there must be a gardener who comes to tend it, and the skeptic rejects this idea. This leads to the decision to wait for the gardener, but one never arrives. The skeptic concludes that no gardener exists since no one ever comes to take care of the garden. But the believer suggests that the gardener cannot be seen, smelled, or detected in any way at all. Then the skeptic asks, "But what remains of your original assertion?"[72] Perhaps the assertion of the believer has died the death of a thousand qualifications, "so eroded by qualification that it was no longer an assertion at all."[73] I tell this story to say that we must be careful not to allow Christian perfection/polity to die the death of a thousand qualifications.

CONCLUSION

The Wesleyan affirmation of a native form of holiness that comes to characterize a believer's life as a gift of grace in the maturity of faith should not be reduced to an experience. A faithful reconstruction of it will force us to look at the forms of life, the activities that engender a native form of holiness. It will raise the importance of the church, as a community of incarnation, to emerge as that form of life that engenders Christian polity. It will guard against the tendency to rationalize, overly structure, reify in our attempt to qualify and otherwise preserve the doctrine. Perhaps, it might remind us that after all we are part of a great crowd of people who walk together toward a land that God is showing us. We are together because we come to enjoy the grace of God in a way that would remain closed to us otherwise. There can be no assurance on this journey together other than the hope that comes from the presence of God in the community, but "we" are shaped and formed into the image of God by this very hope.

72. Flew and MacIntyre, *New Essays*, 96.

73. Flew and MacIntyre, *New Essays*, 98.

CHAPTER 4

The Apocalyptic Wesley

A Dogmatic Sketch

Henry Walter Spaulding III

Blessed are the pure in heart, for they shall see God.—Matthew 5:8 NRSV

INTRODUCTION

IN THE FIELD OF systematic theology, eschatology is traditionally a much-neglected topic. Eschatology is often treated at the end of any work of systematics. The traditional assumption, with some notable exceptions, is that eschatology comes at the end of our theological reflection. However, in the recent century generally and the past decade specifically, a new emphasis has risen to prominence in the academy, namely apocalyptic theology. This school of thought confesses that in the incarnation, life, death, resurrection, and ascension of Christ, the fallen powers of the world are defeated. This established the Lordship of Christ over all creation and inaugurated a struggle against the powers that will culminate in Christ's eschatological return and renewal of all creation. This movement has reinvigorated eschatological thinking and firmly positioned it at the beginning of all theological knowledge.

John Wesley is not typically recognized as a systematic theologian in the modern academic sense. He never developed a formal system of theology, nor did he attempt to outline Christian doctrine in a rigidly structured framework. Yet this raises a crucial question: can Wesley's theological writings be approached in such a way that allows for a systematic account of eschatology? I argue that Wesley is best understood not as a systematic theologian in the modern mold, but rather as a dogmatic theologian—one who engages ecclesial dogma pastorally and theologically within the lived faith of the church. Specifically, Wesley offers a profound engagement with the dogma of the beatific vision, not as abstract speculation, but as a theological reality interwoven with his doctrine of Christian perfection and shaped by an apocalyptic key.

Apocalyptic theology has arisen primarily within Reformed and Lutheran confessional circles, with its emphasis on divine disruption, unveiled judgment, and the inbreaking of the eschaton. This study explores whether this largely non-Wesleyan theological emphasis can speak meaningfully into a Wesleyan account of eschatology. I contend that it can. Apocalyptic theology offers a corrective to tendencies in Wesleyan thought that render sanctification as a closed, immanent moral process. Instead, by recovering the apocalyptic shape of Christian hope, Wesley's doctrine of perfection can be re-situated within the dogmatic horizon of the beatific vision—a gift that lies beyond human striving, granted by God at the eschatological consummation. Such a dogmatic reading opens Wesley's theology to renewed engagement with classical Christian eschatology and offers a richer, more theocentric rendering of sanctification as participation in divine glory.

DOGMATIC THEOLOGY

Dogmatic theology is not simply a system of doctrines but an ongoing event—a spiritual, historical, and liturgical process in which the church contemplates the mystery of God revealed in Christ. Dogma, in this sense, is not a finalized set of eternal propositions but a lived response to divine revelation, expressed and unfolded through the church's life across time. As theologian Karl Barth notes, Dogmatics is "the self-examination of the Christian Church in respect of the content of its distinctive talk about God," and it presupposes that such talk occurs only in response to God's self-revelation in Christ.[1] For Barth, dogmatics is neither a detached academic exercise nor a mere repetition of established truths. It is, fundamentally, the church's critical self-examination of its talk about God in light of the revelation of Jesus Christ. This means that dogmatics

1. Barth, *Church Dogmatics* I/1, 12.

belongs intrinsically to the church. It is not simply a theological discipline that happens to be Christian, but an act of the church as it seeks to speak truthfully and responsibly in response to God's self-revelation.

Barth insists that theology, and especially dogmatics, emerges because the church knows itself to be fallible in its speech about God. Although the church speaks as a community summoned by grace, it must not presume that its speech is automatically correct. Instead, theology arises from the church's recognition that it "must give an account to God for the way in which it speaks."[2] The word of God is divine speech and the church, in faithful witness, offers an account of that speech in dogmatic theology. Dogmatics, then, is an act of obedience—an effort to bring the church's proclamation into greater conformity with its true source and standard: the person of Jesus Christ. Barth's point is clear: the church's speech about God must always be measured by its own being, which is grounded not in itself but in God's gracious address.

Sergius Bulgakov offers a complementary vision of dogmatics, one deeply rooted in Orthodox theology yet attentive to the Spirit's ongoing activity in history. He argues that dogma is not simply given but *sought*, a product of the church's creative and liturgical life. He writes that dogmatics "must inevitably be supplemented from sources other than the clear and obligatory dogmatic definitions," such as "the living tradition of the Church," doctrinal development, and metaphysical reflection.[3]

Dogma, for Bulgakov, emerges through the prayerful and theological consciousness of the church. It is "not only static in its given character," Bulgakov insists, "but . . . dynamic in its role, or its development."[4] This dynamic character moves believers toward eschatology, not as a final chapter of theology, but as its structuring horizon. Theology must look forward; it must speak from within history but in light of what Bulgakov calls the "fullness of the divine life which is inherent to the Church."[5] The eschatological vision essential to dogmatic theology in general finds its dogmatic expression in what many Christian traditions have called the *beatific vision*, namely the final consummation of divine-human communion in which the faithful "see God." While Bulgakov does not use the Latin phrase *visio beatifica*, his theology of dogmatic development orients itself around this very reality. He insists that theology must be

2. Barth, *Church Dogmatics* I/1, 4.

3. Bulgakov, *Dogma and Dogmatic Theology*, 42.

4. Bulgakov, *Dogma and Dogmatic Theology*, 56.

5. Bulgakov, *Dogma and Dogmatic Theology*, 55.

contemporary, not in the sense of novelty for novelty's sake, but because it must "express religious thought about eternity in time, the supratemporal in the temporal."[6] This requires that theology be liturgical, mystical, and eschatologically open—never closed off to new expressions of truth.

From this perspective, dogma is not simply a repetition of the past, but a spiritual labor carried out "in the element of the eternal," even as it must express itself "in the categories of time."[7] Dogmatics, for Bulgakov, is not a scholastic summary but a form of theological pilgrimage—"on the way," always reaching forward in hope and in thought toward what has not yet been fully seen.

Barth and Bulgakov both understand that dogma is not static content but a dynamic, Spirit-led exploration of the divine mystery. Barth similarly insists that dogmatics is always *on the way*, not because truth is inaccessible, but because human knowledge of God is always mediated through grace, faith, and creaturely limits. Thus, while dogmatics aims at truth, it does so as an act of faith, trusting that in obedience to revelation, theology may speak rightly even in its weakness. "Dogmatics is possible only as an act of faith," Barth writes, "in the determination of human action by listening to Jesus Christ and as obedience to Him."[8] The faithfulness of human action defines not just the content of dogmatics, but also its method. Because theology begins and ends in obedient hearing, its standards cannot be borrowed wholesale from other disciplines.

As such, dogmatics is not a neutral science in the modern sense. It cannot be judged by the standards of coherence, verifiability, or rational neutrality demanded by contemporary scientific disciplines. Barth explicitly denies that theology must conform to a general concept of science. Instead, theology becomes a "science" only insofar as it remains faithful to its own object and method—namely, God's revelation in Jesus Christ. In this sense, dogmatics is "scientific" not because it follows universal laws of reason, but because it follows the logic of grace, engaging in disciplined inquiry grounded in faith, Scripture, and the church's being.

In harmony with Bulgakov's emphasis on theology as doxological and liturgical, Barth also insists that dogmatics is never an autonomous or purely rational task. It is undertaken in prayerful dependence on God's continuing self-revelation and in expectation of the Spirit's illumination. As Barth emphasizes, it is only within the context of the church's

6. Bulgakov, *Dogma and Dogmatic Theology*, 58.

7. Bulgakov, *Dogma and Dogmatic Theology*, 45.

8. Barth, *Church Dogmatics* I/1, 18.

obedience and hope that theology can become what it is called to be: a human witness to divine truth. Both Barth and Bulgakov, from their distinct traditions, affirm that theology is not speculation but a form of faithfulness—rooted in the church, reaching toward God, and animated by the living presence of Christ.

Barth shares the eschatological drama of dogma. Barth presents a similar tension between the givenness of God's revelation in Christ and the unfinished character of theology's grasp of it. For Barth, the word of God is the reality of God's continued speech and act of revelation. Barth's emphasis on revelation as event means that all theological language is responsive, summoned into being by the word of God. Theology cannot capture God in concepts; it can only confess the grace by which God has spoken. In this way, Barth too insists that dogmatics must be undertaken with humility and urgency, as Bulgakov would say, "with the full strength of creative daring."[9] Such urgency stems from a deep awareness that theology, if unmoored from its living source, can easily mistake its language for its object.

Both thinkers reject the tendency to confuse theological formulations with the fullness of truth. Bulgakov warns that much of modern theology, especially in its polemical forms, creates what he calls "illusory dogmas or quasi dogmas" which "are mistaken for ready dogmas."[10] These arise not from contemplation but from reaction—from theology reduced to confessional correctness or ideological defense. Barth issues similar warnings against treating theology as an abstract science, rather than as the church's continual re-hearing of the word of God.

Therefore, in both Barth and Bulgakov, dogma points beyond itself. It is the language of faith spoken in the direction of the God who is coming. Its task is not to master divine truth, but to bear witness to it—and, ultimately, to prepare the church for communion with the One who is its final end. In Bulgakov's terms, this means that theology must arise from the "charismatic life" of the church and must be shaped by its "prayerful inspiration and revelation."[11]

9. Bulgakov, *Dogma and Dogmatic Theology*, 57.
10. Bulgakov, *Dogma and Dogmatic Theology*, 52.
11. Bulgakov, *Dogma and Dogmatic Theology*, 45.

WESLEY AND DOGMATIC THEOLOGY

John Wesley was not a dogmatic theologian, but to say that he did not engage in a theological method similar to the one outlined by Barth and Bulgakov would be a stretch. Wesley's theological vision, particularly as retrieved by Randy Maddox, offers a dogmatic framework that resonates with and responds to both Karl Barth's account of dogmatics and Sergius Bulgakov's mystical ecclesiology.[12] At the heart of Wesley's theology is the conviction that salvation is neither solely a divine monergism nor a human achievement, but a cooperative process grounded in grace and embodied in the life of the church. As Maddox emphasizes, Wesley understands divine grace as *responsible* grace, namely grace that not only precedes and enables human response but also holds humanity accountable for that response.[13] This dynamic interplay of divine initiative and human participation provides a distinctive theological grammar for engaging in dogmatic reflection. For Wesley, theology is not primarily a speculative science but a practical discipline rooted in the church's mission of forming faithful, holy lives.[14]

This practical orientation does not exclude Wesley from the dogmatic tradition; rather, it locates dogmatics precisely within the living reality of ecclesial existence. Wesley's sermons, hymns, and liturgical practices are themselves theological performances—ecclesial acts of speech shaped by Scripture, tradition, reason, and experience. In this way, Wesley anticipates Bulgakov's claim that theology arises from the "charismatic life" of the church and must be shaped by its "prayerful inspiration and revelation."[15] For Wesley, theological reflection is always inseparable from the Spirit's sanctifying presence in the community of faith. The church, in Wesley's view, is not simply a recipient of theological truths but the living context in which grace is encountered, doctrine is discerned, and discipleship is cultivated.

Moreover, Wesley's account of grace and salvation bears a striking resemblance to Barth's claim that theology must be a response to God's revelation in Jesus Christ. While Wesley does not frame his theology in Barth's Christocentric idiom, his emphasis on prevenient grace reflects a deep conviction that all true knowledge of God begins in divine

12. Maddox, "Responsible Grace."

13. Maddox, "Responsible Grace," 12–13, 15–16.

14. Maddox, "Responsible Grace," 8–9.

15. Maddox, "Responsible Grace," 16–17.

initiative. As Wesley writes, "There is no power in man, till it is given him from above," and yet this gift of grace does not negate human agency but calls it forth in gratitude and obedience.[16] Theology, then, is not a neutral exercise in rational coherence but a response to God's address—a labor undertaken in the fear of God, as an act of faithful obedience. This harmonizes with Barth's insistence that dogmatics is possible only as an act of faith, and that it must proceed under the authority of God's self-revelation rather than the methodological constraints of modern scientific rationalism.

In Wesley's framework, then, theology is shaped by the eschatological horizon of sanctification—the goal of being made perfect in love. This teleological vision provides dogmatics with its proper orientation: not toward the closure of doctrinal systems but toward the transformation of the church into the image of Christ. This is where Wesley most clearly aligns with Bulgakov's eschatological mysticism. Wesley's understanding of salvation is not merely juridical or forensic but ontological and participatory; it involves a real change in the believer wrought by the Spirit through means of grace, communal accountability, and liturgical formation. Theology, in this context, serves the church's journey toward beatific communion with God. It is not the possession of truth but participation in it.

Thus, to read Wesley through a dogmatic lens is not to force him into a scholastic mold he resisted, but to recognize the systematic coherence and spiritual depth that animate his practical theology. Wesley's vision of responsible grace offers a rich and distinct contribution to the church's dogmatic task—one that is responsive to Barth's call for obedient speech and Bulgakov's plea for theology to arise from the liturgical and mystical life of the church. In Wesley, we find a dogmatics not of abstract propositions, but of grace-infused formation, shaped by Christ, empowered by the Spirit, and oriented toward the glory of God.

DOGMATIC THEOLOGY AND FINAL ENDS

Such a theology is inherently oriented toward what lies ahead—it not only remembers the past but leans forward in hopeful discernment. As such, the dogmatic question before us concerns final ends, namely, eschatology. As Barth insists, dogmatics must constantly keep exegetical

16. Wesley, "Sermon 53."

theology in view. Throughout Scripture, vision of God is a constant desire of creatures, but these desires hardly provide a comprehensive picture of our final ends. Vision of God, namely the beatific vision, is an essential dogmatic account of the fulfillment of God. As Bulgakov contends, theology must not only systematize truths but must be "directed toward the contemplation of divine glory," which finds its consummation in the beatific vision.[17]

Utilizing the recent work of Hans Boersma, there are three key Scriptural reasons that vision is essential to a dogmatic account of our final ends. First, vision—namely, sight of God—is a key metaphor in Scripture. In the final two chapters of the New Testament, for example, several passages point to the light of God's glory that gives light to the New Jerusalem (Rev 21:23–24). Directly after this, John even explicitly appeals to the beatific vision: "And they will see his face, and his name will be on their foreheads" (Rev 22:4 DBH).[18] In addition, the overwhelming impression of the New Jerusalem as radiant with golden streets and "transparent glass" (Rev 21:21 DBH) reinforces the centrality of seeing God as a telos of Christian life.

For Bulgakov, this eschatological dimension of dogma is not a supplement to theology but its very core. Dogma is not only a symbol of truth but a mystery pointing beyond itself. This means that every dogmatic affirmation must point toward the ineffable, toward that vision of God in which the church and the world will be transfigured in light. In short, dogma is both the articulation and the anticipation of God's self-disclosure.

Second, vision is given priority over other senses in Scripture. Paul argues that our present state is "by way of a mirror, in an enigma, but then [we shall see] face to face" (1 Cor 13:12 DBH). Paul prioritizes vision as a means to fulfill knowledge and as a final end of faith, hope, and love. In the present, signs (sacraments) mediate and help us see and hear God. Yet, as Boersma and Bulgakov both suggest, these mediations direct us toward a final encounter—where the form is no longer mediated but fully revealed in the person of Christ. The beatific vision is not the possession of truth, but being possessed by it.

Finally, the beatific vision requires a movement of transfiguration—a dogmatics of becoming rather than mere knowing. Theology must be

17. Bulgakov, *Dogma and Dogmatic Theology*, 38.

18. Any Scripture citation marked DBH is from David Bentley Hart's translation of the New Testament (see Hart, *New Testament*).

eschatological because it is liturgical: it prepares the soul for the final doxology of seeing God. In this sense, dogma prepares the church not just to speak about God, but to receive the vision of God that completes all theology.

In summary, to speak dogmatically is not to presume the full possession of divine truth, as though theology could exhaust the mystery of God through conceptual mastery. Rather, to engage in dogmatic theology is to participate—humbly and obediently—in the church's ongoing contemplation of the divine mystery as it has been revealed in Jesus Christ. Dogma, in this sense, is not a terminus but a signpost; it points beyond itself to the ineffable reality of God, always drawing the church deeper into the mystery it confesses but cannot fully comprehend. To speak dogmatically, then, is to speak in faith—not with the presumption of final knowledge, but with trust in the One who has made himself known and continues to be known in the life, worship, and mission of the church.

Dogma is always ordered toward vision. It does not seek to capture God in propositions but to attune the church's language, imagination, and practice to the beatific reality toward which it journeys. In this sense, dogma anticipates its own fulfillment not in the clarity of human articulation but in the eschatological unveiling of God's glory. It is provisional speech rooted in promise—speech that bears witness to a future that has already broken into the present through the life, death, and resurrection of Christ. That future, which the church names as the beatific vision, lies beyond the reach of language but not beyond the reach of faith. In faith, the church dares to speak, knowing that its words are upheld not by their precision but by the grace of the One who calls it to see, to know, and to love. Thus, dogmatics is a discipline of hope—hope that what we now know in part will one day be known fully, even as we are fully known.

The dogmatic work inherent in eschatology, then, is a movement into proper sight and specifically sight of God. Therefore, our theological exploration of the dogma of final things in a Wesleyan spirit must consider how Wesley contributes to such a discussion. I believe that Wesley has much to offer dogmatic theology and especially on Boersma's final dogmatic perspective, namely the movement from speech to vision.

PAUL'S APOCALYPTIC THEOLOGY: THE ALREADY AND THE NOT YET

To speak dogmatically, as we have seen, is not to claim final possession of divine truth but to participate in the church's unfolding and faithful contemplation of the mystery of God. Dogma functions as a provisional, yet Spirit-breathed response to divine revelation—a confession that points beyond itself toward a reality it cannot fully contain. In this sense, dogma is always eschatologically oriented. It speaks in hope, not closure. It is ordered toward vision—toward the beatific encounter with God in which faith will become sight. Karl Barth reminds us that dogmatic theology is always speech under judgment and grace, an act of obedience to the revelation of Jesus Christ, rather than a human mastery of sacred truth. Likewise, Sergius Bulgakov emphasizes that dogma emerges from the charismatic and liturgical life of the church—it is the Spirit-bearing word that prepares the church for her transfiguration in divine light. For John Wesley, as interpreted by Maddox, this unfolding movement is governed by *responsible grace*, in which God's initiative summons and empowers human response, leading the church not only into holiness but into ever-deepening communion with God.

Into this theological framework, Pauline apocalypticism offers an essential deepening. It names the crisis, rupture, and unveiling that stand at the heart of the Christian confession. In Paul's epistles—especially Romans, Galatians, and 2 Corinthians—revelation is not information about God but the apocalypse of God in Christ: a disruptive inbreaking that reconstitutes all human knowing, judging, and speaking. "Paul's apocalyptic theology," as Pauline scholar Beverly Roberts Gaventa understands,

> has to do with the conviction that in the death and resurrection of Jesus Christ, God has invaded the world as it is, thereby revealing the world's utter distortion and foolishness, reclaiming the world, and inaugurating a battle that will doubtless culminate in the triumph of God over all God's enemies (including the captors Sin and Death). This means that the gospel is first, last, and always about God's powerful and gracious initiative.[19]

In this light, the "truth" that dogmatics seeks is not a timeless metaphysical principle but the unveiling of Jesus Christ, who reveals both God and the true creature in a single act. Christ is not simply the object of

19. Gaventa, *Our Mother Saint Paul*, 81.

theological reflection but its living subject—the One in whom God's self-revelation and humanity's renewal converge. Therefore, dogmatics does not pursue clarity by rising above history, but by standing within the disruptive and redemptive event of Christ's death and resurrection, through which all speech about God must now be measured. The apocalyptic vision undergirds the eschatological shape of dogmatics. It reminds us that the church's speech is always caught up in the dialectic of the *already* and the *not yet*, where we proclaim what we have seen in Christ even as we long for its consummation in the beatific vision. "Now we see through a mirror, in an enigma; then we shall see face to face" (1 Cor 13:12 DBH). Dogmatic theology, then, is neither speculation nor system but a cruciform discipline of watching and waiting, of proclaiming the mystery that has been revealed even as it continues to unfold.

In this way, Pauline apocalyptic strengthens the dogmatic arc from speech to vision. It secures the orientation of theology in revelation—not as static doctrine, but as event. And it clarifies the church's vocation: not to possess the truth as a finished product, but to testify to it as gift, to be grasped only in faith and finally consummated in sight. Dogma, therefore, is not an end in itself; it is an ordered response that prepares the church for her final end—beatific communion with the triune Lord. And this response, always imperfect and partial, is nevertheless sanctified by grace, taken up into the Spirit's work of leading the church into all truth. Thus, theology is a kind of doxology on the way—a labor of love that speaks while it waits, names what it has seen while yearning for the fullness of what is to be revealed.

Defining Apocalyptic

This unveiling of Jesus Christ as both divine and human truth has shaped not only dogmatic theology but also contemporary biblical scholarship, especially in Pauline studies. With Barth, our dogmatic exploration of the beatific vision much never depart too far from exegetical theology. One influential trajectory of exegetical theology is the apocalyptic vision that can be seen in the work of New Testament scholars who seek to understand Paul's gospel as the disruptive inbreaking of God's reign over the powers of sin and death. Among these, Beverly Gaventa's definition arises from a particular school of thought most indebted to the debate between Rudolf Bultmann and his student Ernst Käsemann. Bultmann's existential interpretation of the New Testament famously de-emphasized cosmic apocalyptic elements, focusing instead on individual decision in response to the kerygma. Käsemann, however, responded by insisting that Paul's theology is inseparable from the apocalyptic expectation of the Lordship of Christ and the final subjugation of the powers. This framework would deeply inform the later apocalyptic readings of Paul in which Gaventa's work is situated. As Käsemann writes,

> Christian apocalyptic . . . was released on the Church by the experience of the Spirit in the time after Easter, preserved as a living phenomenon by those endowed with the Spirit, nourished theologically from the tradition of Jewish apocalyptic, and finally accompanied by enthusiastic hopes and manifestations . . . of advancing post-Easter enthusiasm.[20]

Here Käsemann locates apocalyptic as the early Christian enthusiasm for God's reign made possible by the events of the incarnation, crucifixion, resurrection, and ascension of Jesus of Nazareth, which provides the clearest vision of God. This enthusiasm is accompanied with "the expectation of an imminent Parousia," or rather the coming reign of God, which is *not yet,* but provides hope to the individual and all of creation still trapped within the powers of sin and death.[21] In his exploration of historical Christianity, Käsemann notes the disappointment arising from the fact that the imminent Parousia did not occur in the timeframe envisioned by early Christians.

In light of this perceived failure, as Käsemann notes, apocalyptic begins to wane. In its place, Christianity developed a grammar of Jesus's divinity somewhat divorced, in Käsemann's mind, from the original apocalyptic hope of early Christianity.[22]

Bultmann would answer Käsemann's query with a resounding yes. For Bultmann, apocalyptic is a mythology of the ancient world of the prophets and apostles. Though it is a myth, Bultmann argues that there is an integrity in the myth that must be preserved existentially. Bultmann succinctly refers to this myth, and all mythology of this sort, as a thing of the past.[23] Apocalyptic must be demythologized in order for the Christian message to remain authentically eschatological and, thus, not rely

20. Käsemann, "On the Subject of Primitive Christian Apocalyptic," 109n1.

21. Käsemann, "On the Subject of Primitive Christian Apocalyptic," 109n1.

22. Käsemann, "On the Subject of Primitive Christian Apocalyptic," 115.

23. Bultmann, "New Testament and Mythology," 2.

on the mythological *Weltbild* of Paul predicated on an apocalyptic, imminent end. By eschatological, Bultmann means "not . . . that God's Reign is already here; but . . . that it is dawning."[24] The weakness of apocalyptic, according to Bultmann, is the expectation of an end within chronological history. "Eschatology," on the other hand, "is the notion of the end of the world; it is a notion which as such does not intend to include a concrete picture of the end-occurrence, which does not even think of the end as chronologically fixed."[25] Such a claim would betray the non-objective nature of his dialectical theology. As a dialectical theologian, Bultmann expresses God's activity outside the realm of observable fact. God's acts can only be preserved by faith in the moral response of the individual. Bultmann argues, "If the lordship of Christ and the subjection of the cosmic forces are understood only as apocalyptic statements, then, although they occur in the relation of the already and the not-yet, they are not in a dialectical relation. They do this only if they are oriented toward the individual."[26] Over against apocalyptic accounts that center on a fixed, future end-time, Bultmann argues that the saving event of Christ is encountered and responded to in the present as realized eschatology. In this reading, eschatology ceases to be a concept and is opened to the advent of grace, in which the individual responds in obedience to the demand of God. This is firmly Lutheran, namely that one must respond to the demand of God in faith. Only by this faith is one justified and one's self-love and private interest put off. This is how God delivers humanity from captivity to sin and death.

THE "ALREADY" AND "NOT YET": A WESLEYAN SYNTHESIS OF PAUL'S APOCALYPTIC THEOLOGY

Paul's apocalyptic theology is a hotly debated position in the academy. There remains a debate, however, whether the *already* or the *not yet* is individually efficacious, but historically they belong together. Most figures who approach Paul with an apocalyptic interpretation are Lutherans. These Lutherans have a specific hermeneutical orientation to apocalyptic as a means to describe justification by faith alone, that the righteousness

24. Bultmann, *Theology of the New Testament*, 7.

25. Bultmann, "Ist die Apokalyptik die Mutter der christlichen Theologie?", 476.

26. Bultmann, "Ist die Apokalyptik die Mutter der christlichen Theologie?," 480–81.

of God is a means to overcome the self-centered, prideful human in the face of sin.

John Wesley holds a hermeneutic of sanctification, which does not exclude Luther but rather extends the necessity of the *already* and *not yet* in Paul.

> Who has wrote more ably than Martin Luther on justification by faith alone? And who was more ignorant of the doctrine of sanctification, or more confused in his conceptions of it? In order to be thoroughly convinced of this, of his total ignorance with regard to sanctification, there needs no more than to read over, without prejudice, his celebrated comment on the Epistle to the Galatians.[27]

Wesley offers a hermeneutic of sanctification as a critical response to Luther's hermeneutic of justification by faith. Despite Wesley's criticism, he was very much appreciative of Luther's work.

Wesley's praise of Luther comes from personal experience. It was during a reading of Luther's commentary of Romans on May 24, 1738, that Wesley experienced an assurance of his salvation. Wesley upholds much of Luther's understanding of justification by faith, but with some minor augmentations.[28] Most notably, and apparent in the above quote, is Wesley's emphasis on sanctification. For Wesley, justification is not only a matter of faith but exemplified in good works. Wesley believes that justification is fundamentally a gift by grace and agrees with Luther that justification by faith speaks directly against prideful humanity that was produced in the Fall. But Wesley extends this to sanctification in order to move the focus from sheer obedience to gracious transformation to enabling the willing of the will of God.

To illustrate the difference between a Wesleyan interpretation of apocalyptic and the Lutheran standard interpretation, I return to Bultmann's Lutheran commitments. Bultmann's demythologizing project is a result of a Lutheran hermeneutical commitment to justification by faith alone.[29] Bultmann's main critique of apocalyptic is its objectifying capture of the future. Rather than the believer objectifying the future, Bultmann writes,

27. Wesley, "On God's Vineyard," 204.

28. See Maddox, *Responsible Grace*, 148–51.

29. I thank Charles Cosgrove for his assistance in helping me recognize this Lutheran element of Bultmann.

> [The believer] who is open to all that is future as the future of the coming God, death has lost its terror. He will refrain from painting in the future which God bestows in death, for all pictures of a glory after death can only be the wishful images of imagination and to forego all wishful images is part of the radical openness of faith in God's future.[30]

This eschatological posture is an act of faith, which does not seek a literal picture but walks into death faithfully.

Faith in Bultmann's interpretation of Luther is an act of obedience.[31] This is clear in Bultmann's de-objectified, demythologized eschatological faith, which calls for radical obedience. Wesley's account of eschatology, justification by faith, and the interim between differs. Wesley faulted Luther in his lack of theology of sanctification. This is Wesley's alternative to demythologization for the sake of obedience. Wesley believes that the Holy Spirit's therapeutic presence heals our damaged humanity. Like the apocalyptic Paul, Wesley argues that as a result of the Fall, humanity is now subject to an alien power, though Wesley understands this more as an infirmity in our tempers. The consistency between the two, however, is that something infringes on our ability to obey God.

Rather than a hermeneutic of demythologization and justification by faith, Wesley argues, through a hermeneutic of sanctification, that the presence of the Holy Spirit enables a renewing of the human condition itself. This is the difference between Luther and Wesley. Wesleyan scholar and theologian Randy Maddox writes, "If fallen humanity were left to respond to God's initiative from our own resources, we would never overcome our spiritual infirmity, because our faculties are debilitated. For this reason God has graciously provided not only pardon but also a renewed empowering presence in our lives."[32] This is crucial because such a presence creates a "habitual disposition of soul . . . [which] is termed holiness."[33] The Holy Spirit encourages love in the believer that enables love of God, but this love of God must be taken up in the believer in practice or, as Wesley argues, in the means of grace. This is the process of sanctification whereby fallen powers are overcome in concrete practice and the therapy of the Holy Spirit. Maddox contends that Wesley

30. Bultmann, "Christian Hope and the Problem of Demythologizing," 278

31. Consequently, this is also a key element of Käsemann's demythologization, that all ideology and mythology is demythologized for the sake of radical obedience in faith.

32. Maddox, *Responsible Grace*, 119.

33. Wesley, "Circumcision of the Heart," 25.

"became convinced that we *can* love God only in response to our awareness of God's salvific love for us."[34]

Wesley's account of sanctification is apocalyptic in its ability to resist the powers through an ever-increasing love of God in the present. The Spirit of the Son breaks into the hearts of believers so that we might cry "Abba Father!" (Gal 4:6 NRSV). This is already an apocalyptic disruption of the sinful order of the world that enables the love of God. In addition to the Spirit's apocalyptic disruption, Wesley also emphasizes the *not yet* eschatological transformation of the cosmos through this same hermeneutic of sanctification. Wesley articulates a therapeutic recuperating of sinful humanity that sanctifies the believer for the *amor Dei* that does not justify the sinner alone. One can be free of sin in the present as one grows in love.

> One is called to obey and put off selfishness in faith and will grow in grace in sanctification. However, this does not mean that Wesley has no use of eschatology. Wesley also argues that sanctification is incomplete without the new creation and the resurrection of the dead. It will not always be thus: these things are only permitted for a season by the great Governor of the world, that he may draw immense, eternal good out of this temporary evil . . . It is enough we are assured of this one point, that all these transient evils will issue well, will have a happy conclusion, and that "Mercy first and last will reign" . . . And we have strong reason to hope that the work he hath begun he will carry on unto the day of his Lord Jesus; that he will never intermit this blessed work of his Spirit until he has fulfilled all his promises; until he hath put a period to sin and misery, and infirmity, and death; and reestablished universal holiness and happiness, and caused all the inhabitants of the earth to sing together, "Hallelujah! The Lord God omnipotent reigneth!" "Blessing, and glory, and wisdom, and honour, and power, and might be unto God for ever and ever!"[35]

Wesley is clear: the work of sanctification culminates in a new creation. This new creation is determined by God's reign and frees creation from sin and death. Wesley operates with an apocalyptic eschatology where three things are assured. First, evil is temporary. Second, God reigns. Third, all things will be fulfilled in the new creation. Wesley believes that

34. Maddox, *Responsible Grace*, 174.

35. Wesley, "General Spread of the Gospel," 499.

God will remove that which impinges upon the created order, that which prevents universal holiness and happiness.

This Wesleyan hermeneutic operates by connecting the apocalyptic *already* to the *not yet*. In the *already*, the Holy Spirit sheds the love of God abroad in our hearts and makes love of God possible. It is not obedience, but the actual rehabilitation of our capacity to love God. This is sanctification. Wesley places, then, sanctification as a unique work of the Holy Spirit and ontologically locates our action within the action of another. In other words, the Holy Spirit is now the active power of God's eschatological reign.[36] Our activity comes to completion not in our work, but from the God who draws creation to its completion. Wesley describes it in a manner much akin to the apocalyptic thinkers of the *not yet*. He writes, "And to crown it all, there will be a deep, an intimate, an uninterrupted union with God; a constant communion with the Father and his Son Jesus Christ, through the Spirit; a continual enjoyment of the Three-One God, and of all the creatures in him!"[37] For Wesley, the entirety of the Christian life is a slow drawing of creation into the very triune life. First, as the Spirit renews the human heart for love of God and, second, when the entire created order is drawn into the life of the trinity, a new uninterrupted intimate center between God and creation.

THE BEATIFIC VISION: A DOGMATIC SKETCH IN A WESLEYAN, APOCALYPTIC KEY

Käsemann and Wesley offer compelling accounts of eschatology, and also compelling accounts of the vision of God. For Käsemann our vision becomes interrupted by the apocalyptic incursion of Christ into the cosmos as our gaze is lifted heavenward awaiting God's immanent return. For Wesley, it is a gradual growth in grace that culminates in the new creation. Though these two emphases do not exclude each other, they have not been placed in conversation on the beatific vision. Wesley, through his hermeneutic of sanctification, unites the already and not yet in a gracious character rather than constant assault.

The preceding section argued why apocalyptic needs Wesley because it places before Christians the interruptive face of God, namely an expectation of the beatific vision. However, Wesley is also in need of

36. See Zeigler, *Militant Grace*, 72.

37. Wesley, "New Creation," 500.

apocalyptic. The issue in Wesleyan theology is an attempt to define holiness without a thoroughgoing eschatology. Bultmann subverts this by always walking non-objectively in faith. As Käsemann argues, this faith "is only to be had on earth as a pledged gift, always subject to attack, always to be authenticated in practice—a matter of promise and expectation."[38]

This expectation is essential for Wesleyans, who oftentimes, absent the expectation of God's immanent return, think they have attained an adequate lingustic structure. Take for example the now infamous position of Wesleyan scholar J. Kenneth Grider, that racial prejudice is not purged in entire sanctification.[39] When holiness lacks an expectation of the beatific vision it collapses into a linguistic structure as the realization of entire sanctification. Recalling Boersma, the collapsing of the Christian life into a closed linguistic system is the inversion of the beatific vision, which conversely celebrates an expectancy and need of the vision of God as the source and fulfillment of the Christian life.

In the persistent presence of fallen powers, Christians must recognize our incompleteness and need of God's face. Wesley, correctly understood, articulates this need. However, Wesley's progressive eschatology makes this an underdeveloped theme. Wesley believes, at least in one sermon, in an immanent expectation for an apocalyptic fulfillment of time. Wesley's Christian perfection and eschatology need each other. Holiness and Eschatology belong together, precisely because the Christian life finds its end in the beatific vision. Dogmatics arises not from perfect language or linguistic system, but rather in their interruption. Apocalyptic expectation reminds the Christian that they have yet to arrive, and only do so when they can no longer speak. The purpose of interruption does not merely place the Christian in crisis, but rather reminds the Christian that her life exists in anticipation of the fulfillment of the beatific vision. Furthermore, seeing God is defined not by a more perfect linguistic system but by the very failure to describe what she sees.

Building on this framework, a Wesleyan dogmatic approach to the beatific vision in apocalyptic key would begin by affirming that holiness and eschatology are inseparable—not merely because holiness points forward to an eschatological goal, but because the telos of sanctification is nothing less than participation in the unveiled glory of God. For John Wesley, the process of sanctification is already oriented toward a

38. Käsemann, "'Righteousness of God' in Paul," 170.

39. Grider, *Wesleyan-Holiness Theology*, 414.

final consummation: perfect love made complete in union with God. Yet when placed in conversation with Käsemann's apocalyptic realism, Wesley's vision of gradual sanctification is not rejected but intensified. That is, holiness is not a linear ascent, but a life lived in *expectant rupture*—a sanctification under siege by the powers of sin and death, and a self shaped in perpetual anticipation of God's transformative self-disclosure.

A Wesleyan apocalyptic dogmatics would thus conceive of the beatific vision not as the terminus of doctrinal development, but as the very disruption of its supposed completion. Drawing from Käsemann's insight that faith is always a "pledged gift" on earth, authenticated in practice and under threat, Wesleyan theology must renounce any static or triumphalist definition of entire sanctification that loses sight of the eschatological tension that marks all Christian existence. In this sense, the beatific vision is not merely the reward of the sanctified but the interruption that keeps sanctification from devolving into ideological complacency. Entire sanctification, then, is not the possession of divine likeness, but the intensification of the soul's hunger for the vision of God—a hunger that renders all present holiness provisional.

In this view, dogmatics itself becomes a doxological anticipation of that final unveiling. Rather than forming a closed system of propositions, Wesleyan dogmatics becomes a grammar of longing—an unfolding articulation of faith that knows it must ultimately fall silent before the face of God. The beatific vision, therefore, reorients theology from a pursuit of precision to a posture of praise. Insofar as theology speaks truth, it does so as a response to the God who speaks first in Christ and will speak last in glory. The Wesleyan emphasis on spiritual formation, when placed under the apocalyptic horizon, means that theology must form a people who not only speak rightly of God, but who are being made ready to behold God. This is a dogmatics of transfiguration.

The beatific vision also resists the reduction of theology to ethics. While Wesley is rightly concerned with holiness of life, a Wesleyan apocalyptic dogmatics reminds us that the end of the Christian life is not simply moral improvement, but divine communion. Apocalyptic expectation keeps this truth alive by insisting that the Christian life is fundamentally about seeing what we cannot yet see. As David Congdon has argued, eschatology is not the end of history, but the invasion of time by eternity. In a Wesleyan register, this means that grace does not merely elevate or perfect what is already present, but arrives as the inbreaking of a future that undoes and remakes the present. The beatific vision is not the result of moral progress, but of divine mercy.

In sum, a Wesleyan dogmatic approach to the beatific vision in apocalyptic key must reclaim eschatology as the grammar of holiness. To speak dogmatically is not to close the question of God but to keep it open in faith, hope, and love—awaiting the day when our eyes shall see, and we shall know as we are known. Until then, theology lives by promise, prayer, and the longing that can only be satisfied when faith becomes sight.

CONCLUSION

This chapter has sought to sketch a dogmatic theology in a Wesleyan, apocalyptic key—one that retrieves eschatology not as a mere appendix to theological reflection, but as its very grammar. By reading John Wesley in conversation with the apocalyptic tradition—particularly as developed by Barth, Bulgakov, Käsemann, and contemporary Pauline scholarship—we have seen that Wesley's theology possesses deep dogmatic potential. Far from being an unsystematic moralist or pietistic revivalist, Wesley offers a vision of grace that is both theologically robust and spiritually generative: a vision in which sanctification is not a closed system of virtue but a dynamic participation in the life of God, always ordered toward divine consummation.

This apocalyptic reorientation of Wesleyan theology opens new dogmatic possibilities. It resituates the doctrine of Christian perfection not as a final arrival but as an eschatological pilgrimage—a sanctification under interruption, awaiting the beatific vision. Wesley's emphasis on responsible grace, when illumined by the apocalyptic grammar of divine disruption and future hope, yields a dogmatics that is both realist and hopeful, both humble and bold. It calls the church not to speak as those who possess the final word on God, but as those who have heard the word and await the vision.

To speak dogmatically, then, is not to build a tower of theological certitude but to lift the church's eyes toward the One who comes. It is to bear witness, in broken and provisional words, to a glory that will one day break through every veil. The beatific vision is not the end of theology because all has been said, but because nothing more needs to be said—because the church shall see God, and in seeing, be made like God.

Until then, Wesleyan dogmatics remains a theology of transfiguration: ever reforming, ever yearning, ever praising the God who interrupts, redeems, and draws all creation into communion. In that hope, we see dimly now—but not forever.

PART II:

Christian Ethics and Wesleyan-Holiness Thought

If holiness is the heart of Wesleyan theology, then its vitality depends on resisting the temptation to reduce it to mere moralism. Too often, holiness has been misinterpreted as a system of behavioral rules—a collapse into moral thinking that aligns more closely with fundamentalist impulses than with the dynamic vision of sanctifying grace in the Wesleyan tradition. Yet holiness is not a set of prohibitions or a checklist of moral achievements. Rather, it is a divine enticement—a summons into the transforming life of God that awakens and sustains moral imagination. As such, holiness transcends rigid categories of ethics and piety, broadening the theological conversation into matters of beauty, justice, communion, and love. This section explores how Wesleyan-Holiness theology continues to expand its moral horizon—not by abandoning holiness, but by recovering its deeper rhythm as a response to divine grace.

Chapter 5 explores the eschatological shape of ethics by examining how holiness functions as a political imagination that resists domination and individualism. Chapter 6 expands this vision into the realm of justice and liberation, especially how sanctification empowers the church to confront structural sin and offer a counter-cultural witness. Finally, chapter 7 presents a groundbreaking dialogue between Womanist theology and Wesleyan-Holiness soteriology. It argues that reimagining atonement through the lens of racial reconciliation and holy love not only addresses systemic injustice but also deepens our understanding of holiness itself.

Taken together, these chapters invite readers to imagine Christian ethics not as moralism or abstract duty, but as participation in the life of God—a life made visible in Jesus and made possible through the sanctifying work of the Spirit. They offer a Wesleyan ethic that is as rigorous as it is hopeful, as communal as it is personal, and as attuned to justice as it is to joy.

CHAPTER 5

Good Conscience or Good Confidence

A Postmodern Re-Thinking of Ethical Reflection in the Holiness Tradition

Henry Walter Spaulding II

INTRODUCTION

One horizon of the engagement between postmodernism and Wesleyan-Holiness theology concerns the relationship between holiness and morality. All of which raises a question—Can a holy person be a moral person? For many within the Wesleyan-Holiness tradition, the relationship between holiness and morality assumes a nearly self-evident status. Such a conclusion renders the term "holiness ethics" redundant. Yet, if I am right, it may not be redundant, but contradictory. Philosophically, this fact becomes clear with a more rigorous and creative engagement with postmodernism, especially in its postliberal form. There is also a theological consideration that may question the association between holiness and morality. Specifically, holiness comes by grace; it is received as a gift. It flows from a pure heart empowered by a vision of the triune God. Morality is constructed from choices directed by reason, either as a response to duty or toward a good end. When holiness and morality are linked, it can turn the gift into a mere human product. When this happens, holiness is reduced to a human construct devoid of the consciousness of the gift of a holy God. Then, holiness becomes preoccupied with standards, principles, and human achievement. It is no longer holiness, it is morality, a place where no grace is needed and none can be found.

John Milbank makes a distinction between conscience and confidence, which relates to our attempt to rethink moral practice. Conscience refers to ethical reflection and the effort to secure virtue by appeal to reason, end, or duty. It refers to the capacity to make a moral decision, which is the end of moral reflection. This is problematic for holiness. Milbank also talks about confidence, which is less about security and more about faith. It is, in fact, a contradiction to the morality arising from conscience.[1] Here Milbank sets the precise issue which informs any attempt to re-think moral practice in the Wesleyan-Holiness tradition. The purpose of this chapter is to examine this question in some detail with the hope that it will lead to a richer appreciation for the resources within the Wesleyan-Holiness tradition for engaging postmodernism and re-thinking the time-honored association of holiness and morality.

THE POSTLIBERAL CRITIQUE

The postmodern era has challenged those within and outside the church to reconsider their paradigmatic commitments. Postmodernism is a multifaceted discussion that encompasses various disciplines and perspectives. It affects not only philosophical and theological reflection but also biblical studies, historical studies, and even pastoral practice. One of the most interesting and helpful members of the postmodern family is post liberalism. Three individuals, Alasdair MacIntyre, Stanley Hauerwas, and John Milbank, can be generally associated with the postliberal critique of modernity. Together, they point to a version of moral reflection that might allow Wesleyan-Holiness theologians to "think again" about the most fundamental aspects of the Christian faith, specifically moral practice.

Alasdair MacIntyre, a relentless critic of the failed Enlightenment project, has written numerous books and articles that have contributed to a reconsideration of moral theory.[2] He argues against the attempt to ground morality in universal or rational principles. People holding such principles separate morality from culture, occasion, and history, among

1. Milbank, *Word Made Strange*, 231.

2. See MacIntyre, *After Virtue*, 39.

other factors. This leads to an unhealthy climate for making critical moral choices. According to MacIntyre, some theorists following universal principles conclude that the only possible form of ethical theory is emotivism. MacIntyre argues that this kind of moral thinking will not work; it has failed as a viable theory.

MacIntyre offers an alternative approach; he argues, "man is in his actions and practice, as well as his fictions, essentially a storytelling animal. He is not essentially, but becomes through his history, a teller of stories that aspire to truth."[3] This suggests that morality emerges from those habits and practices which guide life through its many twists and turns. The disembodied principle, which has nourished the individualism of modern ethics, cannot be finally justified according to MacIntyre. If he is right, then another account of moral theory must be suggested. He argues that habits and practices offer such a pathway.

Stanley Hauerwas is one of the most provocative voices in the church today. His energy and insight have unquestionably changed the theological landscape of the church. Hauerwas is also a vigorous critic of the way in which many have unconsciously or carelessly bought into the assumptions of liberal/democratic society. He finds these assumptions, even in liberation theology: "to make the metaphysics of liberation central or overriding as a description of the nature of Christian existence, as is done in much of liberation theology, is a mistake, given the background of much of our recent intellectual and political history."[4] He doubts these assumptions will be of much service to the church, they may in fact, be quite dangerous. He looks instead to the underlying narratives of the Christian community for the formation of character. He asserts the importance of a truthful narrative that will help engender the kind of character capable of freedom, justice, compassion, and liberation.[5] The truthfulness of the Christian claim about virtue is not dependent upon rational justification, but the kind of character emerging from Christian community. Virtue emerges from the character of a person formed by truthful narrative. This is the task of the church as a community of character.

Hauerwas writes eloquently regarding his understanding of the church:

3. MacIntyre, *After Virtue*, 216.

4. Hauerwas, *After Christendom*, 55.

5. Hauerwas, *Christian Existence Today*, 29.

> the truthfulness of Christian convictions resides in their power to form a people sufficient to acknowledge the divided character of the world and thus necessarily ready to offer hospitality to the stranger. They must be what they are, i.e., the church, precisely because the story of God that has formed them requires them to understand and acknowledge the divided character of the world. The task of Christians is not, therefore, to demonstrate that all possible positions are false through critical questions, but to be a witness to the God that they believe embraces all truth.[6]

This suggests the alternative epistemology that Hauerwas embraces. Rational grounds do not justify virtue; instead, the lives of those people who are formed by the truth are the justification. The church is the community called into being by the Spirit and the preaching of the word and nourished by the habits and practices to form the character of those willing to embrace the adventure.

John Milbank moves with ease through theology, philosophy, and sociology. He points to an "ontology of violence" that lies at the root of secular reason. This is problematic to the extent that much theology, and in particular liberalism, has bought into the assumptions of secular reason. To overcome secularism's influence, Milbank calls for the theologian to perform the task "of redeeming estrangement; the theologian alone must perpetuate that original making strange which is the divine assumption of human flesh, not to confirm it, but to show it again as it surprisingly is."[7] His point comes through clearly in the last chapter of his *Theology and Social Theory* where he says:

> The task of such a theology is not apologetic, not even argument. Rather it is to tell again the Christian *mythos*, pronounce again the Christian *logos*, and call again for Christian *praxis* in a manner that restores their freshness and originality. It must articulate Christian difference in such a way as to make it strange.[8]

He goes on to talk about "Counter-Ethics," which challenges the attempt to conform moral practice to the theoretical tendencies of secular reason. Instead, he argues for an Augustinian point of view, which acknowledges the difference between the City of Man and the City of God. He can make this claim because, "it implies both that the part belongs to the whole,

6. Hauerwas, *Community of Character*, 93–94.

7. Milbank, *Theology and Social Theory*, 1.

8. Milbank, *Theology and Social Theory*, 381.

and that each part transcends any imaginable whole, because the whole is only a finite series which continues indefinitely towards an infinite and unfathomable God."[9]

These three important theologians have pointed to some of the obstacles that stand in the way of moral practice. Their analysis points to the way in which the search for an adequate moral theology within the church is subverted by alien assumptions. Consequently, the church can run the risk of making moral practice a liberal notion of universally established ideals. These men also suggest that often our moral theory can rest upon rational justifications, instead of the habits and practices that finally engender virtue. These men also question the autonomous self, which is assumed by modern ethics. They point to the socially constructed self and the accompanying need for community. Finally, they question the tendency of the church to make sense of the world. They wonder if such a task is a worthy goal at all.

THE TRAJECTORIES OF WESLEYAN-HOLINESS ETHICS

The historical relationship between "Methodist perfection and . . . moral ability"[10] seems indisputable. Yet, larger questions remain—Does this mean that Wesleyan-Holiness theology is wedded to a particular ethical scheme? Is there a danger in linking the holy life with the moral life? Is there a difference between an association of holiness and the discipline of ethical reflection? Is there a difference between the expectation of a holy life and a commitment to moral theology? These questions reach beyond how moral practice has been engendered in the Wesleyan-Holiness tradition. They go on to say how this tradition has attempted to "think itself" and thus to "go on."[11] In order to more fully appreciate the dilemma and the possibilities of these "theological" questions, we will need to look at the trajectories of Wesleyan-Holiness ethical reflection. Since, the "holiness movement," even with the qualifier "Wesleyan" added, is quite diverse, we will only be able to examine the debate in its broadest terms. I

9. Milbank, *Theology and Social Theory*, 405.

10. Smith, *Revivalism and Social Reform*, 114.

11. The term "go on" is used in the Wittgensteinian sense of solving a philosophical problem.

hope to show that a careful analysis of the theological issues at stake point an impasse and suggest a way to "go on."

Wesleyan-Holiness Deontology

One way in which moral reflection has proceeded in the Wesleyan-Holiness tradition can be linked to deontological ethics. This is clear in the theology of H. Orton Wiley, who says, "As theology is the science of God and the mutual relations of God and man, so ethics, as the science of duty, has to do with the end, the principles and motives of obligatory conduct."[12] He thinks of Christian ethics as revealed in the sense that it is centered in Divine Revelation.[13] This is important for him because it separates "Natural" and "Revealed" ethics. It grounds the demand, which becomes a duty in God. Out of this, he attempts to locate the principles of Christian ethics in liberty, love, and conscience. The business of ethics is the "application of moral principles in the regulation of human conduct."[14] As Wiley expands his discussion of Christian ethics, he carefully connects the concept of duty at all levels. He discusses duties to God, duties to oneself, and the duties we owe to others.[15] Wiley's ethical reflection centers on duty, principles, and right.

Charles Carter is another Wesleyan-Holiness theologian who develops a fundamental deontological vision for ethical reflection. He begins his treatment by noting the importance of principles in Judeo-Christian ethics.[16] He also discusses the business of ethics as the application of the absolute tenets to specific situations. Carter also reveals his deontological commitments by his reference to the Decalogue, which "was designed by God to be the *objective moral norm and directive* for man in his fallen, perverted, subjective moral state."[17] Carter looks at the Scripture as "the grace of God in Christ that saves, supports, and directs the believer in the way of right conduct toward God and one's fellow human beings."[18] Partially because of his interpretation of Christian/Wesleyan ethics as

12. Wiley, *Christian Theology*, 3:7.
13. Wiley, *Christian Theology*, 3:24.
14. Wiley, *Christian Theology*, 3:36.
15. Wiley, *Christian Theology*, 3:68.
16. Carter, "God's Ethical Ideal for Humanity," 955.
17. Carter, "God's Ethical Ideal for Humanity," 963.
18. Carter, "God's Ethical Ideal for Humanity," 993.

deontological, he views the works of Joseph Fletcher and John A. T. Robinson as damaging. He feels that these works profess to be Christian but turn out to be "subjectivistic."[19] It is more than a little interesting that Carter juxtaposes objective and subjective, associating the objective with Christian ethics. Carter goes on to observe, "Out of the contemporary ethical situationism produced by these and other influential relativistic thinkers, a general moral revolution resulting in the near collapse of much of Western society is taking place."[20] He laments the lack of ultimate norms in situation-based ethical reflection. He says, "In fact, there can be no right or wrong where this philosophy is accepted."[21] While Carter transitions from biblical to situational ethics in this article, his fundamental understanding of moral reflection remains clear. He finds that any ethical system, which is Christian, much less Wesleyan, must work from ultimate, objective, universal norms. He finds that these are contained in the Scripture. Perhaps these are found in the Christian tradition, but all moral norms must be measured against the righteous character of God, as revealed in Scripture through the Holy Spirit.

Richard Taylor is another prominent Wesleyan-Holiness theologian whose moral reflections are deontological in character. He talks about the "ethical standard that is to mark holy living."[22] Even Taylor's talk of liberation from the law is couched in a higher moral expectation. He warns, "Professors and exponents of holiness, above all, should be absolutely blameless in ethical practices."[23] Taylor urges that "It is the duty of the Church to set ethical standards and raise ethical issues, if for no other reason than to discharge its teaching responsibility."[24] He looks at the life of holiness as living out of the duty inherent within the Christian faith.[25] The language of duty, fixed landmarks, standards, etc., indicates that moral reflection for Taylor, and thus holiness, is deontologically conceived.

19. Carter, "God's Ethical Ideal for Humanity," 998.

20. Carter, "God's Ethical Ideal for Humanity," 999.

21. Carter, "God's Ethical Ideal for Humanity," 999.

22. Taylor, *Theological Formulation*, 208.

23. Taylor, *Theological Formulation*, 209. While Taylor uses the term 'practice' it is clear that he is using it in a way that is rather disembodied, thus it does not connote the moral practice as it is used in this chapter.

24. Taylor, *Theological Formulation*, 210.

25. Taylor, *Theological Formulation*, 212

These are but a few of the theologians who have attempted to delineate Christian ethics within the Wesleyan-Holiness tradition. They share a commitment to clear, objective standards that define their duty. Each is suspicious of any attempt to allow the situation to influence moral choice overly. They each think that the self is capable of conceiving Christian duty in the context of the revelation of God, Scripture, and the church.

Wesleyan-Holiness Teleology

The work of H. Ray Dunning is an example of Wesleyan-Holiness teleological ethical reflection. He suggests in *Reflecting the Divine Image* "the necessity for a theologically based ethic . . . that grows out of and is informed by a comprehensive theological vision."[26] He thinks, "The Wesleyan vision is peculiarly fitted to provide such a theological underpinning."[27] Dunning suggests that this is the case because "Wesley himself . . . recognized sanctification to be a thoroughgoing ethical concept."[28] Dunning offers a brief section on Christian ethics in his book *Grace, Faith, and Holiness*, where he discusses three approaches to ethics within the holiness movement. First, he talks about those who seek to identify rules for conduct in the Bible and then apply these in a literalistic way to contemporary life.[29] Second, he talks about ethical reflection in the Wesleyan-Holiness tradition that "centers in law, obligation, and duty . . . Since when dealing with divine commands, it is claimed that the Christian ethic fits this model."[30] Third, Dunning discusses the teleological vision within Wesleyan-Holiness theology, which emphasizes goals, ends, and happiness. He summarizes this discussion in the following: "Historically, the holiness movement has utilized all three of these approaches, but the most adequate attempts to justify the holiness lifestyle used some version of the teleological approach."[31]

According to Dunning, it is crucial to define an ethical principle for moral reflection. Such a principle is necessary so that the difference between right and wrong will be clarified. He also suggests that the

26. Dunning, *Reflecting the Divine Image*, 21.

27. Dunning, *Reflecting the Divine Image*, 21.

28. Dunning, *Reflecting the Divine Image*, 21–22.

29. Dunning, *Grace, Faith and Holiness*, 500. I tend to think that this way of moral reflection is a naïve form of deontology, but it can be argued the way Dunning suggests.

30 Dunning, *Grace, Faith and Holiness*, 501.

31. Dunning, *Grace, Faith and Holiness*, 502.

principle should be transcendent, so that the standards of contemporary culture will not shape our ethics. Dunning states his point of view, "I have concluded that Christian ethics, especially when viewed from a Wesleyan perspective, is thoroughly teleological."[32] The shape of ethical reflection within the Wesleyan-Holiness tradition is developed under the rubric of relation to God. One way this becomes evident is that Dunning prefers the term obedience to duty. This means that "The end of obedience is communion, not obedience."[33] Such an understanding avoids the legalism that often attaches itself to deontological schemes. Dunning further suggests that this understanding of "image as relation to God," opens toward two moral principles. First, "a principle of discrimination concerning which aspects of life should be avoided and which should be embraced."[34] Relation to God is the substantive element, which "umpires", "arbitrates", and "guides" one's life toward holiness.

Second, a principle of separation, which Dunning puts this way, "Since in my relationship with God I acknowledge him as absolute sovereign and loving Father, any activity that compromises that relation must be avoided."[35] These two principles offer Dunning the matrix to develop a Wesleyan-Holiness ethic.

One more idea is vital to moral reflection, according to Dunning—the church. He begins by noting, as many have before, that individualism tends to diminish the importance of the church and the meaning of moral reflection in general. While this is a short chapter, it does at least show an interest in linking ethical reflection to the church in a way that allows it to be more than a "museum for moral norms." The importance of practice and sacramental life is largely missing, but Dunning does attempt to link ecclesiology within the moral life.

Although Dunning is the only theologian we have treated under this category, it is possible to draw a few conclusions regarding the point of view. It construes Christian ethics as directed toward particular ends. Wesleyan-Holiness teleology tends to think that it captures the genius of Wesley more fully. It is linked to principles, which inform the moral agent regarding decision-making. This position is no less convinced of the authority of the Scripture or the clarity possible for moral decision-making than the deontologists.

32. Dunning, *Reflecting the Divine Image*, 35.

33. Dunning, *Reflecting the Divine Image*, 81.

34. Dunning, *Reflecting the Divine Image*, 81.

35. Dunning, *Reflecting the Divine Image*, 83.

Preliminary Assessment

The trajectories of Wesleyan-Holiness moral reflection, as we have treated them to this point, tell us a great deal about its paradigmatic commitments. Stanley Hauerwas and David Burrell make an interesting observation that is relevant for our investigation:

> It is our contention, however, that the standard account of moral rationality distorts the nature of the moral life by: (1) placing an unwarranted emphasis on particular decisions or quandaries; (2) by failing to account for the significance of moral notions and how they work to provide skills of perceptions; and (3) by separating the agent from his interests.[36]

Whether it is deontology or teleology the question becomes an examination of paradigms.

An examination of those Wesleyan-Holiness theologians whose moral reflection is shaped by the deontological tradition leaves one with several impressions. First, moral reflection when it is shaped by duty implies a particular understanding of Scripture. Perhaps, at its most naïve level it implies a "biblical positivism," which is the attempt to lift from Scripture moral prescriptions and apply them directly to life. But no one we have looked at in this section would agree with this form of moral reflection. Rather, we encounter this understanding in more nuanced ways in what J. Kenneth Grider calls "A homing instinct for the moral."[37] I am not arguing here that Grider is a deontologist, much less a "biblical positivist" at the point of morality, for it is not clear from his *magnum opus* that he develops either a deontology or a teleology. Indeed, his brief discussion of a homing instinct could be interpreted either way. What I do want to suggest is that deontology within the Wesleyan-Holiness tradition treated here is linked to an understanding of Scripture that allows for, if not encourages, a reduction of the Scripture to disembodied moral norms. It encourages a separation between moral theology and systematic theology.

A second observation is that deontological moral reflection in the Wesleyan-Holiness theologians we have treated seems preoccupied with locating and defending a foundation. It is most clear in Carter, but it is evident in Wiley and Taylor as well. There would be no real problem with

36. Hauerwas and Burrell, "From System to Story," 163.

37. Grider, *Wesleyan-Holiness Theology*, 36.

this if it were not for at least two things. First, it forces moral reflection to become preoccupied with producing epistemologically grounded proofs for moral standards. This almost guarantees that the rich diversity of the Scripture will be reduced to a catalog of publicly defensible norms. Second, there is also the inevitable wedding of moral reflection with modern philosophy. The irony of this merging of modern epistemology and holiness theology is the general antipathy of modern philosophy for revelation.

Wesleyan-Holiness moral reflection in the teleological tradition is clearly a very profitable avenue for ethical reflection. It seems to best capture the genius of Wesley. The principles that move this teleology become disembodied in the same fashion as duty in the deontological tradition. Further, the same kinds of critique suggested regarding deontology apply to teleology. Specifically, it is not at all clear that a different hermeneutic is employed, although teleology moves in the right direction. It is also not clear that the foundational tendencies are avoided; instead, they seem to be merely relocated in consequences and ends.

As we have already observed, there are limitations with either tradition of moral reflection in the Wesleyan-Holiness tradition. While at some level it may seem that the choice between deontology and teleology is the only choice, it is worthwhile to look more carefully at the options. The two traditions may share a great deal more than initially appears. For example, they are both dependent upon some rational grounding or justification for moral decision-making. The deontologist looks for objective norms, and the teleologist looks for a transcendent principle, which is no less knowable. One is left to consider the real difference.

Another issue worth considering is the distinction between deontology and teleology. The first sees a self that chooses by knowing the universal norms at stake. The second considers a self that is no less rational in its selection of appropriate ends. For both, the self is capable, albeit with the Holy Spirit's help, of grasping the duty or end toward which a person is called to live. The deontologist resists the temptation to get lost in the situation for many reasons, most notably because it makes it less likely that a sentimental understanding will cloud the vision of the objective norm. The teleologist embraced the situation but feels that the transcendentally secure principle will guide the moral agent through the maze with more compassion, but similar results.

It is, perhaps, at this point that the issue becomes the clearest. It seems to boil down to a conservative perspective versus a liberal one.

For some, Wesleyan theology is inescapably and most appropriately conservative. That is, Wesleyan-Holiness moral reflection rests on certain irreducible truths, which can be known and defended. For others, Wesleyan-Holiness theology is more open in its engagement with the world; it is liberal in the best sense of the word. That is, Wesleyan-Holiness moral reflection builds bridges to contemporary culture. Thus conceived, Wesleyan-Holiness theology expresses itself in modern idiom. One approach of Wesleyan-Holiness moral reflection is conservative, the other is liberal; yet, with all the differences, the persuasiveness of either option is unclear. We are left to consider why this is the case. The answer may be found not in the difference between deontology and teleology, but in the construal of the moral enterprise itself.

An examination of the trajectories of Wesleyan-Holiness moral reflection indicates the dependence of each on the modern paradigm. Perhaps, this is part of what lies behind Milbank's provocative question; "Can morality be Christian?"[38] He answers, "Let me tell you the answer straightaway. It is no. Not 'no' there cannot be a specifically Christian morality. But no, morality cannot be Christian."[39] This startling answer calls into question the point of locating the problem with Wesleyan-Holiness moral reflection in either deontology or teleology, but with the moral enterprise itself. He goes on to talk about the five marks of morality: reactive, sacrifice, complicity with death, scarcity, and generality.

Milbank critiques morality as reactive. In other words, virtue is seen only in the face of the greatest adversity. He says, "virtue is always reactive, it always secretly celebrates as its occasion a prior evil, lives out of what it opposes."[40] Milbank also talks about sacrifice, "In morality there is no love for the other nor opening to the other, but always and everywhere a principle of self-government, whether of the soul or the city."[41] The third mark of morality for Milbank is complicity with death. He says, "If Reaction requires Sacrifice, then both concern death: in fact a threat of death repelled by a willing to die."[42] Milbank adds to this, "So ethics must covertly celebrate death, for only our fragility elicits our virtue."[43] The fourth mark is called scarcity, which is linked to death and sacrifice.

38. Milbank, *Word Made Strange*, 219.

39. Milbank, *Word Made Strange*, 219.

40. Milbank, *Word Made Strange*, 221.

41. Milbank, *Word Made Strange*, 223.

42. Milbank, *Word Made Strange*, 223.

43. Milbank, *Word Made Strange*, 223.

Milbank observes, "because life is in short supply, because it might run out on us, sooner or later, we must invest, we must insure."[44] The fifth and final mark of morality for Milbank is generality. He observes, "It is this generality which ensures that the moral command is a law or general prescription, including a prescription of virtue."[45] The impasse of moral reflection that plagues all deontology and teleology is illuminated by this analysis. In other words, it does not matter so much whether it is a norm, duty, end, or principle; the problem does not reside there. It goes far deeper to the difference between the nihilism and ontology of violence that is present in secular reason and even in liberal theology, perhaps in conservative theology as well. This suggests the need for a third option, one that emphasizes character over principles, social formation as opposed to resolution of conflict of duty, and one that recognizes the significance of liturgical practice. Herein lie the formative factors for a Wesleyan-Holiness moral theology capable of engaging postmodernity while avoiding its nihilism.

CHARACTER AND HOLINESS: THE GRAMMAR OF FAITHFUL PRACTICE

This section intends to offer a preliminary reflection on the possibilities for moral theology within the parameters of the Wesleyan-Holiness tradition.[46] Perhaps, such an investigation will be capable of engaging postmodernism. Two underlying convictions guide this reflection. First, theology and moral practice must be understood together. It is impossible that either can function without the other. This fact is evident by the understanding of theology, which informs it, a disciplined reflection upon the forms of life engendered by Spirit, word, and the sacramental life of the church. Milbank is a powerful voice in this discussion when he calls for a *counter-ethics*. He means by this that the Christian faith "implies a critique not only of the prescriptions but also of the formal categories of antique ethics of art, *phronesis*, telos, 'the mean' and so forth."[47] He gives specific shape to this counter-ethic when he talks about the five

44. Milbank, *Word Made Strange*, 224–25.

45. Milbank, *Word Made Strange*, 226.

46. I am using the term "moral theology" as an attempt to broaden the meaning of moral reflection to include a theological reflection.

47. Milbank, *Theology and Social Theory*, 399.

notes of the gospel, which are to be distinguished from the five marks of morality discussed in the previous section. These five notes are gift, end of sacrifice, resurrection, plentitude, and confidence. They suggest the radical difference between moral theology and ethical reflection, even in its theological mode. For example, gift emphasizes a "divine creative act."[48] The note "end of sacrifice" is shaped by the understanding that "I exist and persist also in giving, which is prior to any sacrificial loss."[49] The third note is resurrection and it is "the sustaining of joyful, non-reactive giving, by a hastening of death as the only way of continuing to give."[50] The fourth note is plentitude, which is "to believe in the already commenced and yet-to-come restoration of Creation as Creation."[51] The final note of the gospel is confidence, which places moral reflection squarely in the "sufficiency of God, and actions excessively out of this excess."[52] Thus, theology and moral practice share a common pathway. Re-thinking moral practice in the Wesleyan-Holiness tradition is congenial to this proposal.

The second conviction, which informs this project, involves what Ludwig Wittgenstein calls grammar. This is a strategy for confronting and creatively appropriating the nonfoundationalism of postliberalism. When we do this, two things will happen: first, we will understand, and second, we will be able to go on. Wittgenstein says, "But there is also this use of the word 'to know': we say 'Now I know it!'—and similarly 'Now I can do it!' and 'Now I understand.'"[53] Understanding is the result of a "grammatical investigation." The point he wants to make is that understanding is more than just grasping a formula. He says, "Try not to think of understanding as a 'mental process' at all—For that is the expression which confuses you. But ask yourself: in what sort of case, in what kind of circumstances, do you say, 'Now I know how to go on,' when, that is, the formula has occurred to me."[54] Theology is grammar according to Wittgenstein. I take this to mean that theology and for that matter understanding takes place within a complex of activities. Therefore, any consideration of moral reflection requires a grammatical projection.

48. Milbank, *Word Made Strange*, 228.

49. Milbank, *Word Made Strange*, 228.

50. Milbank, *Word Made Strange*, 228.

51. Milbank, *Word Made Strange*, 229.

52. Milbank, *Word Made Strange*, 231.

53. Wittgenstein, *Philosophical Investigations*, 59.

54. Wittgenstein, *Philosophical Investigations*, 60.

Re-thinking moral practice requires a consideration of the habits and practices of the Christian faith. Finally, a focus on grammar will help us to go on, to re-order our lives around Christian practices. This means that understanding moral practice in the postmodern era is not purely a matter of thinking, but of life, it is embedded in the forms of life.

The interrelation between theology and moral practice as well as the constructive possibilities of a grammatical focus are the two underlying convictions of this project. We will now turn to a consideration of three elements that together point to a new way of "going-on" for Wesleyan-Holiness moral theology. Hopefully, the appropriateness of the subtitle "The Grammar of Faithful Practice" will become evident in the following paragraphs.

1. Doxology

All theological reflection begins and ends in the worship of a triune God. Therefore, moral theology is, first of all, the worship of Father, Son, and Holy Spirit. The life of the trinity serves as the clue for understanding all other aspects of the Christian tradition. Since moral practice is doxological in character the first question concerns God. This fundamental assertion that the God we worship is triune is the first reality of the Christian life. It is the affirmation that God is related as triune without coercion, competition, and as eternal love that informs all moral practice. The worship of God is first initiatory and then recapitulatory and one without the other weakens its meaning. Worship as doxology includes sacrifice and praise, initiation and recapitulation. The very meaning of theology as doxology is that it begins as a reflection of the ever-present triune God, continues in the outpoured love made incarnate in the Christ, and it reaches outward as that creative moment engendered by the Spirit. This conception of theology has clear moral significance. According to Geoffrey Wainwright, "Christian ethics is the confession of faith in praxis."[55] It is the fundamentally Christian affirmation that God exists as a being-in-communion, which offers vision and conviction to the Christian life. Moral practice, therefore, begins in the life of a God who "lives as the loving friendships, the self-giving relationships, of Father, Son and Holy Spirit."[56] Grammatically considered, moral theology is first a doxological practice centered on the God who exists with humankind.

55. Wainwright, *Doxology*, 431.

56. Jones, *Embodying Forgiveness*, 112.

This means, in part, that moral theology is not in its first act a human construction, which rises to meet the challenges presented to it. Rather it reflects the gracious move of God toward us; it is the reception of gift and the thanksgiving, which follows. Moral theology, in order to be genuine, arises from our need for God to sustain our life together. Christian virtue does not exist as some disembodied duty or holy *telos* for the Christian, instead it is embedded in the worship of God. It is the grammar of faithful practice. The first act of moral theology is the worship of a triune God. Moral theology within the Wesleyan-Holiness tradition will not be found in a therapeutic model of Christianity, which can only be sustained by an association of persons seeking to find vision in human need or Christian responsibility. Such a situation is really an attempt to treat virtue as a duty, which comes from the outside. A grammatical understanding begins to see that moral theology arises in the worship of Father, Son, and Holy Spirit.

The worship of the triune God is not an attempt to deny the reality of the world, rather it is an attempt to see through "the storied practices of the church . . . the ultimate realism."[57] Of course, the ultimate story of the world is the God who creates, redeems, and sanctifies through the power of grace. Milbank suggests, "Christian belief belongs to Christian practice, and it sustains its affirmations about God and creation only by repeating and enacting a metanarrative about how God speaks in the world in order to redeem it."[58] This is according to Milbank a "counter-ontology" and we understand its significance in the practice of worship. Yet, it is often easy to miss the doxological dimensions of faith and practice to react appropriately to the challenges presented by secular reason. It is just because of this that the beginning of a reconstructed Wesleyan-Holiness moral theology must arise out of the worship of God.

Following the analysis above the difference between the "reactive" in morality and the "gift" of the gospel suggests something significant about the way we "go on." The former makes ethics an attempt to answer secular reason, the latter is the joyful note in the midst of the secular which calls it to conversion. Stanley Hauerwas says, "Trinity is the story that all that is, including us, is part of God's story."[59] He adds, "It is in worship that we learn to tell the story of creation as part of God's Trinitarian

57. Hauerwas, *Dispatches from the Front*, 180.

58. Milbank, *Social Theory*, 422.

59. Hauerwas, *Sanctify Them in the Truth*, 255.

life."[60] Perhaps, this is the pathway to re-thinking our ethics in a way, that avoids what Milbank calls complicity with the secular.

2. Character Formed by Truthfulness

The truthfulness of the gospel cannot be justified by an appeal to some exterior criterion. It cannot be demonstrated as a public reality in a way that is not circular. The character that arises out of its proclamation and its life within the church can justify the truthfulness of the gospel, including moral practice. This may sound strange, but what it suggests is fundamental to the meaning of moral theology. Moral reflection as it is usually understood tends toward a preoccupation with decisions made by an individual. Moral practice looks beyond principles, to those forms of life capable of social embodiment. According to Hauerwas, "The self that gives rise to agency is fundamentally a social self, not separable from its social and cultural environment."[61] Moral practice has no meaning when separated from one's character. There is a tendency, especially in modernity, to reduce ethics to decisions. The key to moral practice is to be found in a character formed by the truth. In order that truth not become one more disembodied principle, it is essential that it be understood within the complex of activities engendered by the faithful practice of proclamation and sacrament.

This is from the very start a rejection of the autonomous self. Going back to the importance of seeing God as a being-in-communion who creates humankind as a being-in-relation, it becomes abundantly clear that autonomy is a dangerous illusion. The truth comes to human beings when they are lost in the illusion of self-sufficiency. It is that strange word that Milbank says is the fundamental task of the theologian in our time. The strangeness is in part to be accounted for in the call to community in a time of alienation. It is also evident in the willingness to look beyond the façade, which often hides the truly important. The truth is not always pleasant, at least at first, but it is part of the redeeming presence that is evident in the first movement of moral practice.

Truthful narrative is more than words, it refers to those gestures of truth that form the heart of the church, i.e., baptism, Eucharist, friendship, prayer, preaching, etc. According to Hauerwas, "Choice is the center

60. Hauerwas, *Sanctify Them in the Truth*, 255, 256.

61. Hauerwas, *Character and the Christian Life*, 33.

of our action, but character is the determination of choice as well as its continuing result."[62] Character gives a person a nose for the truth. One is prepared for moral discernment by being formed in truthfulness. Such a commitment to truthfulness requires courage and patience.

Several important issues come into focus in this statement. First, we come into our humanity, not as a natural endowment, but through the truthful narrative. Second, we are given in the church God's way of forming us in the truth. Third, the Scripture must be heard again as that narrative which reminds us that we are not the object of the story, rather it is God. Fourth, the importance of the preacher is affirmed and with it the work of helping people see again the primary task of ministry, that is, helping others see the truth. Finally, while it is not explicitly said, it is the Spirit who moves in the church as the envisioner of grace and as the movement toward moral reflection.

The practice of the truth that helps us embody moral practice is sustained in the instituted sacramental life of the church. It is in this way that we begin to "unlearn our habit of sin."[63] Baptism teaches us who we are, and the Eucharist reminds us of our past as it points to our real hope. The sacramental life of the church is shaped in the recognition of divine grace. It is the way in which our identity becomes evident as our destiny is envisioned.

The sacramental life of the church embraces the truth. It is because of this that it reaches to a world that needs to know that it is the world. Hauerwas says: "For the church to be, rather than have, a social ethic means we must recapture the social significance of common behavior, such as acts of kindness, friendship, and the formation of families."[64] In other words, the sacramental life of the church is an important key to the grammar of moral theology. It is the visible re-narrating of life through the lens of a triune God. Milbank talks about Christian "moral practice embedded in the historical emergence of a new, and unique community . . . situated in the re-narration of Christian emergence."[65] Of course, the narrative is an outgrowth of the story of a triune God sustained in the church and sustained by its sacramental life.

62. Hauerwas, *Character and the Christian Life*, 112–13.

63. Jones, *Embodying Forgiveness*, 76.

64. Hauerwas, *Community of Character*, 11.

65. Milbank, *Theology and Social Theory*, 381.

3. Sanctification

The final movement in our consideration of moral theology is an examination of sanctification. The importance of this grand doctrine of the Wesley-Holiness tradition may in fact turn out to be our true genius. It may help us realize the best of our theological heritage as it points to the future. The Holiness movement has continued to believe that the grace of God is sufficient to cleanse the heart, nourish our relationship with God, and empower us to service. Suppose there has been a fault line in this theological affirmation. In that case, it has been the tendency to be captured in the liberal democratic assumptions regarding selfhood, along with its implications for moral reflection. Hauerwas points to this in the following comment: "The problem with the language and practice of holiness in modernity is that it has been far too spiritual. To become holy had been presented as something we will, something we could become if we just tried hard enough."[66] When the self is construed atomistically, especially regarding sin and grace, the real genius of sanctification runs the risk of being lost. Hauerwas reflects this in his reading of Paul, "Holiness is not, for Paul, a matter of individual will. Holiness is the result of our being made part of a body that makes it impossible for us to be anything other than disciples."[67] When we continue to think of sanctification as a personal victory over a mountain of sin, inherited and actual, we lose sight of what is vital about holiness.

All too often, it seems "holiness folk" tend to get locked into holiness ethics and lose sight of a holy God, thus exchanging holiness for moralism. We tend to seek security in lifestyle and miss our mutual dependence on God. We begin to seek an experience instead of a God who is being-in-communion. We may seek our confidence in rigorous standards, then through time place the standards first, instead of Spirit-engendered praxis. Sanctification is an important key to understanding moral theology in the Wesleyan-Holiness tradition.

Sanctification is crucial for the plain fact that in a "post-age" there is no doctrine, no dictionary, and no foundation sufficient to establish the truth claims of the Christian faith. This surely means that a grammatical investigation of moral theology will require a full accounting of holiness. Milbank says, "The Church, to be the Church, must seek to extend the

66. Hauerwas, *Sanctify Them in the Truth*, 89.

67. Hauerwas, *Sanctify Them in the Truth*, 84.

sphere of socially, aesthetic harmony."[68] Grammatically formed holiness will take full regard of the triune God and the truthful narrative, or put more plainly the Spirit-engendered culture that is the church.

The emphasis on holiness for understanding moral theology is essential for many reasons. First, it reminds us that as the people of God, we are pilgrims on the way to God's future. We are not seeking to establish a kingdom on earth. Liberty, fraternity, and equality, which seem so obviously linked to the Enlightenment, cannot hope to engender moral practice beyond some intellectual or moral consensus. As exodus people, we know that our conscience may mislead us, but our confidence when placed in the triune God can form us into a peculiar people. Second, it reminds us of our eschatologically framed journey.

It is not hope that presumes, nor is it a hope lost in despair. It is not a strain understanding the Christian life, which detaches one from the difficulties of life. An eschatologically informed faith understands that the hope of the gospel does not deny the present as much as it frames it in an optimism of grace. Third, it reminds us that worship is not merely a segmented span of time when we sing, pray, and listen/preach. Rather worship is a description of the character of life when it is lived in community. Wainwright reminds us that "the world is not an easy place in which to live doxologically."[69] Yet, when life is so lived it is the best, if not only justification of our moral practice.

Understanding the importance of Christian Perfection, entire sanctification, and the many cognates of holiness within the Wesleyan-Holiness tradition indicates one resounding conviction. The optimism of grace or trajectory of hope unites all Wesleyan-Holiness moral theology. Theodore Runyon reflects this conviction: "What the renewal of the creature in the image of God requires is participation in the 'energy of God, an energy that transforms and creates anew. Thus what is called for is nothing less than a conscious encounter with grace!"[70] This kind of statement can be located throughout the Wesleyan-Holiness tradition. It expresses the insight that holiness extends to the many relationships that characterize life, including the cosmos.[71] Finally, it is in moral practice that the doctrine of sanctification joins the grammar of faithful practice.

68. Milbank, *Theology and Social Theory*, 422.

69. Wainwright, *Doxologyy*, 415.

70. Runyon, *New Creation*, 151.

71. See Marquardt, *John Wesley's Social Ethics*, 120–21. It seems clear that Marquardt is talking about moral practice as we are developing it in this chapter.

It is shaped by grace, engendered by the word, Spirit, and sacrament as it reaches toward the brokenness of the world.

Moral practice arises out of the worship of a triune God, finds embodiment in truthfulness, and is finally justified in holiness. If we are to sustain moral theology in our time it will be through our worship of the triune God that is formed by the truth and incarnated in a community of character as it returns to the God who is Father, Son, and Holy Spirit. Virtue does not hang in empty space, and it is not a rationally defined and justified virtue. It is not about securing self-worth or individual rights, neither is it about how we feel. This is only possible when we understand that embodying moral reflection is a doxological enterprise.

CONCLUSION

The question must be raised again—Can a holy person be a moral person? The answer depends upon whether one seeks a pure conscience or good confidence. It comes down to whether virtue is an appropriate reaction to a moral challenge or a response to a gift of grace. All else follows from this distinction and the answer will go to the future of holiness theology in the next millennium. The holy person lives out of the grace of God and knows that no human action can produce a good conscience. Therefore, a holy person depends on the grace of God who patiently and courageously responds with confidence. The holy person does not look for or need generality, for such a person dares to respond to God amid the contingencies and possibilities of a particular practice, which engenders character. The holy person can celebrate life instead of secretly celebrating death as a moral person does. The holy person knows the plenitude engendered by grace as opposed to the scarcity, which characterizes a moral person. So the answer to the question becomes clear—No, the holy person is not a moral person. Yet, a holy person is so much more for such a person lives with the confidence engendered by the triune God.

Thus, moral theology is not about pointing to proofs, or building carefully crafted arguments based on rationality, nor it is about saying "look there is moral virtue." Moral practice introduces a person to a new way of being in the world engendered by Word and Spirit as truthfulness, patience, and sacramental life nourishes it. It is not about isolating a word and linking it to some transcendentally secure meaning. Moral theology will only be able to "go on," as it is understood to be a gesture of a truthful story shaped by the practice of the grace of God.

CHAPTER 6

Practicing Holiness

Considering Action in the Theology of John Wesley

Henry Walter Spaulding II

INTRODUCTION

RECENT DISCUSSION REGARDING A "practiced" Christianity may prove to be fortuitous for Wesleyan-Holiness theology. The connection between holiness and practice is both obvious and difficult. It is obvious because the general exteriorization of inward holiness amounts to the practice of holiness. Describing precisely what exteriorizing holiness means presents a challenge. Practice can easily be understood apart from grace. Since practice is a particular species of action, a thoroughgoing analysis of practicing holiness will require a consideration of Wesley's theology of action.

Such an analysis will no doubt evacuate the usual juxtaposition of "being" and "doing." In fact, it shows such a dichotomy to be false, one that denies the very heart of Wesleyan-Holiness theology. Clearly, Wesley's call to practice the faith constitutes action. He refused to allow the Christian faith to be a "mere" inward experience. Instead, he consistently called for action and defined this as "real" Christianity. The central argument of this chapter will be that Wesley not only calls for such action but provides a theology that renders such action intelligible.

ARGUMENT

The chapter will be organized into three general tasks. First, the philosophical and theological issues presented by action will be considered. This analysis is complicated by the way modern philosophy has understood the self and, by extension, action. Part of what must be done here is to trace the broad contours of the self in modernity and its demise in some postmodern philosophy. Agency, moral choice, decision-ism, and intentionality are not unique to modernity, but they have certainly been shaped by it. According to Catherine Pickstock, "the Cartesian gaze is inward and reflexive; gazing only at its own projection of order and sign, as if in its own mirrored reflection."[1] The second task of the chapter will be to examine the specific parameters of Wesley's understanding of action. For example, what is the relationship, if any, between the "Cartesian gaze" and Wesley's call for an embodied holiness? The final task of the chapter will take up the larger constructive attempt to embody Christian practice from a Wesleyan-Holiness perspective. Specifically, I will suggest that gift, participation, and practice combine to transform the meaning of action in Wesley to something that challenges the modern conception of the self and the nature of action itself. Further, the chapter will argue that a Wesleyan re-narration of action and self will provide a much more helpful place for addressing the concerns of practicing the faith.

ACTION, SELF, AND CHARACTER

Part of the story of Western thought and thus Christianity can be told by a consideration of action, self, and character. These three have shaped the intellectual traditions of the West and in turn have helped to define Christian theology. After all, the self has been present as the actor or sometimes the acted upon throughout history. People have deliberately chosen ends and in that way stitched together culture. In other words, human agents have intended and acted as they have embodied character. The story told through the lens of action, self, and character comprises the very fabric of human civilization. Sometimes human agents have proudly claimed to be the measure and other times they have lamented human failure. Friedrich Nietzsche, when reflecting on some of this

1. Pickstock, *After Writing*, 69.

says: "What a mad, unhappy animal is man!"[2] While the mood of human agency changes, its presence in the very fabric of things cannot be dismissed. All of this presents a special problem for comprehending and articulating the Christian faith.

A basic definition of human action is the capacity to envision and the power to accomplish certain ends. According to Maurice Blondel "the will could not find its entire completion in the intention alone; that is why it turns to action; to equal itself, it needs to produce itself."[3] Action reflects both desire and energy. Comprehending the meaning of action requires understanding what desire and energy come to mean. The problem, then, is with the weakened power to act on intentions. Perhaps, the often-repeated words of Paul reflect this dilemma, "I do not understand my own actions. For I do not do what I want, but I do the very thing I hate" (Rom 7:15 NRSV). Yet, the Scripture often urges action, "Keep alert, stand firm in your faith, be courageous, be strong. Let all that you do be done in love" (1 Cor 16:13–14 NRSV). At other places Paul reflection on the relationship between a husband and a wife. He goes on to talk about the relationship between a master and his slave. He gives advice to Timothy and Titus. The epistles often call to action, thus the tension between desire and energy is present in the entirety of the Scripture. This is all the more important in light of the words of Blondel: "Action is the cement with which we are fashioned; we subsist only to the extent that we act."[4] There is no honest way to read the history of faith apart from a history of sanctity. The idea of a disembodied faith is foreign to the Scripture and especially to the Wesleyan-Holiness tradition.

Part of the argument of this chapter is that, in order to talk about Christian practice, either as baptism, communion, prayer or visiting the sick, it is necessary to reflect upon a theology of action. Christian practices at some level must be intended/desired and accomplished. Dykstra and Bass define Christian practices as "things Christian people do together over time to address fundamental need in response to and in the light of God's active presence for the life of the world."[5] A self acts/practices, but what is this self? A full answer to this question requires a broad look at Western philosophy. It is my contention that the theological

2. Nietzsche, *Genealogy of Morals*, 226.

3. Blondel, *Action*, 152.

4. Blondel, *Action*, 178.

5. Dykstra and Bass, "Theological Understanding,"18.

resources found in Wesley's theology provide a creative place to engage these very issues.

To tell this story adequately, it is best to begin in the middle and then move backward and then forward. The analysis will begin in the emergence of modernity and then move back to the ancient/medieval world, finally coming to rest in what some call an *ancient* postmodernity. The modern shift as it is sometimes called is a complex event that cannot be fully captured in one philosopher or strand of modernity, but the general shift from practical to the theoretical has significant impact on the understanding of action. No one philosopher more clearly captures the shift than Descartes. He determined to begin again, thus dismissing experience, what he had learned from tradition, and all that appeared to be common-sense knowledge. He resolved to doubt and was left with a clear and distinct intuition. It is one that serves as the basis for modern philosophy: the self. He explicitly describes what kind of self: "But what, then, am I? A thinking thing it has been said. But what is a thinking thing? It is a thing that doubts, understands [conceives], affirms, denies, wills, refuses, that imagines also, and perceives."[6] This characterization plays itself out in Continental Rationalism and with slight mutation in British Empiricism. Yet, a strong argument could be advanced that the autonomy of the self is not a sixteenth-century move as much as it is a further advance of a late thirteenth-century move. Catherine Pickstock observes that "the theology of Duns Scotus (1265–1308) is perhaps the first definite theoretical symptom of the destruction from within of the liturgical city."[7] Therefore, any helpful discussion of action and practice will require some attention be given to the place that self takes in the divine economy/liturgical city.

Charles Taylor reflects on the meaning of agency in the modern world by calling attention to its central themes: inwardness, freedom, individuality, and being embedded in nature.[8] Any attempt to understand the issues that inform a discussion of action will require that we understand these themes as formative. Immanuel Kant makes this clear: "The concept of freedom, in so far as its reality is proved by an apodictic law of practical reason, is the keystone of the whole architecture of the system of pure reason and even of speculative reason."[9] Later in the same work

6. Descartes, "Meditations on First Philosophy," 388.

7. Pickstock, *After Writing*, 121.

8. Taylor, *Sources of the Self*, ix.

9. Kant, *Critique of Practical Reason*, 3.

Kant adds, "The autonomy of the will is the sole principle of all moral laws and of the duties conforming to them."[10] The positing of freedom is central to the idea of the practical reason necessary for morality. Yet, this presents a problem, one that is at the center of modern philosophy. According to D. Stephen Long, "This poses an irremediable contradiction in Kant's ethical system. The validity of the moral law requires something like God. But the moral law is known from and achieved through freedom alone, separate from any object of the good."[11] Such a contradiction forces freedom to be either arbitrary and/or absurd. The will is loosened from the metaphysical connections of the ancient/medieval world and left to defend itself in a world where freedom is the sole proprietor of action.

Kant reflects this in another work as well: "A good will is good not because of what it performs or effects, not by its aptness for the attainment of some proposed end, but simply by virtue of the volition, that is, it is good in itself."[12] Action thus conceived becomes self-defeating. Not long after Kant's observation, Nietzsche made this perfectly clear: "There is nothing of life that has value, except the degree of power—assuming that life itself is the will to power."[13] This very insight finally led Nietzsche to affirm that there is in fact no freedom of the will.[14] Yet, again for Nietzsche, "The will is a creator."[15] The subtle question of modernity that began with Descartes's assertion that the self is a "thinking, willing thing" becomes this hollow affirmation of Nietzsche: "Nothing more delightful grows on earth, O Zarathustra, than a lofty, strong will, that is the earth's most beautiful plant."[16] This story could be told over and over again as we hear the twin moves of affirming the priority of the will and fearing that it is simply not enough.

Modernity's growing awareness that human beings cannot bring themselves to happiness gives rise to a conception of the agent whose will is isolated within its own inwardness. Nietzsche says, "The sad truth is that we remain necessarily strangers to ourselves."[17] In other words,

10. Kant, *Critique of Practical Reason*, 33.
11. Long, *Goodness of God*, 64.
12. Kant, *Fundamental Principles*, 18.
13. Nietzsche, *Will to Power*, 37.
14. Nietzsche, *Will to Power*, 342.
15. Nietzsche, "Thus Spake Zarathustra," 253.
16. Nietzsche, "Thus Spake Zarathustra," 392.
17. Nietzsche, *Genealogy of Morals*, 149.

positing freedom of the will is the first note sounded toward nihilism. Those who understand the Scripture know exactly why this is the case. Adam and Eve were created for one another. Humans are together as co-humanity. We are called together in the word through the Spirit to be the body of Christ. The practice of baptism amounts to the Christian identity performed in the Eucharist. Yet, such a reality is impossible apart from fellowship with God. The anthem sounded by Nietzsche combines both the freedom of the will and its corollary, nihilism.[18]

Perhaps, Nietzsche illustrates more clearly than any other modern philosopher that the love of man is not enough, even if he wishes that it were enough. The primary focus of action as self-creation, without the resources of the Christian faith, is to be finally isolated on a path of inwardness. If modernity makes nothing else clear, such a path is one of alienation and erring. Catholic theologian Maurice Blondel reflects explicitly on Kant with these words, "What does this mean, if not that human action, by its own strength, pretends to assimilate, even to the point of exhausting it, all that knowledge cannot attain or that the will cannot fully embrace."[19] The hopes of modernity must finally be understood as vain. In other words, Descartes's often-repeated maxim, "I think, therefore I am," cannot sustain itself. A human being cannot ground itself any more than it can free itself.

According to Nietzsche, "God died: now we want the overman to live."[20] Yet, the truth that plays itself out in late modernity and early postmodernity is that, when God dies, so does the overman. Charles Taylor puts it this way: "There is a large element of hope. It is a hope that I see implicit in Judeo-Christian theism (however terrible the record of its adherents in history). In its central promise of a divine affirmation of the human, more total than humans can even attain unaided."[21] Action cannot be fully understood by looking for the will to power, but in a will saturated in the grace of God. The words of the Scripture ring true: "Those who find their life will lose it, and those who lose their life for my sake will find it" (Matt 10:39 NRSV). It is of at least some interest how modernity, in its affirmation of the self, ends up surrendering it and the will to the forces of the arbitrary, isolated, voluntarist journey into inwardness.

18. See Nietzsche, *Genealogy of Morals*, 177–78.

19. Blondel, *Action*, 293.

20. Nietzsche, "Thus Spake Zarathustra," 399.

21. Taylor, *Sources of the Self*, 521.

Before moving on to the sources out of which the newly freed, yet isolated self emerges, it is important to assess the central conclusions of modern philosophy regarding action. First, action is essential to the self. Second, to comprehend such action, it is necessary to posit freedom. Third, because this freedom is posited largely without metaphysical resources or least through the resources of epistemology loosened from metaphysics, action becomes arbitrary. Fourth, such arbitrariness posits a self that is lonely and isolated; it is a self without a face, one that begins to fear the pointlessness of action. Finally, the self that remains is not a self at all, and all action, either as sensation or will to power, can only exist emotively. The fate of this move can best be seen again in the horizon of the twentieth century. The words of Nietzsche can be heard at the close of modernity with a celebration that sounds more like a dirge: "Dead are all gods: now that we want the overman to live—on that great noon, let this be our last will."[22]

When Socrates stands before the men of Athens to defend himself against the charges of atheism and corrupting the youth, he makes a statement that all students of philosophy know: *the unexamined life is not worth living*. This phrase, when understood in its native Athens, is far different than when it is heard by the modern person. Socrates would never have considered this as an inward quest. Rather, he would have understood an examined life to be one that has come to understand itself in light of the "forms." Therefore, when he reflects on the education of the guardians, those who will rule the city, he considers character. Socrates says in Book II of *The Republic:* "The love of wisdom, then, and high spirit and quickness and strength will be combined for us in the nature of him who is to be a good and true guardian of the state."[23] Socrates is arguing in this work that the character of the guardian is the assurance of the will being directed to what is good, noble, and prudent. The distinction made by Socrates between knowledge and opinion is essential for understanding the will and thus the nature of action. He thinks that it is possible to educate a person who will come to see this distinction and therefore be able to live a just life, one where the will immediately attaches to the truth. Augustine presents a clear image of how desire becomes action and finally character:

22. Nietzsche, "Thus Spake Zarathustra,", 191.

23. Plato, *Republic*, 623.

> The same appetite with which one longs open-mouthed to know a thing becomes love of the thing known when it holds and embraces the acceptable offspring, that is, knowledge, and joins to its begetter. And so, you have a particular image of the trinity, the mind itself and its knowledge, which is its offspring and its word about itself, and love as the third element, and these three are one [1 John 5:8] and are one substance.[24]

Here we can see the will and the self united to the source of being; thus, action is defined not by arbitrary assertion but by an ordered love.

Robert Jenson underscores this insight: "But I do not arrive at that perfection by a journey of self-realization. I arrive at that perfection by never budging from baptism."[25] From this point of view, human doing is always a prayer. Jenson adds: "The Eastern Church's language about 'divinization' is the message that the final fulfillment of human being is to become not merely spectator but participant in the triune life of God."[26] There is a fixed reference for action in the ancient world, one that the Christian faith comes to see as Christian character or holiness. The fundamental insight of Wesleyan-Holiness theology is that action engenders character and character frames action. The touchstone for action is not self-creation, but participation in God. This point is spelled out by Augustine: "For before I was, you were, and I was nothing to which you could grant being. Yet, behold! I am, because of your goodness which preceded all that you made me to be, and all out of which you made me."[27] The emphasis upon character and ordered love apparent in much of the ancient/medieval world suggests the importance of tradition. As it was given to me, so I give to you becomes a standard way in which this takes place. Doctrines are, therefore, vehicles that define how Christians are to think, but more importantly how they are to be/act. The attempt to separate doctrine and ethics is foreign to the Wesleyan-Holiness tradition.

D. Stephen Long calls attention to the fact that modernity gave priority to ethics over theology.[28] This is possible only when the autonomy of the will/good will is assumed to be the most appropriate pattern of life. This leads to a disembodiment of virtue from the life it seeks to inform. So that, for example, justice becomes an ideal distinct from its

24. Augustine, *Trinity*, 283.

25. Jenson, "Doctrine of Justification," 110.

26. Jenson, "Doctrine of Justification," 112–113.

27. Augustine, *Confessions*, 335.

28. Long, *Goodness of God*, 18–20.

embodiment and its narrative history. We no longer have the saints to show us what virtue is; rather we have replaced it with an abstraction—a disembodied ideal without a narrative history. Yet, this turns out to be insufficient for the full kind of life that discipleship requires. The will becomes an abstraction and in that way is detached from particular action. An emphasis upon tradition gives us a history and a narrative by which we are to interpret life and to act. This is something that modernity has in large part forgotten and it something to which the Wesleyan-Holiness tradition leans.

The emphasis upon character, ordered love, and tradition is finally located most clearly in the recognition of God. Finally, it is not being toward which the Christian faith reaches, but God. When the will is considered in this light, its true nature is radically re-narrated:

> For will, in God or in creature, names neither a spontaneous arbitrary reduction from indeterminacy, nor even strictly speaking, the relation of cause to effect. Will, which cannot be a composite or contingent relation to God's essence, rather names, paradoxically, the infinite determinism of the Trinity to itself, the threefold determinism of love to the act of love: the lover's loving the beloved who himself fully and simply is the lover loving the beloved.[29]

This analysis makes it rather clear that it makes little sense to posit an inner self that is completely distinct from the outer self. Therefore, the will is both desire and power. Any other conclusion commits the modern mistake of the extended/unextended self, thus contributing to the unhelpful dualism of mind/body and body/soul. Blondel puts this idea forth with great clarity: "Every act tends to become a communion."[30] This same idea can be found in Aquinas according to Randy Maddox: "Aquinas came to value the way that Aristotle's model implied an ever deepening co-operation of God and humanity in the spiritual life, and the way that it made sense of how living in spiritual disciplines provides persons with a progressive freedom for Christian action."[31] The relation between action and recognition of God is essential to a re-narration of

29. Hanby, "Desire," 113.

30. Blondel, *Action*, 378.

31. Maddox, "Visit the Poor," 38.

action. Jenson makes this same point: "God *crucifies* human personality in order thereby and only thereby to bring it to fruition."[32]

Character, ordered love, and an emphasis on tradition all depend on an understanding of the way in which action is made coherent in the reality of God. This is a God who finds us in our disordered love in a condition of ill-being (sin) and by grace orders our love toward the Triune God. This results in correct desire and grace-enabled energy to engender the kind of character that is capable of freedom. In order to maintain this, certain skills or practices must be defined. This is, in part, the business of a practiced faith. This provides one grammar by which Wesleyan-Holiness theology and practice can be understood. Aristotle puts it this way: "It must, then, be remarked that every virtue or excellence (1) renders good the thing itself of which it is the excellence, and (2) causes it to perform its function well."[33] Finally, from a Christian point of view in general and a Wesleyan-Holiness point of view in particular, everything is to be understood as gift. Hanby reflects on Augustine in the following way: "The doxological self is thus able to participate in the life of the Trinity by virtue of a doxological character which it cannot escape, but can only pervert."[34] Therefore, action is rendered intelligible only by reference to character, ordered love, tradition, and recognition of God. Action exists in this sense as the overflow of gift.

Now that we have considered the issues and themes of action in modernity and the ancient/medieval world, the precise problem comes into focus. The self of Kant and others depends upon freedom to act but fails to provide a conception of the self that is adequate to engender a character capable of that freedom. Therefore, action is reduced to an arbitrary and/or pointless act, one without a real criterion for meaningful action. The quandary of modernity is unnecessary considering the resources already present in the ancient medieval world. For example, Plato provides an argument for character and an understanding of participation in the eternal forms sufficient to engender it. Aristotle develops a political understanding of humankind considering association and friendship to facilitate moral action. He specifically raises the issue of character because of habit. These ideas are further developed by Augustine and Aquinas as they are integrated into a Christian understanding. For Augustine it is the conception of *caritas* and *cupidity,* whereas for Aquinas it is the location

32. Jenson, "Doctrine of Justification," 109.

33. Aristotle, *Nicomachean Ethics*, 41.

34. Hanby, "Desire," 115.

of this worldly end considering the world to come. According to Aquinas: "And since man is rational man must have free choice . . . But free choice is the subject of grace."[35] It is this understanding that needs to be told again considering the modern dilemma.

Action is linked to self, and both are made coherent through an understanding of character. The comparison of the modern shift with the ancient/medieval starting place can be approached through the resources of intellectual history. We can, for example, see the results of positing a principle of freedom apart from a sense of the divine or at least a Platonic or Aristotelian conviction regarding metaphysics. Such a circumstance cannot but result in deep anxiety both intellectually and spiritually. Rowan Williams puts this in perspective: "A culture which tolerates the loss of a sense of damage to the moral identity, the loss of shame and remorse, is bound to be one that dangerously overplays the role of the will in the constitution of human persons."[36] His book is about the losses that seem to accompany late modernity. Here he is referring to the loss of moral identity as it becomes evident in the loss of shame and remorse, but there is a deeper problem. This is specifically addressed toward the end of Williams's book:

> The "lost icons" of this book have been clusters of convention and imagination, images of possible lives or modes of life; possible positions to occupy in a world that is inexorably one of time and loss. But as the discussion has developed, it has hinted more and more at a single, focal area of lost imagination—what I have called the lost soul. And this loss, I've suggested, is inextricably linked with the loss of what is encoded in the actual icons of Christian tradition and usage—the Other who does not compete, with whom I don't have to and can't bargain; the Other beyond violence, the regard that will not be evaded or deflected, yet has and seeks no advantage.[37]

Here is the problem (the loss of reference) and the solution (the re-narration of life as participation in the divine) that I will argue Wesleyan-Holiness theology and practice provides at the dawn of the postmodern world. It is the forward look from the backward glance that some call *ancient postmodernity*. Before this can be addressed in a fuller manner,

35. Aquinas, *Summa Theologica*, 437–38.

36. Williams, *Lost Icons*, 102.

37. Williams, *Lost Icons*, 186.

it will be important to address the basic themes of Wesley's theology of action.

THE SINGLE EYE: WESLEY'S THEOLOGY OF ACTION

John Wesley's theology of action affirms that human doing is a response to the grace of God. Theologically construed, it is necessary to understand that the currents of the Latin and Greek fathers flow in his theology. This fact helps to explain the theological genius of his theology, but it also illustrates some of its diversity of interpretation. Most of all, however, it provides a theological basis for holding together faith and sanctity as they shed light on the nature of action. H. Ray Dunning locates a Wesleyan distinctive in the doctrine of prevenient grace: "It could even be argued that this teaching was the most far-reaching and pervasive aspect of Wesley's thought."[38] Dunning consistently seeks to show how a Wesleyan theology avoids the trap of fundamentalism on one hand and liberalism on the other. He argues that Wesleyan theology offers a relational theology capable of sustaining the central claims of Christian perfection.

J. Kenneth Glider argues that the distinctive of Wesleyan-Holiness theology[39] comes down to doctrines that are "peculiarly suited to our homing instinct for the moral."[40] His agenda is to show that the American Holiness Movement corrected Wesley in certain ways, especially at the point of "Christ's Spirit baptism." He says, "It remained for the American Holiness Movement to elucidate the teaching."[41] Walter Klaiber and Man-ford Marquardt note: "Despite Wesley's efforts to promote sanctification . . . there remains a tension between the striving for a clearly established perfection and the abiding awareness of one's dependence upon God."[42] Kaliber and Marquardt are less interested in the tensions apparent between classical Wesleyan theology and the American holiness tradition and more concerned to provide the United Methodist Church

38. Dunning, *Grace, Faith, and Holiness*, 49.

39. It should not escape our attention that Grider consistently uses Wesleyan-Holiness theology where Dunning uses Wesleyan. This reflects a theological battle that informs some "camps" within those Wesleyans who particularly emphasize entire sanctification.

40. Grider, *Wesleyan-Holiness Theology*, 36.

41. Grider, *Wesleyan-Holiness Theology*, 434.

42. Klaiber and Marquardt, *Living Grace*, 307.

with "a clearer exposition of its theological stance."[43] These three comments illustrate some of the range present within Wesleyan theology. The concern of this chapter is to show that, considering the recent interest in a "practiced" faith, a Wesleyan-Holiness tradition provides a theology ready-made for such an emphasis.

The concern of this chapter has been to define and finally to argue for a theology of action in the Wesleyan spirit. It is also important to understand the unique intellectual space occupied by John Wesley. It is a lack of understanding this issue that often makes the Wesleyan-Holiness position seem untenable or even anti-intellectual. This is not the place to fully engage this issue, but it is essential to sketch the broad parameters of this intellectual space as a way of locating Wesley's theology of action. The basic parameters of this space are as follows: (1) a vigorous Triune metaphysic of gift; (2) an understanding of knowing as participation: and (3) a practical rationality defined by the means of grace. It should be clear from this basic outline that Wesleyan-Holiness theology is catholic in the broad sense of the word. It should also be noted that Wesleyan-Holiness theology is evangelical in the sense that it understands grace as instantaneous. All of this leads to an optimism of grace, one that holds out hope for humankind's restoration in the saving/sanctifying grace of God. A fuller treatment of these broad parameters will need to wait for later development, but these parameters do locate Wesley's theology of action as gift, participation, and practical rationality in the means of grace.

The larger grammar sketched in the previous paragraph suggests a strong link between action, self, and character: "Let all those who are real members of the Church, see that they walk holy and unblameable in all things."[44] The argument of this section is rather straightforward. First, Wesley consistently calls for Christians to act, that is, to embody or exteriorize their faith. Second, this action is always understood in conscious dependence upon God. This makes it abundantly clear that Wesley construes the self and thus Christian character in dependence upon the ever-present help of the Holy Spirit. Therefore, action is envisioned/shaped and empowered by God. This means that Wesley offers a theology of action and not a philosophy or psychology of action. The re-narration of action found in Wesley presents a challenge to the modern construal of the self and thus conceives of action only in reference to the divine.

43. Klaiber and Marquardt, *Living Grace*, 11.

44. Wesley, "Of the Church," 6:400.

Wesley talks about action as a man who knew the current debates in philosophy and theology. He is a post-Descartes and pre-Nietzsche theologian. Wesley breathes the air of empiricism, especially the influence of John Locke.[45] But it is central to the argument of this chapter to understand that, while Wesley was an eighteenth-century person, his deepest debts were not to the modern paradigm, but to a re-narrated ancient post-modernity. I am not arguing that Wesley was a postmodern thinker. Rather, my argument is that Wesley understands the issues at stake in the modern self and intentionally interprets them through the lens of the ancient faith. Several interesting insights into Wesley's understanding should be noted in this passage. First, God made human beings "thinking beings" capable of perception of present and past. There is only a hint of Descartes (or the Cartesian gaze) in this description. While Wesley notes the importance of thinking, he is clear that it is a gift of God. Therefore, it is not difficult to see that, for Wesley, even sensation is to be comprehended as gracious gift. Second, human beings can place themselves in history as a way of connecting *inward* perception and *outward* behavior. While on the face of it this may sound like a modern separation of the inner and outer, nothing could be further from the truth for Wesley. He says, "Some late writers indeed have given a name to this and have chosen to style it a *moral sense.*"[46] He prefers "conscience" to "moral sense" because it is scriptural, "because it is the word which the wisdom of God hath chosen to use in the inspired writing."[47] He adds to this by further clarifying the meaning of conscience. It is "a faculty or power, implanted by God in every soul that comes into the world, of perceiving what is right or wrong in his own heart or life, in his tempers, thoughts, words, and actions."[48] Wesley is not afraid to talk about behavior or even morality, but he is clear that such is not an autonomous activity. We have a conscience capable of action, but the only way to understand this is from a theological frame.

Wesley understood the conscience as first and foremost a way of understanding the Scripture and self. He also connects this to an agreement of our attitudes and conversations in light of the Scripture. Conscience is the way our inner self conforms to an outward rule.[49] The link between

45. Maddox, "Reconnecting the Means to the End," 39.

46. Wesley, "Witness of Our Own Spirit," 5:135.

47. Wesley, "Witness of Our Own Spirit," 5:136.

48. Wesley, "Witness of Our Own Spirit," 5:136.

49. Wesley, "Witness of Our Own Spirit," 5:137.

conscience and Scripture or inner perception and outward behavior is of greatest interest in Wesley: "What the eye is to the body, the intention is to the soul. As the one guides all the motions of the body, so does the other those of the soul."[50] There is no sense that one can navigate these waters in an appropriate manner apart from the grace of God. According to Wesley:

> From those which are commonly termed religious actions, and which are real branches of true religion, where they spring from a pure and holy intention, and are performed in a manner suitable thereto—our Lord proceeds to the actions of common life; and shows that the same purity of intentions is as indispensably required in our ordinary business as in giving alms, or fasting or prayer.[51]

Every good action comes from God and every evil action is a perversion of the good that God desires for us.

Wesley understood that action is made even more difficult in light of the temptations of the world, that is, sin. Apart from God there is no hope for right action, and it is equally futile to retreat into some inner self that remains pure in a godless world. Wesley so links the inner and the outer that it is best to talk about Christian character. When Wesley refers to the "Character of a Methodist," he makes this clear. "Whether he lie down or rise up, God is in all his thoughts; he walks with God continually, having the loving eye of his mind still fixed upon him, and everywhere 'seeing Him that is invisible.'"[52] Action for Wesley is a response to the grace of God. Apart from this graciousness we would by our own action build a personal "Tower of Babel" and the result would be the confusion that can be easily documented in the modern world.

Wesley suggests many ways to talk about action, but none of these ways is better than his expression: the single eye. He talks about the single eye "in simplicity and godly sincerity."[53] He adds, "This is what our Lord recommends, under the name of a 'single eye' . . . If therefore this eye of thy soul be single, all thy actions and conversation shall be 'full of light,' of the light of heaven, of love, and peace, and the joy of the Holy Spirit."[54] He

50. Wesley, "Upon Our Lord's Sermon on the Mount—Discourse VIII," 5: 362.

51. Wesley, "Upon Our Lord's Sermon on the Mount—Discourse VIII," 5: 361.

52. Wesley, "Character of a Methodist," 6:343.

53. Wesley, "Witness of Our Own Spirit," 5:138.

54. Wesley, "Witness of Our Own Spirit," 5:139.

further defines this single eye as "a steady view," "a single intention," and the "constant spring of all our thoughts, desires, and purposes."[55] At one level such a description makes no sense at all. It seems that any description of human consciousness as *single* flies in the face of what we know about the unconscious mind or even the multitude of influences in the world. How could one hope to think one thing when the many voices of life call from every corner of the world? Wesley had to know that the memory plays a role in present decisions and thus actions. Yet, he calls for a single eye, one that is simple and sincere. He makes the distinction between these: "Simplicity regards the intention itself, sincerity the execution of it; and this sincerity relates . . . to our whole conversation."[56] Wesley links intention and execution in such a way as to completely evacuate the false dichotomy between being and doing.[57] Once again, Wesley makes it clear that action and the resulting holiness as justice, mercy, and truth is a gift of God. For him, action is an expression of the divine ground of selfhood. It is this conviction that keeps Christian action from sinking to "the beggarly elements of the world."[58] He can say, then, "that all my works are wrought in him. Yea and that it is He who worketh all my works in me. I rejoice in seeing through the light of God, which shines in my heart, that I have power to walk in this way; and that, through his grace, I turn not therefrom, to the right hand or to the left."[59] Wesley's understanding of the single eye, therefore, must be understood as suggesting that action tends toward the divine. Freedom in this sense is in dependence, that is to say, it is obedience. Action can never be thought of in the grammar of Wesley's theology as "works righteousness," but it is equally true that human action is the active, not merely the passive response to the grace of God.

Wesley says, "I am conscious to myself of one more property, commonly called liberty."[60] In order to be clear, he adds, "This is very frequently confounded with the will, but is of a very different nature."[61] This clarification is connected to Wesley's attempt to describe the self in relation to God. He does not recognize any attempt to completely

55. Wesley, "Witness of Our Own Spirit," 5:139.
56. Wesley, "Witness of Our Own Spirit," 5:139.
57. Wesley, "Witness of Our Own Spirit," 5:139.
58. Wesley, "Witness of Our Own Spirit," 5:139.
59. Wesley, "Witness of Our Own Spirit," 5:142.
60. Wesley, "What Is Man?" 7:228.
61. Wesley, "What Is Man?" 7:228.

separate the self and God. In fact, human life as God intends it can only be understood in light of the divine. Speaking of the will, he always connects it to the soul, which governs all the motions of the body.[62] According to Randy Maddox, "The technical way what Wesley expressed this general conviction was by equating the human faculty of the 'will' with our 'affection'. Since the will is usually understood to be the springboard of human action, Wesley's equation allowed him to stress that we must be 'affected' before we can act."[63] This further argues that Wesley saw action holistically, that is, springing from a character responding to the work of God in the heart.

Wesley reflects on the importance of the will and its need to be broken in children in a sermon entitled, "On the Education of Children,"

> Indeed it may be said that every man is by nature, as it were, his own God. He worships himself. He is, in his own conception, absolute lord of himself. He seeks himself in all things. He pleases himself . . . *His own will* is his only law; he does this or that because it is his good pleasure.[64]

Because of this, it is crucial as the first order of business in the education of children is "to break their will the first moment it appears. In the whole art of Christian education there is nothing more important than this."[65] The parent is to "teach them to submit to this while they are children, that they may be ready to submit to His will when they are men."[66]

Several things arise from a consideration of Wesley's understanding of self in relation to action. First, the will as it is affected by the grace of God will determine, in at least a soft sense, the nature of action. This goes back to the idea of the single eye, "It is by faith that the eye of the mind is opened, to see the light of the glorious love of God."[67] Second, it is essential to distinguish between the will and the tempers. Wesley talks about the will in light of the single eye. The will can respond to the Holy Spirit; therefore, it can be instantaneously re-oriented by faith. The tempers are historical dispositions and as such are subject to the more gradual re-narration by attending the means of grace and the process of

62. See Wesley, "What Is Man?" 7: 226–27.

63. Maddox, "Visit the Poor," 17.

64. Wesley, "On the Education of Children," 7:89.

65. Wesley, "On the Education of Children," 7:92.

66. Wesley, "On the Education of Children," 7:92.

67. Wesley, "Upon Our Lord's Sermon on the Mount—Discourse VIII," 5:362.

being healed by the Spirit. Strictly speaking, even the process is instantaneous for Wesley. The logic of this is guided by the idea that the healing of the tempers is still a gracious gift and as such it comes in an instant. This safeguards Wesley from allowing the process of healing to be a subtle opening to human effort separate from the gift of grace. This is, of course, the paradox Top of Form of Wesleyan-Holiness theology. All we do is a response to the grace of God, but, apart from the response, the grace is ineffectual. Therefore, we act by way of a response, yet apart from the response good is not done.

The quandary of a Wesleyan-Holiness theology is how to maintain the centrality of the graciousness of God in light of an appropriate understanding of human agency. I am arguing that this is much less a problem for Wesley than it is for many Wesleyans. The reason is that Wesley understood selfhood only as a relation to God, and therefore human agency was always a response to grace. This means that action is not a striking out on one's own; it is always a response either as obedience or disobedience to a gracious God. Understanding this will make it clear that sin is a disordered act of love in the thought of Wesley. In other words, we are made in the image of God and we are restless until we come to rest in God. A renewed will is an instantaneous gift of a gracious God. The reordering of the affection is the continually gracious endurance of a person who has fixed his/her eye on God.

Because of the way Wesley understood action, especially in light of the graciously related self, he thinks of zeal as crucial to all action, "for without zeal it is impossible either to make any considerable progress in religion in ourselves, or to do any considerable service to our neighbor, whether in temporal or spiritual things."[68] Yet, it is crucial to see that Wesley understood that "true Christian zeal is not other than the flame of holy love."[69] The breadth of this statement effectively links all the elements of action in Wesley. First, the key to action is that love sits on the throne of life and in the fullness of that presence guides all behavior. Second, the holy tempers, that is, those historical dispositions that determine much of our lives as they are linked to the love on the throne of life, are manifest as fruit of the Spirit. Third, from these holy tempers proceed the works of mercy. It is in this way that faith connects to the needs of other people. It is the way in which the earth is renewed by the presence of the faithful.

68. Wesley, "On Zeal," 7:57.

69. Wesley, "On Zeal," 7:59.

Fourth, after the works of mercy, which touch the lives of the hurting, the works of piety follow and the means of grace become the vehicle for a further provocation to action. Finally, all of this comes to rest in the church as the community instituted by God to engender the life and thus actions of the faithful. This is the expression of zeal for Wesley. Therefore, we come to see that zeal is the expression of the gracious leading of the Holy Spirit.

It is the single eye that describes Wesley's understanding of the relationship between action, self, and character. It suggests that for Wesley the autonomous self is a perversion of God ordered love. Singleness and purity of intention are less a testament to the rationality of human agency and more to the capacity of the self to be doxologically framed. Given that fact, the self is construed not only as a thing that *thinks*, but as a thing that *acts*. Yet, it is crucial that both thinking and acting be understood as tending toward the divine. In fact, for Wesley, it can be put more forcefully than that. Our entire existence, either as a prodigal or as a son/daughter, is defined by the gracious presence of God. The basic logic of Wesley's theology of action is that a single eye engendered by the grace of God defines a doxological self who, throughout life, comes to rest in a Christian character. Maddox points to a crucial point for our discussion. Therefore, the process that results in the gracious gift of a Christian character is ultimately defined by grace.

The general argument of this chapter is that the recent emphasis upon a "practiced" Christianity is probably a fortuitous event. The reason for this is that, at the very core of Wesley's theology, a grammar, there exists that which is compatible with a move away from theology as metaphysics to a theology as action. No one would argue that core doctrinal convictions are unrelated or unimportant for theology. Still, too much modern theology has been content to hammer out doctrine without truly engaging life. When we turn to Wesley, we find a clear sense that faith is both an intellectual endeavor and a matter of faithfulness in life and ministry. At every point, behavior is linked to faith, and this is in part the meaning of holiness. The tension between faith and action need not complicate Wesleyan-Holiness theology. The reason for this is apparent: Wesley provides a theology with the parameters to encourage attending to the means of grace and visiting the sick. His emphasis on character argues against reducing the Christian life to a moment but encompasses all moments within the endurance that defines character.

Wesley talks about the single eye, but he refuses to make it our work alone. Still, he holds to the conviction that faith is a response to gracious invitation. Wesley reflects on the self, but he refuses to allow it to become the lonely self-willing itself to be. Therefore, Wesley can largely avoid making faith to be merely the "courage to be" that is so attractive to many in modern theology. Because of this, he can ground the self in gracious gift and still talk about working out our salvation. Clearly, he does not mean that we do the saving any more than personal faith means that I have designed myself or put God in a box. Finally, it all comes down to the kind of character that is capable of freedom, which knows the freedom that comes in obedience to the Holy Spirit. It is in just this way that Wesley avoids the trap of the modern self and arbitrary action and turns his attention to the single eye caught up in the Triune music of peaceful flight.

GIFT, PARTICIPATION, AND PRACTICE

Understanding the issues involved in a theology of action against the horizon of modern theology suggests that the rupture between self/God, self/world, and self/other is avoidable. In other words, it is possible and even advisable to challenge the viability of the autonomous self. Wesley talks about this in terms of the character of a Methodist. He defines such a person as one that is happy, prays, has a pure heart, keeps the commandments, presents his soul and body as a living sacrifice, and understands that all doing is to the glory of God. A Methodist is "inwardly and outwardly conformed to the will of God, as revealed in the written word."[70] He also says, "All the commandments of God he accordingly keeps, and that with all his might."[71] These comments illustrate that a Wesleyan theology of action is about a living faith, one that offers an option to a sterile and abstract faith. It is a practiced faith, one that is constituted as gift, participation, and practice. Wesley's theology of action demonstrates that resources exist within the Wesleyan-Holiness tradition for addressing the rupture that appears to be inherent in modern philosophy and theology.

My final task is to present a constructive proposal for reclaiming the intellectual space for an authentic Wesleyan-Holiness theology, with special reference to action. This will involve three spheres, each of which

70. Wesley, "Character of a Methodist," 6:346.

71. Wesley, "Character of a Methodist," 6:344.

intersects at the point of action. The first sphere involves a Triune metaphysic vigorous enough to engender a theology of gift. At the most basic level, this first move is a challenge to all attempts to understand action autonomously. Likewise, it challenges all decisionistic conceptions of the self. It suggests a theonomous ground for all human action, one that is dependent upon revelation. It is as God as revealed himself as Father, Son, and Holy Spirit and as that life has overflowed to all creation that we come to understand gift. We act not because we are powerful enough to act, but because we have received a gift unexpectedly from a gracious God. It is in the power of God that we are empowered to decide and to act.

Blondel makes this very point: "Action is not completed in the natural order."[72] Contra Kant, Blondel makes it clear that action cannot be fully understood until it comes to rest in communion. Milbank confirms this analysis by saying that "Blondel's phenomenology concludes negatively, with the paradox that human will, from its most native desire, demands a completion that goes beyond its resources. In its immanent impulses, it requires the transcendent, which, though necessary to it, can only be superadded, freely given."[73] Since all action arises in response to and finds completion in the divine life, it is vital to consciously understand that the doctrine of the Trinity is the fundamental Christian narrative. It is the reference to the sacred that challenges modern theology to heal the rupture. Central to any consideration of a choosing self is the conviction that all choice is predicated upon gift. Crucial to this observation is the understanding of the self as doxological.

Augustine says, "Your works praise you, to the end that we may love you, and we love you to the end that your works may praise you."[74] Action is praise and such a life is a prayer. A Christian life is one that is uttered in the presence of a God who has called humanity in the word to participate in him. Hanby observes, "Thus on Augustine's terms, nihilism can arise only when doxology fails, and all that is not doxology is nihilism."[75] A doxological self is one that is framed by a prayer uttered to God that in turn spills over into the world of associations as invitation. Therefore, action is a prayer, one that is first a doxology.

72. Blondel, *Action*, 358.

73. Milbank, *Theology and Social Theory*, 210.

74. Augustine, *Confessions*, 367.

75. Hanby, "Desire," 116.

What does it mean to be an acting self? The place to begin this reflection is on the God who exists in everlasting donation and return. It is as the Father loves the Son and as that love is returned in the Spirit that the life of God is constituted as being-in-communion. It is in this way that the persons of the Trinity act. We know as we are known and the only real way to understand this is as a prayer. God has shown us how to be and at the same time evacuated the idea that being is separate from doing. The response in time is the church. Human beings are called by the Spirit through the foolishness of preaching to be enacted in the world. According to John Milbank: "Finally in Christianity, God is thought of as asking only for the offering of our freewill, in the return of love to him. This is no longer in any sense a self-destructive or self-division, but rather a self-fulfillment, an offering of the fullness of Being. It is receiving God: 'deification.'"[76] According to Milbank, "Every action, proceeds, outwards, away from ourselves hitherto, and back into a public domain, as something in principle appropriable by others."[77]

The second sphere involves participation. Augustine helps us to see part of the meaning of participation: "God is the only source to be found of any good things, but especially of those which make a man good and those which will make him happy; only from him do they come into a man and attach themselves to a man."[78] Understanding that the starting place for a theology of action is the Triune life of God leads one to see the importance of participation. The subject/object split is part of the grammar of the modern world, but what is often lost in this process is a deeper insight regarding participation. We are able to act because we participate in God. Knowing is not a wrapping of the mind around some exterior reality. Rather, knowing is being known and allowing that participation to define life. Understanding the interpenetration of life in the Spirit helps us to understand the nature of action more clearly.

The self that participates is not the self-authenticating self of much modern philosophy/theology. There is a real sense in which the self is lost only to be found again in a new and better reality. Stanley Hauerwas suggests: "The loss of the 'self and the increasing appreciation of the significance of the body, and in particular the body's permeability, can help us rediscover holiness not as an individual achievement but as the work

76. Milbank, "Postmodern Critical Augustinianism," 271.

77. Milbank, *Theology and Social Theory*, 357.

78. Augustine, *Trinity*, 350.

of the Holy Spirit building up the body of Christ."[79] Hauerwas is pointing to an inconsistency in much holiness theology at this point. He observes: "The 'self' that theologians now rush to save is the 'sovereign self' that sought to be its own ground."[80] Action, when it is understood through the lens of a Wesleyan-Holiness theology, will always be constituted by participation.

The third sphere involves practical reason through the means of grace. The means of grace become a way of engaging the world. For example, baptism is a way of coming to see ourselves as owned by God. When it functions this way, it is a practical rationality. The same could be said for hospitality to the stranger, visiting the sick, or even discernment. There is a sense in which the means of grace are ways to "reason" the world. They locate the self as recipient while at the same time driving us to act. According to Serene Jones, the means of grace free us and form us.[81] It is in this rationality that the church can embody holiness.

All three spheres considered as part of this constructive proposal intersect at action. The Triune metaphysic frames the centrality of gift. Participation drives the human agent to act and invites all other agents as well as creation to join in transformative action. Thus, the agent is transformed and transforms in the economy of grace. Practical rationality through the means of grace becomes the way the world is construed and engaged. The rationality engendered by the means of grace re-narrates all of life, including action. Graham Ward makes this point:

> If the Church is to speak in and to the present *Zeitgeist,* then it must recover its deliberations of desire and articulate again its theology of eros. It must do so in a way that learns from, but goes beyond, the contractualism of Hobbes and Spinoza, and the hierarchical teleology of Hegel. It must do so in a way that maintains corporeality and emphasizes the formation of substantial communities through shared practices.[82]

These shared practices are the rationality that defines the Christian faith. They serve as a way of engaging the world, whether in doxology or invitation. The means of grace are a practice and as such they represent a way of engaging life, of acting.

79. Hauerwas, *Sanctify Them in the Truth,* 78.
80. Hauerwas, *Sanctify Them in the Truth,* 98.
81. Jones, "Graced Practices," 58.
82. Ward, *Cities of God,* 151.

The three spheres set out in this section (gift, participation, and practice) are the first steps to a larger endeavor. Milbank approaches this in the following comment: "For a polity based on virtue, the goal of authority is not simply an effective peace or order, nor the representation of majority will, nor the liberty and equality of individuals, but rather the education of individuals into certain practices and states of character, regarded as objectively desirable goals for human beings as such."[83] The interesting part of this observation is the connection between virtue and character. A Wesleyan-Holiness theology of action is much more connected to character than decision. No doubt there are many decisions that a human agent will make, but the interesting thing is not a decision, but the endurance of those moments into a character. A Wesleyan-Holiness theology of action will seek to comprehend those through the lens of gift, participation, and practice.

I began with the observation that recent discussion of a "practiced" Christianity may prove to be fortuitous. The reason for this is the natural tendency, especially in the modern world, to compartmentalize. When this happens, "orthodoxy" and "orthopraxy" can be separated into self-justifying theological camps. Yet, this separation is unhealthy and unnecessary. I have attempted to argue that sufficient resources exist in Wesleyan-Holiness theology to heal this rupture. A theology of action has been used to illustrate how this might happen, but the same logic can be extended to a wide range of theological concerns. In fact, Wesleyan-Holiness theology requires that faith and sanctity be held together. When this happens the doxology will ring from the actions of those who have been saturated in the everlasting grace of God.

83. Milbank, *Theology and Social Theory*, 326.

CHAPTER 7

Sanctifying Atonement

Womanist Theology, Wesleyan Ethics, and the Future of Wesleyan-Holiness Atonement Theology

Henry Walter Spaulding III

INTRODUCTION

As theologian Hans Urs von Balthasar writes, "God's truth is, indeed, great enough to allow an infinity of approaches and entryways. And it is also free enough subsequently to expand the horizon of one who has chosen to narrow a starting point and to help him to his feet."[1] Thus, differing theological perspectives not only approach the infinite nature of God, but when read in harmony with one another, illuminate and deepen our understandings of certain theological positions on which we have been too narrow-minded. This is especially true of the Church of the Nazarene where the doctrine of atonement is concerned. The doctrine of the atonement has not been integrated in the way we understand theological ethics and holiness. This is because the Article of Faith of the Church of the Nazarene on atonement has focused on a certain theory of the atonement (namely satisfaction theory) and not on how our entire theological reflection has a hole in it, lest we make connections between the various ways we see atonement fitting within our views of sanctification. What is missing is how both atonement and sanctification help inform our ability to be creatures in the way God intended, namely the *imago Dei.*

1. von Balthasar, *Glory of the Lord,* 1:17.

This paper will consider three subjects (i.e., atonement, sanctification, and ethics) together as uniquely informing a holistic understanding of the Wesleyan perspective on the economy of salvation and our participation in the life of God. This is partially in response to two major events at the 28th General Assembly. One is the response to JUD-802 and JUD-816 by the committee on the study of Scripture by the General Board that requested to expound "the concept of atonement, thereby enriching the Church's comprehension and faith."[2] To this end, I suggest a serious exploration of the work done by Womanist theologians on the atonement provides such an enrichment. This paper will also answer the conundrum of the rejected USA-920 on racial reconciliation from the North American Caucus of the Church of the Nazarene. The previous consideration of Womanist theology might provide an avenue for a theologically robust language of reconciliation that can emerge from preexisting confessions in our tradition. This might seem like an odd choice with an immense task for theological discussion, but the promise of such an engagement should prove valuable to both our reconciliatory efforts and theological confession. If nothing else, I would hope that this chapter may spark conversations about our article of faith on atonement and the language of racial reconciliation. My argument will be that when Womanist theologies of atonement are read next to Wesley's own views on holiness, a certain type of moral theology—centered on a concrete participation in the work of Christ—emerges.

IMAGO DEI

To understand the work of atonement from Womanist thinkers, we must understand what type of atonement we need. Thus, it would be important to note not what humans were created in (i.e., *imago Dei*) but what they fell into (i.e., *sicut Deus).* What *we* will notice from such a comparison is that humans have fallen from their relationships with God and others. Thus, the sin that needs to be redeemed is our loss of vision of what it means to be creatures. Instead, we have become trapped by bent and disordered desires.

The reality of *sicut Deus* comes to pass through the promise of having a better relationship with God. It happens in the fall when Adam and Eve eat the fruit, which prompts humanity's reorganization. This

2. King and Varughese, "Report of the Scripture Study Committee," 11.

reorganization comes to Adam and Eve via the serpent's promise over and against the statement of God that eating the fruit would lead to their death (Gen 2:17).[3]

The promise to be like God is a promise for a deeper relationship. However, it is a relationship that is coded under death. For as long as the serpent tries to rearticulate in a more positive light the stipulation that if they eat of the fruit they will die, it is still the end result of the fall.[4] When Adam literally ingests the fruit, he ingests death.[5]

In addition to digesting death, Adam and Eve birth a tangential mode of being human not intended for them in the original creation. When humanity becomes *sicut Deus* they cease to be *imago Dei.* To be in the image of God means to be free, like God is free.[6] The human as *imago Dei* is free, but it has limits imposed upon it; namely, it is not the creator and it must rely on God for its existence and freedom. Now, these realities still exist, but they are hampered. It is not that the creature becomes closer to God, but rather denies his/her limit and creates life for him or herself. Thus, the central problem in *sicut Deus* is not that a person has ceased to be a creature, but that she has ceased to let God create her life. This means that *sicut Deus* creates life for herself and attempts to exist as an unprepossessed reality by which she can remain creator of her life and world. In this creation, it is essential to realize the disastrous result for other humans who live with the *sicut Deus.*

It is important here to briefly summarize the positive side of the Image of God. In short, the Image of God means that we were made to have freedom with God and not to rely on our own resources. This "freedom is," as Bonhoeffer writes, "a relation between two persons."[7] This is "likeness," note, not "like God" We only know of this freedom to be in proper relation (to God, people, and creation) because of Jesus Christ.[8] It means that to be restored is to be visited with a new vision. Our freedom is not understood in terms of substance—in which we receive a new substance in the coming of Christ—but rather as something that happens through

3. See Bonhoeffer, *Creation and Fall*, 113.
4. Bonhoeffer, *Creation and Fall*, 112.
5. Bonhoeffer, *Creation and Fall*, 135.
6. Bonhoeffer, *Creation and Fall*, 62.
7. Bonhoeffer, *Creation and Fall*, 63.
8. Bonhoeffer, *Creation and Fall*, 62.

Christ.[9] Ultimately, this is the result of the anhypostatic union of Christ uniting himself to us.[10]

If the atonement is meaningful then it must seek to restore what was lost in humanity, namely this freedom. This is in fact what it means to be made in God's image, to be free in relationship. The term Bonhoeffer uses is *analogia relationis*.[11] We share in God's nature through this ability to be free for relationship. As Bonhoeffer writes, "Only where God and the brother, the sister, come to them can human beings find their way back to the earth. Human freedom for God and the other person and human freedom from the creature in dominion over it constitute the first human beings' likeness to God."[12] Two things must be noted here: 1) the relationship of original humanity and 2) that we have lost this ability to be in relationship.

SOCIOPOLITICS OF SATISFACTION THEORY OF ATONEMENT

The satisfaction theory of atonement was born out of a certain sociopolitical reality in the eleventh century. Amid the bloodshed that arose at the beginning of the feudal period, cultural leaders were forced to try and find a theopolitical answer to the problem.[13] Among the places being ravaged were holy places such as churches and monasteries. To respond, bishops and leaders began, among other councils and ecclesial initiatives, emphasizing the death of Christ as that which bound Christians together.[14]

Rita Brock and Rebecca Parker note that, "Christianity [already had begun] to lose its grip on the sinfulness of killing. A new age began—one in which the execution of Jesus would become a sacrifice to be repeated, first on the Eucharist altar and then in the ravages of a full-blown holy war."[15] Thus, we see a shift taking place in the element of the blood of the cross as not only salvific in itself, but an action that demands repetition

9. Bonhoeffer, *Creation and Fall*, 63.
10. See Bonhoeffer, *Creation and Fall*, 63.
11. Bonhoeffer, *Creation and Fall*, 65.
12. Bonhoeffer, *Creation and Fall*, 67.
13. Brock and Parker, *Saving Paradise*, 254–57.
14. Brock and Parker, *Saving Paradise*, 252–53; 258–306.
15. Brock and Parker, *Saving Paradise*, 252.

through the spilling of the blood of others. This was promoted as a salvific act as humanity was increasingly reminded of their guilt for the execution of Jesus. Therefore, to achieve peace in the eleventh century Holy Roman Empire, the cross became a central aspect for political peace.

The feudal theology of crucifixion increasingly began to be read as a salvific, peace-giving source and was ultimately taken up not just as a political tool, but as central to the theological account as well. This is no clearer than in the theology of St. Anselm of Canterbury, chief architect of the satisfaction theory of atonement. In Anselm's time the cross had already begun to be venerated as a sign of peace between people. However, Anselm had unique life problems of his own surrounding his role as bishop. As Brock and Parker write,

> [Anselm] was called to Canterbury as archbishop in 1093, during a lull in a long-standing conflict between the church in England and King William Rufus. Rufus wanted the churches and monasteries to swear allegiance and donate their revenues to him rather than to the pope. Anselm opposed Rufus and became embroiled in the fray, which erupted intermittently through two popes, two kings, and two periods of exile. During his exiles, Anselm struggles to find resources to meet his community's needs. The conflicts trapped Anselm in a lifelong struggle with debt.[16]

Anselm was embroiled in a particularly difficult problem with the feudal order. He was left with the choice to give honor (i.e., pay allegiance) to a feudal king or to the vicar of Christ. Thus, debt imagination ruled his thought as he turned to his work on the atonement.[17] As Brock and Parker write,

> Anselm did not base his theology on scriptural interpretation and disputation with other thinkers . . . Rather he drew his analogies of sin and recompense from an emerging monetary system that, for many, resulted in crushing debt and the desperate struggle to pay it off. The obedient loyalty and honor due to feudal lords provided the framework of values for his thinking.[18]

Thus, in Anselm's thought God serves in place of the feudal lord, but instead of paying him honor through monetary means we pay God through

16. Brock and Parker, *Saving Paradise*, 266.
17. Brock and Parker, *Saving Paradise*, 266–67.
18. Brock and Parker, *Saving Paradise*, 267.

pious actions.[19] However, we are incapable of paying God honor and thus sin against God. Furthermore, since the one we sin against is God, we incur an infinite debt that we can never repay. Therefore, as Anselm writes, "The life of this man [Christ] was so sublime, so precious, that it can suffice to pay what is owed for the sins of the whole world. Did he not give up His life for the honor of God? . . . He freely gave to God his honor [to] make compensation for all the debts of all human beings."[20] Anselm provides the church with a full-fledged account of the atoning work of Christ in relation to feudal monetary systems. To be freed from sin someone must satisfy the debt. We cannot satisfy this debt, but Christ does. This may not be the first time debt language has been used to express the atonement.[21] However, Anselm provides a system based on a specific economy. Therefore, this is the first systemic account of monetary recompense for salvation. Thus, Anselm gave Christianity a theological and economic account for a certain social order. This is an order in which certain members of a sociopolitical class/status must live their lives based on the life of another. Furthermore, this order is coded through death. Rather than the atonement being about the restoration of the *imago Dei,* it became about the satisfaction of a monetary debt.

WOMANIST THEOLOGY OF ATONEMENT

The Image of God as right "relationality" is of chief concern for Womanist theologians. Womanist theology was born out of a close examination of the experience of African American women. As Katie Geneva Cannon, Emilie M. Townes, and Angela Sims sum up,

> Womanists share extensive stories full of contextual complexities. . . . We speak from a bittersweet place that is informed by our daily reorientation in a race-, sex-, class-conscious society. We talk about African American women's multiple labels—some self-applied, others culturally imposed. As daughter, sister, niece, cousin, mother, lover, wife, friend, girl, woman-child—each of us speaks from a place that has been turned upside down and inside out by inequities in a social system that is anything but just.[22]

19. Brock and Parker, *Saving Paradise*, 267.
20. Anselm of Canterbury, *Cur Dens Homo?*, 155–56.
21. See for example Athanasius, *On the Incarnation*, 33.
22. Cannon et al. *Womanist Theological Ethics*, xv.

Womanist theology then is a project that addresses the social situation of African American women and their unique experience of the unjust nature of society. Womanist theologians rightly recognize that many of the social constructs that oppress African American women are theologically mediated, and were especially so during the time of antebellum slavery. Thus, the critique of the Womanist theological movement is both theological and social.

One such theological position that is critiqued from its theological confession and social construction is that of atonement and redemption. The reason for the concern for this doctrine is the way that the slave owner articulated his relationship to the slave, similar to the popular theory of atonement, namely, satisfaction theory. For the female slave, the social embodiment of this theory of the atonement was surrogacy.[23] In short, the way that Jesus is portrayed as humanity's surrogate—by paying the price for our sin on the cross—is recapitulated in African-American women's experience through the fact that their masters become the surrogates through which they are granted life on earth.[24] Specifically, this entailed their lives being lived through the master who guaranteed their life by contract. Traditionally, in ancient slavery the master would commute a death sentence of a slave who was normally procured through an act of war. In the antebellum period, the master, rather than assuming the salvific relationship by commuting the death sentence, would assume a debt through payment of the "price" for the slave. Either way the slave owner was the avenue of life for the slave. Either in the case where the slave's life is spared in times of war, or if a slave owner frees a slave in the antebellum period, the legitimacy of their freedom is guaranteed through the slave owner. This was generally how the language of surrogacy played out in slavery.

Certain roles for African American women were also forced through a relationship of surrogacy. For example, Delores Williams offers an anamnesis to modern culture, in that, during the slave period, African American women were forced into roles of forced labor to substitute for their white masters in the field as well as their white female masters by cooking.[25] Even more troubling was the fact that black women were subject to the sexual lusts of white men in the fields as they served in these

23. See specifically Williams, "Black Women's Surrogacy Experience," 19–32.

24. See Weaver, *Nonviolent Atonement* and Williams, *Sisters in the Wilderness*, 161–62.

25. Williams, "Black Women's Surrogacy Experience," 19–27.

roles. In some Christian households, wives of plantation owners would force specific female slaves into roles as sexual surrogates to their husbands so that the wives could maintain their consecrated virginity.[26] Even after the end of the Civil War, the end of the coerced surrogacy of enslavement gave rise to "voluntary" surrogacy in the role of the "mammy," where African American women became surrogates of white mothers at the cost of caring for their own children.[27] Williams and other Womanist scholars deeply question the strict satisfaction theory of atonement that much of the church confesses. In fact, this particular theory of the atonement is the stance of the Church of the Nazarene. Article VI of the Manual of the Church of the Nazarene states,

> We believe that Jesus Christ, by His sufferings, by the shedding of His own blood, and by His death on the Cross, made a full atonement for all human sin, and that this Atonement is the only ground of salvation, and that it is sufficient for every individual of Adam's race. The Atonement is graciously efficacious for the salvation of *those incapable of moral responsibility* and for the children in innocency but is efficacious for the salvation of those who reach the age of responsibility only when they repent and believe.[28]

The proposed amendment, JUD-802, to the Articles of Faith in the Manual of the Church of the Nazarene sought to reinstate the word "meritorious" before death in the article as it has been previously left out.[29] The rejection of this, and the call for an exploration of new ways of articulating the atonement in the Church of the Nazarene, should be greeted as a chance to service a more robust account of the atonement that considers the full humanity of all individuals who are lovingly freed from the effects of sin by Jesus Christ.

Womanist theologians recognize that theories of the atonement and redemption have been at the forefront of the Christian imagination since its earliest days. These early Christians (from Irenaeus to Anselm) utilized their sociopolitical language to express the nature of how the atonement could be achieved. Williams writes, "so the Womanist theologian uses the sociopolitical thought and action of the African American woman's world to show black women that their salvation does not depend upon

26. See Glancy, *Slavery in Early Christianity.*

27. Williams, "Black Women's Surrogacy Experience," 23.

28. *Manual of the Church of the Nazarene*, 30–31. Emphasis original.

29. King and Varughese, "Report of the Scripture Study Committee."

any form of surrogacy made sacred by traditional and orthodox understanding of Jesus's life and death."[30] Thus, it is a critique levied against the lived experience of African American females and thus a uniquely liberative language for how death and sin are defeated in Jesus Christ. This takes place in three general shifts: a general shift from the death of Jesus to his life, a shift of the blood of the cross to the empty cross, and a shift from the execution of Jesus to the resurrection of Jesus.

First, Delores Williams helps us see what is at stake in shifting perspectives from the death of Jesus as a coerced surrogacy role for the sins of humanity to the life of Jesus. This is the strongest shift that needs to happen in the Womanist theology of atonement. Williams writes, "salvation is assured by Jesus' life of resistance and by the survival strategies he used to help people survive the death of identity caused by their exchange of inherited cultural meanings for a new identity shaped by the gospel ethics and world view"[31] The ethics of resistance is primarily seen in the temptation account of Jesus in the Wilderness located in the Gospel of Matthew (4:1–11). That Jesus was able to break the power or influence of sin shows that the breaking of the power of sin and death happen in Jesus's life, not death. She writes, "Jesus therefore conquered sin in life, not death. In the wilderness he refused to allow evil forces to defile the balanced relation between the material and the spiritual, between life and death, between power and the exertion of it."[32] Thus Williams understands the root of sin (both individual and corporate) to exist primarily in the playing of life and death off one another. Jesus, as narrated by Williams, refuses to live in that scenario and play by those rules, but reveals those systems as corrupt.

The scene before Pilate in the Gospel of John highlights just this type of scene as well. The choice Jesus is given in this moment is the chance to play into the systemic orders of sin, namely life and death, created by humanity in this situation. However, his response represents the ethic of resistance that is his new "ministerial vision" of right relationships.[33] This means that the life of resistance helps eliminate the identity of those forced to live in systems of sin that claim the power of life over death.[34]

30. Williams, *Sisters in the Spirit*, 164.

31. Williams, *Sisters in the Spirit*, 164.

32. Williams, *Sisters in the Spirit*, 166.

33. Williams, *Sisters in the Spirit*, 164–67.

34. Williams, *Sisters in the Spirit*, 164.

This makes sense of what Karl Barth calls the Judge judged in our place. He writes,

> Why did the Son of God become man, one of us, our brother, our fellow in the human situation? The answer is: In order to judge the world. But in light of what God has actually done we must add at once: In order to judge it in the exercise of His kingly freedom to show His grace in the execution of His judgment, to pronounce us free in passing sentence, to free us by imprisoning us, to ground our life on our death, to redeem and save us by our destruction.[35]

Our destruction is not of us in our particularity, but the identity that sin has created for us. Furthermore, this destruction also defeats the sins that misappropriate humanity's relation to material and spiritual orders.

It is the misrelating to spiritual and material realties that is the systemic order of sin that leads to Jesus's death. In short, because Jesus refuses to relate to the material and spiritual orders in a manner defined by sin, the orders of sinful humanity seek to put an end to his defiance. As Williams writes, "The cross is a reminder of how humans have tried throughout history to destroy visions of righting relationships that involve transformation of tradition and transformation of social relations and arrangements sanctioned by the status quo."[36] This means that the mission of Jesus was not to die to satisfy a debt incurred by humanity, but to provide a means to cure the problem of sin as it is lived by humanity. It is cured because of the hypostatic union, the very nature of humanity is given a path to follow in the Spirit. In the words of Irenaeus, "what He appeared to be, He really was. God recapitulated in Himself that ancient handiwork of His which is man, to kill sin, to destroy death, and to give life to man. These are His true works."[37] The cross then is just the inevitable response to anyone who would challenge the systemic order of sin. Williams will even go so far as to say "there is nothing divine in the blood of the cross" to shift the perspective of Jesus on the cross, not by divine sanction, but by the persecution of innocence.[38]

Second, a shift must take place from the blood of the cross to the empty cross. Picking up on the profound insight of Delores Williams,

35. Barth, *Church Dogmatics* IV/1, 222.

36. Williams, *Sisters in the Wilderness*, 167.

37. Irenaeus, *Against the Heresies*, III.18.7, in *Scandal of the Incarnation*, 58.

38. Williams, *Sisters in the Wilderness*, 167.

Womanist scholar JoAnne Marie Terrell defines the relationship the cross should have in relation to atonement and Womanist theology in general. Terrell begins in affirmation of Williams's view that the crucifixion was not a violence condoned by God.[39] However, Terrell does believe something divine happens in the blood of the cross. She writes, "Thus while there is *something* of God in the blood of the cross, it is not an act of divinely sanctioned violence. Rather, it highlights the egregious nature of every historical crime against humanity and the Divinity, which means that "the cross is about God's love for humankind in a profound sense."[40] The point is that Jesus is raised from this death of innocent suffering, and echoing Williams, this affirms the efficacy of this life.[41] Terrell sees this as a sign of our own resurrection from our own graves. This also means that Terrell does not think that the resurrection is the end of the gospel message. Rather, "Terrell," as Denny Weaver sums up, "will keep the empty cross, saying that it signifies God's continuous empowerment, and the continuous intercession of the spirit of Jesus Christ with God's people."[42] Thus, the atonement is a reality that we are to participate in daily in the Spirit. Christ's intercession brings life from the death of sinful condition. What was said of Williams's account of Christ's atoning work through the breaking of systems of sin that distort our ability to be in relationship with God, creation, and other humans is still true. However, in shifting our attention from the blood of the cross to the empty cross, we begin to see the continual work of Christ through the Spirit so that we can have participation in this restoration of right relationship.

The focus on the cross must also include the resurrection. Probably the most troubling fact of Article VI is that it makes no mention of the resurrection, effectively removing from it a proper understanding of the atonement. This piece is also missing from Delores Williams's account of the atonement. Another Womanist theologian, Karen Baker-Fletcher, helps fill this void for the Church of the Nazarene. Baker-Fletcher does uphold the insights of Williams and the problematic, traditional ways of viewing the atonement. However, she reminds her readers that while, "atonement theory is problematic, we are still left with the historical reality of the cross."[43] Baker-Fletcher argues that we cannot just ignore the

39. Terrell, *Power in the Blood?*, 121.

40. Terrell, *Power in the Blood?*, 123–24.

41. Terrell, *Power in the Blood?*, 125.

42. Weaver, *Nonviolent Atonement*, 201.

43. Baker-Fletcher and Baker-Fletcher, *My Sister, My Brother*, cited in Weaver, *Nonviolent Atonement*, 202.

reality of the cross; instead, we should switch the emphasis to the resurrection rather than on the death of Jesus. She writes, "an emphasis on the resurrected Jesus refocuses the interpretation of Jesus' death as well. We need to rethink *how* we preach Christ crucified, so that preaching glorifies God. Glorifying the cross as though Jesus came to die glorifies the 'human capacity to oppress others.' In contrast, emphasizing the resurrection shifts the focus to the power of God to overcome oppression."[44] This oppression is twofold, but both are intimately intertwined.

JOHN WESLEY'S MORAL THEOLOGY OF HOLINESS

Though John Wesley's view of the atonement is very close to our implications about the view of the atonement detailed by Womanists, it is our intention here to connect this view more to his theology of holiness and his moral theology. This idea needs to be addressed in our discussion of Article VII because it appropriates a Wesleyan understanding of Article X. Also, it answers the charge of Article VII, "The Atonement is graciously efficacious for the salvation of those incapable of moral responsibility.[45] John Wesley's Christian virtue ethic arises out of the plentitudinal reality of God. Wesley's main emphasis is on the love of God that believers experience through the Spirit. Wesley writes, "let us love one another . . . It is by the Spirit that the love of God is shed abroad in our hearts. Everyone that truly loveth God and his neighbor is born of God."[46] The heart of ethics, holiness, and the renewal of the Image of God all lie in this understanding. The believer experiences the love of God in his/her heart. This is essential for Wesley because for Wesley, one cannot do what one has not experienced, namely love. He writes in a letter to one possibly pseudonymous John Smith,

> I believe firmly, and that in the most literal sense, that "without God we can do nothing" . . . What do I mean by saying that faith, hope, and love, are not the effect of any, or all, our natural faculties? I mean this: That supposing a man to be now void of faith, hope, and love he cannot effect any degree of them in himself by any possible exertion of his understanding, and of any or all his other natural faculties, though he should enjoy them in the utmost perfection. A distinct power from God, not

44. Baker-Fletcher and Baker-Fletcher, *My Sister, My Brother*, 79.
45. *Manual of the Church of the Nazarene*, 30–31.
46. Wesley, *Explanatory Notes*, 1 John 4:7.

> implied in any of these, is indispensably necessary, before it is possible he should arrive at the very lowest degree of Christian faith, or hope, or love . . . he must be created anew, thoroughly and inwardly changed by the operation of the Spirit of God by a power equivalent to that which raises the dead, and which calls the things which are not as though they were.[47]

This quote illustrates what Wesley scholars understand as Wesley's articulation of his "Spiritual Senses." We sense the love of God "shed abroad in our hearts" experiencing the inward power to love in a way distinctly Christian.[48] Thus, the love of God experienced in the heart of the believers initiates a process of transformation in them. This is what Wesleyans should understand as the beginning of Wesley's view of holiness and moral theology.

The work of the love of God spread abroad in our hearts achieves the forming of holy tempers from unholy tempers. The Holy Spirit and grace work persuasively in order to shape *bent, unholy* tempers (i.e., those bent towards sinful inclinations) and reshapes/redirects them to holy ones. As Wesley writes,

> We are inwardly renewed by the power of God. We feel the "love God shed abroad in our heart by the Holy Ghost which is given unto us," producing love to all mankind, and more especially to the children of God; expelling the love of the world, the love of pleasure, of ease, of honour, of money; together with pride, anger, self-will, and every other evil temper—in a word, changing the; "earthly, sensual, devilish" mind into "the mind which was in Christ Jesus."[49]

This is a work of God and of grace in the heart of the believer. It is a therapy and a work of the Holy Spirit which regenerates the believer. This grace is not unilateral; it is responsive. Thus, grace is "responsible grace" in the sense that we are encouraged to cultivate and respond to the work of God in us.[50] The combination of our response and God's grace leads to the creation of holy tempers (i.e., virtues).

We can begin to see here through Wesley's emphasis on holy tempers the connection with the life of Jesus and his vision of renewed, positive relational life. Utilizing the insight of Jesus's atoning work in defeating

47. Wesley, "Letter to John Smith," 12:75.

48. Wesley, *Explanatory Notes*, 1 John 4:7.

49. Wesley, "Scripture Way of Salvation," 373.

50. I borrow this phrase from Randy Maddox and his monumental work.

sin through his life, specifically in encounters with the devil, Pilate, and others attempting to define life with death, the holy tempers serve as a habituation into that life through the Spirit. Since it is the Spirit (i.e., the power of God) who communicates this life to us, then it is Christ who provides a continuing vision of abundant relational living. In short, in the Spirit we are given the power to participate in the ways Christ has righted relational living from sin. Of course, doing this requires practices that leave their mark in the formation of holy tempers as mediated by the Holy Spirit. This is the quintessence of holiness, moral theology, and the insight of atonement at work in everyday life.

These practices help cultivate holy tempers in what he calls "attending to the means of grace" Chief among the means of grace is the Lord's Supper. He writes, "all who desire an increase of the grace of God are to wait for it in partaking of the Lord's Supper."[51] This is a way of daily remembrance of the passion, but also of a visible sign before God.[52] This is a very practical, embodied way of experiencing the love of God. Now, one could raise the point about the Lord's Supper being broken body, and shed blood. This might call to mind Delores Williams's insistence that there is nothing divine in the blood of the cross, so why venerate it in this study? I think theologically we can lift both of these up, namely the Eucharist and the womanist theology of atonement, if we understand what the Eucharist actually does. The body of Jesus is displaced in the resurrection and now made available to all through the mediation of the Holy Spirit. As Graham Ward writes,

> What had throughout the Gospel story been an unstable body is now to be understood as an extendable body. For it is not that Jesus, at this point, stops being the physical presence. It is more that his physical presence can extend itself to incorporate other bodies, like bread, and make them extensions of his own.[53]

This is precisely the *means* of the grace that is communicated. The Eucharistic body is the very real body of Jesus present to us. This is also the body that breaks the power of sin in our lives. Wesley understands that participating in the Lord's Supper is a *means* of grace, because it communicates the grace of Jesus as the *means* by which we can participate in the ministerial vision of relationships restored in our lives. Christ breaks the

51. Wesley, "Means of Grace," 165.

52. Wesley, "Means of Grace," 165.

53. Ward, "Bodies," 167.

power of sin, so it is no longer our ability to do so but to instead focus on how we participate in the life of Christ. This is what it means to partake of the Lord's Supper and the Means of Grace.[54]

In addition to partaking of the Lord's Supper many other practices of the means of grace encourage the forming of the holy tempers. Such examples include: love feast, works of mercy, participating in the class meetings, and bands. These all represent practical examples of exercising one's volition towards the cultivation of the holy temper. It arises from the fullness of God, for in experiencing the love of God we are encouraged to practice that love. The more we practice the love of God and allow the presence of God to continue to work in our hearts, the stronger the holy tempers take root in our hearts. Wesley writes, "deny yourselves every pleasure which does not prepare you for taking pleasure in God, and willingly embrace every means of drawing near to God, though it be a cross, though it be grievous to flesh and blood."[55] Though here Wesley references the cross, it corresponds with what Williams says of the cross, namely its persecution of innocence. If you are drawn near to God you will, through participation in the Means of Grace and the development of holy tempers, find the ministerial vision of life found in Jesus. What Wesley shows here, and I think is affirmed by Williams and the womanists, is that going against the status quo is what it means to grow in holiness and to develop holy tempers (though it may lead to our persecution). Thus, the restoration of the ministerial vision of Christ can be achieved in the development of holy tempers through the Holy Spirit. This is not only the connection between the atonement and sanctification, but between the second and third members of the Trinity, and between all of this and the Christian moral life.

To sum up, the height of Wesley's moral theology lies in the renewing of the Image of God. This is the culmination of our discussion on atonement, holiness, and moral theology. It all begins with Jesus in his own life breaking the powers of sin and death. This is the act of the atonement. This breaking of sin is the power communicated and experienced initially through the Spiritual Senses. This gives us the ability to break the power of sin and wrong relatedness in our life through participation in the ministerial vision of Jesus. This is the beginning of the act of sanctification. This life becomes habituated through the development of holy

54. Wesley, "Means of Grace," 165.

55. Wesley, "On Working Out Our Own Salvation," 490.

tempers. This is what the Christian moral life looks like. From beginning to end, it is about the image of God being restored in humanity. As Wesley writes, "Ye know that the great end of religion is to renew our hearts in the image of God, to repair that total loss of righteousness and true holiness which we sustained by the sin of our first parent."[56] The image of God comes in three forms: the natural image (our original capability with God), the political image (our correct relationship with creation and humanity), and the moral image (the ability to act as God would want). The fall removes the third and distorts the second, leaving the natural image crippled. The process outlined above, from initial experience to the love of Christ to the habituated practice of love, is a process of God drawing us to the image of God. This is the *telos* of the Christian life.

The excellent end in the theology of Wesley is the life of God. The goal is not the satisfaction of a debt but rather habituating ourselves forward and ultimately to regain the image of God, and thus going on to perfection.

CONCLUSION

In conclusion, it has been my objective to show the fruits born from a pairing of Womanist theologies of atonement and Wesleyan virtue ethics/theology of holiness. My hope is that in bringing the pair together we have brought together the economy of salvation and the unity of the work of Christ and the Spirit in sanctification and salvation. The reading explored above presents an opportunity to engage a unique language of liberation to the oppressed, here explored through the liberation of African American women. By bringing together the breaking of powers in the act of sanctification with the breaking of relational powers in oppressive *sicut Deus*, this reading runs counter to the satisfaction theory of atonement the Nazarene Church currently possesses. This language arises from a feudal context in theology and provides legitimacy to the feudal-like order found in antebellum slavery. Thus, a theological critique of slavery is necessary, and the subsequent conditions it creates for African American women means articulating a theology of atonement that confronts the powers of oppression over it. This connects to our restoration of the image of God as likeness to God in relationship. I connected this to the development of holy tempers in Wesley and showed how the unique

56. Wesley, "Original Sin," 334.

moral theology of Wesley mirrors the confessions of womanist theology, but practiced in the very lives of believers. It is a practice of developing the type of tempers that lead to the breaking of the powers of oppression, namely sin. Thus, Wesleyan moral theology has at its heart the reconciliation sought at the heart of the Nazarene USA-920. Our moral theology also participates in the work of Christ in the breaking of power through the work of the Holy Spirit, which leaves its mark, namely sanctification. For a church that has preached freedom to the captive from its inception, it seems that a theological restructuring of its language of the atonement would be attractive. It would be attractive because in promoting Christ-likeness the church needs to answer what that is, and I believe the Womanist language of atonement names that Christ-likeness.

PART III:

Wesleyan Theology and Political Theology

THIS FOURTH SECTION PROBES the intersection of Wesleyan-Holiness theology and political theology, pressing the question: What does it mean to be holy in a world saturated by systems of domination, violence, and inequality? These chapters extend the theological imagination of the Wesleyan tradition into political discourse—not by baptizing political ideologies, but by confronting empire, power, and global injustice with the subversive love at the heart of sanctification.

Chapters 8 through 10 extend Wesleyan-Holiness theology into the realm of political witness, constructing a theological grammar that reframes sovereignty, divine judgment, and forgiveness in light of sanctifying grace. Chapter 8 lays the groundwork by engaging political philosophy to show how holiness challenges worldly power through cruciform witness. Chapter 9 deepens this by contrasting the logic of empire with the radical forgiveness embodied in Trinitarian love—offering real-world examples like the Amish response to violence to reimagine forgiveness as a revolutionary political act. Chapter 10 then broadens the horizon, placing Wesley in dialogue with liberation and decolonial theology to frame holiness as solidarity with the oppressed in a globalized, postcolonial world. Holiness here is not about private moral purity but about public resistance to systemic sin through acts of justice, hope, and prophetic love. Together, these chapters argue that political theology is not peripheral to Wesleyan thought but essential to its faithful expression in a wounded world.

CHAPTER 8

Loophole of Retreat

Charles Wesley's Political Worship

Henry Walter Spaulding III

INTRODUCTION

Charles Wesley, in his now infamous 1781 collection of hymns entitled "Hymns for the Nation," writes this provocative verse,

So shall our happy monarch see
His kingdoms in prosperity,
Through thy uniting power,
The source of all our blessings own,
And prostrate at thy gracious throne,
The King of kings adore.[1]

Wesley was among those most disheartened by the loss at the hand of the American forces and those still loyal to King George. This hymn entitled "For His Majesty King George" reflects well Wesley's indignation. Wesley hoped for a return to prosperity and potential restoration of "treasonous" colonial holdings.[2] Wesley's hymns reflected an undeniable nationalism not uncommon in his day. Therefore, many conclude that Charles Wesley offers no assistance to our contemporary political world.

1. Wesley, "Hymn V," 10.
2. Wesley, "Hymn IV," 8.

Despite this, there is a yet untapped element of Wesley's hymnody that provides helpful guidance in our political times. This element lies in an essential yet somewhat neglected collection of hymns, namely his hymns on the Psalms. In these hymns, unlike other contemporary hymn writers of his day, Wesley provides a theological critique of nationalism and imperialism. Though this does not negate Wesley's larger body of work and personal convictions in support of the divine right of kings and British nationalism, reading Wesley through these hymns provides what Harriet Jacobs calls a "loophole of retreat" from the dominant interpretation of Wesley's work, namely a hermeneutic by which we should read Charles Wesley's politics.

This work will begin, first, with an exploration of the Psalms as a source for both theological and political wisdom for ancient Israel. This engagement will provide the basis for interpreting any hymn that rewords the Psalms. Second, I will focus on three hymns on the Psalms (60, 20, and 47). These Psalms are central to forming Israel's understanding of divine favor and thus are crucial for those transposing through hymnody a similar favor onto their nation. This initial engagement with the Psalms takes place in two parts. First, I interpret each Psalm in the context of ancient Hebrew Scripture. Second, I provide an example of a modern nationalistic interpretation of the Psalms in a modern hymn writer, namely Isaac Watts. Watts's hymns on these selected Psalms illustrate the nationalism of Wesley's era and provide a baseline for Wesley's response. I will conclude this section with the themes most ripe in Watts's interpretation of the Psalms. After extracting Watts's interpretation, I then turn to Charles Wesley. I place Wesley's hymns in the context of theological exegesis and Watts's interpretation in order to determine Wesley's political agenda in his hymns. This process will illustrate how Wesley uses pastoral wisdom to illustrate the original meaning of the text, his critique of imperialism. Wesley's interpretation forms a type of political worship helpful for our own time. Lastly, I will turn to Harriet Jacobs's loophole of retreat in order to locate these hymns as a site of resistance and political insight for our time at the limits of Wesley's politics.

THE PSALMS IN THEIR THEOLOGICAL CONTEXT

Biblical scholar James L. Mays writes, the Psalms have a "double life" as both "scripture and liturgy."[3] This double life served a specific

3. Mays, *Lord Reigns*, 4.

community, namely Israel. Therefore, one cannot deny the potent political service these Psalms performed. They served as a means to encourage these people under one particular rubric, namely *YHWH Malak* (The Lord Reigns). This phrase, as Mays argues, is the "root" of all else that is written about God and God's ways in the Psalms.[4] Mays writes, "The reign of God is God's activity as creator and maintainer of the universe, and as judge and savior who shapes the movement of history toward the purpose of God."[5] All of the topics and functions of "psalmic language" such as prayer, people, place, and instruction all point toward this end of what it means to pray, be, live, and act in the reign of God.[6] The power of these texts lies in their ability to form a specific people, namely the people of God, the reign and providence of God that plays out dramatically in their history.

Such is the power of the Psalter in its ancient Jewish context as well as its place in the Christian canon today. However, such power is also apt to misuse. The danger toward misuse lies in the original kinship between text and the Psalms' audience. It is undeniable that the Psalms formed and shaped not just any people or any land, but the people and land of Israel. Such a context places the theme of the Psalms, namely *YHWH Malak*, deeply inside of historical struggles and political hopes of a people. Therefore, as theologian Willie James Jennings writes, it is "absolutely crucial" to grasp the particular readers of the text and what is read (especially the Psalms). He writes, "It is precisely inside this tender relation that the nationalist vision may grow," and provides the potential of its misuse when transposed onto different nations other than Israel.[7]

According to Jennings, this tender relationship is a curious one because it is fraught with nationalistic peril. Jennings understands this peril to begin at the point of translation. Scholars of the reformation should recognize Jennings's concern, namely that national identity couples neatly with Scripture's translation into a local dialect. As Catholic historian Adrian Hastings writes, "Ethnicities naturally turn into nations or integral elements within nations at the point when their specific vernacular moves from oral to written usage to the extent that it is regularly employed for the production of literature, and particularly for

4. Mays, *Lord Reigns*, 6.

5. Mays, *Lord Reigns*, 7.

6. Mays, *Lord Reigns*, 7.

7. Jennings, *Christian Imagination*, 210.

the translation of the Bible."[8] This process of translation does not merely involve a translation of biblical words into a different language, but into a different idiom altogether. As such, as Hastings continues, the translation of Scripture into the European languages resulted "in strengthening a common language, installing . . . the idea of nationhood."[9] This "vernacularization" of Scripture translates Scripture into the language of "nation-space."[10] To be clear, this is not a simple process, nor does biblical space become national space, but rather, both biblical piety and national piety "inform and energize a new imaginary literary space."[11]

Scripture and national identity become intertwined, especially when we consider the message of the Psalms. The Psalms detail, as already suggested by Mays, the divine movement of history, the chosen people, and the chosen place. In Wesley's day, the Psalms already served the ends of creating a new literary space with Great Britain at the center. This situation is evident most clearly in Isaac Watts's hymnody in the seventeenth and eighteenth centuries.

ISAAC WATTS AND BRITISH VERNACULARIZATION[12]

Isaac Watts (1674–1748) is a well-known English hymn-writer who shaped Great Britain's worship more than any other single hymn writer. In the early eighteenth century, Watts published a series of hymns called *The Psalms of David* (1719) in which he transposed the British Empire over every mention of Israel in the Psalms. The transposition transferred the significance of the Psalter's emphasis on Israel and its priority to the British Empire. Watts is not necessarily in these hymns trying to articulate a political theology, yet as John Hull writes, one sees that "in Isaac Watts' collection, the powers of the Hebrew monarch are transferred to Jesus Christ, and by implication if not always directly to the British King."[13] Readers and hearers of these hymns, then, participate in a shared

8. Hastings, *Construction of the Nation*, 12. Quoted in Jennings, *Christian Imagination*, 209.

9. Jennings, *Christian Imagination*, 24.

10. Jennings, *Christian Imagination*, 210.

11. Jennings, *Christian Imagination*, 210.

12. My reflections on Wesley, Watts, and political theology first occurred alongside my reflections on John Wesley's political theology. For more, see ch. 12 of this volume.

13. Watts, "Psalm 67," 99.

literary space. Watts in these hymns will open up the Israelite story in order to remap Israelite literary space onto British space.

An example of this transposition is Watts's hymn on Ps 67. Here he writes, "Sing to the Lord, ye distant lands. Sing Loud with a solemn voice. While British tongues exalt his praise. And British hearts rejoice."[14] Ps 67 is a call for all nations to worship the God of Israel. Therefore, we might argue that Watts does not perform a controversial reading. Britain is just a modern nation following an ancient mandate. However, Watts "God the Redeemer scatters round His choicest favors here, while the creation's utmost bound shall see, adore, and fear."[15] Watts does not propose an innocent casting of British praise but localizes divine favor in Great Britain. This "casting" appears in all of his hymns on the Psalms, and thus establishes the nationalistic hermeneutic of his interpretation, which we will explore in his interpretation of Pss 60, 20, and 47.

Psalm 60

Psalm 60 illustrates the nationalistic sympathies of Israel, which Watts molded onto Great Britain. This Psalm portrays a prayer in a time of national defeat. The Psalm commemorates David's campaign in 2 Sam 10:15–19 against the Edomites and the Moabites. The Psalm presents Israel's national defeat arising from a perceived loss of God's favor. Written in the opening of Ps 60, "You made the land quake, You cracked it. / Heal its shards, for it has toppled" (Ps 60:2 Robert Alter's translation).[16] The Psalm presents the devastation left by the invading forces in their defeat.

However, though the Psalm presents the discouragement of Israel, its arc bends toward hope. Though the defeat is a sign of divine displeasure, there is hope that God will restore. In verse 4, the psalmist moves to a remembrance of the divine promise, namely a banner in the sky. It moves on to show the power with which God deals with the enemies of Israel. In the final verse, the psalmist moves from reminding Israel of the faithfulness of God to asking God to remember God's faithfulness to Israel.

Knowing Watts's nationalistic hermeneutic, it is not surprising how defeat and God's faithfulness appears in his hymnodic interpretation.

14. Watts, "Psalm 67," 98.

15. Watts, "Psalm 67," 115.

16 Alter, *Book of Psalms*, 208.

He begins his hymn very similarly to the actual Psalm with a lament of defeat. Watts draws the modern British worshiper inside Israel's story in order to make them a part of the narrative. However, the hymn, like the Psalm, shifts from lament. Watts writes,

> Great Britain shakes beneath thy stroke
> And dreads thy threatening hand;
> O heal the island thou hast broke,
> Confirm the wav'ring land.[17]

Watts places British, worshiping voices inside the language of the Psalter and "maps" Britain onto Israel.[18] As Jennings writes, "Israel's history disappears, and the British nation appears as the real history of God with God's people. There is no continuity between Israel's history and that of other nations. All that remains is a kind of parallelism between Israel and Britain."[19] This shift is decisive for the rest of the hymn as the war imagery begins to dominate. Like the Psalm, the hymn speaks of a banner lifted high for those who fear God. Watts's mapping is visible. Instead of Israel asking God to cast out *their* enemies, Watts portrays Britain in this role. Watts ends the hymn with a departure from the Psalm:

> Go with our armies to the fight,
> Like a confed'rate God;
> In vain confed'rate powers unite
> Against thy lifted rod.
> Our troops shall gain a wide renown
> By thine assisting hand
> 'Tis God that treads the mighty down,
> And makes the feeble stand.[20]

The Psalm, which ends in humble supplication for God's unilateral action, is reversed in the hymn. Instead of supplication or a call for God to remember, Watts envisions a call to arms. The renown of British troops exceeds the call to God's remembrance and rings more with an air of presumption. In the end, God's saving work is an aid to Britain's military might. Readers of Ps 60 must reflect on the soteriological elements of space indicated here in Britain's military.

17. Watts, "Psalm 60," 104.
18. Watts, "Psalm 60," 104.
19. Jennings, *Christian Imagination*, 214.
20. Watts, "Psalm 60," 104.

Psalm 20

Psalm 20, much like Ps 60, is closely tied to military struggles. However, in Ps 20, Israel had not yet suffered defeat. Psalm 20 is a prayer for victory in future battles. The Psalm begins with a call upon God's name, which is the first of three petitions. It is an indication that Israelites at this time already professed the power in merely speaking God's name. Most eloquently, this supplication to the divine name contrasts with human ability. "They—the chariots, and they—the horses, / but we—the name of the LORD our God invoke." (Psalm 20:7 Alter) It is a challenge to the assumptions placed before us by Watts in Ps 60. However, this supplication must be inside of Israel's military aspirations. It is naïve to overlook this intention. Such an intention is apparent in the final verse, "O LORD, rescue the king. May He answer us on the day we call" (Ps 20:9 Alter). One can anticipate modern vernacularized translation.

Watts translation does not make all the exegetical moves one would anticipate. For example, Watts quotes almost directly from Ps 20 in verse 5 of his hymn. He writes,

> Some trust in horses trained for war,
> And some of chariots make their boasts:
> Our surest expectations are
> From thee, the Lord of heav'nly hosts.[21]

This reading runs contrary to a later bold emphasis in Ps 60, where military might finds a central place. Watts is far more subtle here. Like Israel, the reader must place this verse inside of higher military aspirations. Watts draws out these aspirations to include the British Army. As he writes in the verses preceding and following verse 5,

> In his salvation is our Hope,
> And in the name of Israel's God
> Our Troops shall lift their Banners up,
> Our navys spread their Flags abroad.
> O may the Memory of thy Name
> Inspire our Armies for the Fight!
> Our Foes shall fall and die with Shame,
> Or quit the Field with shameful Flight.[22]

21. Watts, "Psalm 20," 38.

22. Hull, "Isaac Watts and British Imperial Theology," 65.

Watts links God's salvation to the British Army. Though he does not explicitly name the troops and navy as British, one can assume Britain here since a navy is unique to Britain, not Israel. Though Watts suggests that the salvation of Great Britain lies in part to the British military, he still maintains, like the Psalms, a divine role in war. Thus, Watts aligns himself with the attractiveness of imperial military violence; yet, lacking a more precise distinction, also suggests God's actions coordinate with imperial military violence. Watts, therefore, maintains the close parallel between Britain's military and God's salvation.

Psalm 47

Psalm 47 does not emphasize Israel's enemies or the hope for victory but instead professes God's sovereignty over all the nations. The imagery of the Psalm is God high and lifted above the nations (vv. 1–2). The Psalm celebrates the kingship of the Lord over all people. This Psalm celebrates the openness of Israel's story to include the nations. Watts writes, "God reigns over the nations, and sits on His holy throne. / The princes of peoples have gathered, the people of Abraham's God" (Ps 47:8–9a). In the Psalm, this passage paints a picture of a universal lordship. All nations are subject to God *as* the people of the God of Abraham. In the center of all the nations sits the Lord enthroned.

Watts provides a Christian vision of universal harmony under the Lordship of God. Watts desires Christian worship, capable of forming people. Thus, the Psalms are not Christian enough for Watts, and he performs a Christian translation of this Psalm ordered toward correct worship. Furthermore, Watts brings together the Israelite story and the Christian story into one unified vision of God's Lordship. As Watts writes,

> In Isr'el stood his ancient throne,
> He loved that chosen race;
> But now he calls the world his own,
> And heathens taste his grace.[23]

Watts connects the ancient Israelite story with the continued work of redemption now available in Christ. However, Watts does not stop there.

23. Hull, "Isaac Watts and British Imperial Theology," 65.

The British islands are the Lord's,
There Abraham's God is known;
While powers and princes, shields and swords,
Submit before his throne.[24]

Watts not only includes the British isles under the Lordship of Christ but privileges them in the Lord's work. Watts, as Jennings writes, envisions Britain and God's salvific work as a "single act of divine providence" in this hymn.[25] As Jennings continues, "the Psalm invites its readers to join in the redemptive journey of God to their specific land and their people."[26] The British isle is distinct from the heathens and, like Israel before it, is the site of God's righteousness in the world.

In sum, Watts's hymns on the Psalms of David belong in the intellectual history of Scripture and interpretation. Watts is a talented and theologically trained hymnist who provides culturally appropriated hymns for his contemporaries. Furthermore, these hymns bind communities together in a distinctly Christian translation of the Psalms. Watts, then, is a man of his time. He is caught up in national fervor and imperial hopes. In short, Watts's hymns present worshippers with Israel's fulfillment, namely Great Britain. To summarize Watts, I offer three critical themes for our consideration: 1) Britain as parallel to Israel as a chosen race, 2) expectancy of British military victory because of divine favor, which will increase their renown in the world, and 3) British participation in God's salvific plan in the world. Watts presents in his hymns a vision for Christian nationalism and imperialism bound to doxology.

Charles Wesley and his hymns, such as the "Hymns for the Nations," fit within Watts's general project. As referenced in the introduction, Wesley held nationalist sympathies. However, when we turn to *his* hymns on the Psalms, another pentameter emerges. Though it is not enough to erase Wesley's more considerable sympathies, it forms a loophole or retreat from Wesley's nationalism helpful for Wesleyan political theologians today.

24. Hull, "Isaac Watts and British Imperial Theology," 65.

25. Jennings, *Christian Imagination*, 212.

26. Jennings, *Christian Imagination*, 212.

CHARLES WESLEY'S POLITICAL VERSE

Charles Wesley (1707–1788) wrote on the same Psalms as Isaac Watts, yet with a different purpose. Wesley operated with an appreciation of the Psalms learned from his older brother Samuel Wesley Jr. (1691–1739). Samuel Jr. had a crucial role in raising Charles, and his interpretive perspective influenced Charles. Samuel Jr.'s interpretive key is summed up best in his poem "Upon altering the Psalms, to apply them to a Christian State." In this poem, Samuel Wesley writes,

> His Psalms unchang'd the Saints employ,
> Unchang'd our God applies;
> They fuit th' Apostles in their Joy,
> The Savior when he dies.
> Let David's pure unalter'd lays
> Transmit through Ages down,
> To Thee, O David Lord, our Praise
> To Thee, O David's Son![27]

Samuel Jr.'s poetic proverb played a role as Charles wrote his hymns. Samuel's proverb appears most evident when comparing Charles and his hymns to the hymns of Watts. Samuel Jr. is clear: do not alter the hymns for the sake of a Christian state. Watts does not obey this criterion, as is evident in Pss 60, 20, and 47. Watts sings the praises of the British army and the British Empire as the chosen nation. Unpacking Wesley's hymnodic difference in Pss 60, 20, and 47 will provide a new political vision in light of Samuel Jr.'s hermeneutical key.

Psalm 60

Psalm 60 is a lament in the face of defeat and a call for God's deliverance. Much like the Psalm and Watts's hymn, Wesley begins his hymn with a lament of loss. However, Wesley immediately turns the hymns' attention to the church. He writes, "O turn Thee to thy Church again, / Nor let us seek thy Face in vain."[28] Wesley does not turn back to the nation. He writes,

27. Wesley, "Upon Altering the Psalms," 311.
28. Wesley, "Psalm LX," 157.

In Praises with his People join,
For all his chosen Tribes are mine:
The world shall to my Faith submit,
And Satan fall beneath my Feet.[29]

The culmination of the spread of the gospel is through the cross of Jesus Christ, not national agendas. Furthermore, all people join the saving work of Jesus's cross. All share equally in Christ's salvation.

The hymn ends not with praise of any troops or nation, but with an apocalyptic image. Rather than Britain and her foes, there is a battle between Satan and Christ. The nations, only by relationship to the church, are caught in a cosmic battle where "In Jesu's Strength our Foes tread down, / And win the Fight, and wear the Crown."[30] The foes here are Satan and his works, and the crown, due to his earlier imagery of the cross, is an appeal to martyrdom.

Wesley's appeal to cross, martyrdom, and church shifts the attention from a chosen nation to the one people of God. All are subject to the one cosmic battle between the powers of sin and death and the power of Christ crucified. The arm of God, as the hymn ends, slays the enemy, but the enemy is Satan, not the other nations.

Psalm 20

Psalm 20, as previously mentioned, calls for an ultimate victory for God's people. Wesley, like Watts, focuses on the theme of salvation and war. However, like Ps 60, Wesley focuses on the victory of salvation. Wesley writes in the fourth verse,

Some in Chariots put their trust,
In Horses some confide,
We of GOD will make our boast,
And in his Word abide:
Him we ever bear in mind,
All his faithful Mercies claim,
Life, and Strength, and Succour find
In Jesus conquering Name.[31]

29. Wesley, "Psalm LX," 158.
30. Wesley, "Psalm LX," 158.
31. Wesley, "Psalm XX," 43.

Charles Wesley here does what Isaac Watts cannot. Watts's hymn insists, "Our Troops shall lift their Banners up, / Our navy spread their Flags abroad."[32] The shift, again, is cosmic. The Psalm and Watts both urge reliance on God but believe military might participates in God's salvific work. Wesley, much like the Psalm, appeals to the name of God, and like Watts, Wesley adds the name of Christ.[33] This name carries high power and significance, even more, significant than the armies of Britain or Israel. However, Wesley, unlike Watts, makes this appeal to Christ singular. The name of Christ does not buttress national power but unilaterally works on behalf of all people. Wesley writes, "We will glory in thy Name, / O GOD, thy Conquest sing, / Thee triumphantly proclaim / Our Saviour and our King; / Now I know, the Lord from high / Succours his Anointed One; / Still His Arm shall strength supply, / And send Salvation down."[34] In Watts interpretation, salvation couples with military might, but Wesley tends toward a soteriological interpretation.

Wesley tends in the opposite direction from military struggles, yet not without confusion. As Wesley writes, "All our Foes by thy Righthand / Are suddenly brought down, / We are lifted up, and stand, / And stand by Faith alone; / Still on Thee we cast our Care, / On thine only Love depend, / King of Saints, regard our prayer, / And save us to the End."[35] It is unclear who these foes are. Wesley does not explicitly appeal to British troops (as does Watts) or any military victory for a nation as in the Psalms. The main appeal runs counter to those banners and emphasizes Christ's saving work. Instead, Wesley emphasizes faith. Much like Ps 60, this suggests a cosmic drama, and foes are inside the drama of salvation. This shift is essential for Wesley because it troubles God's cooperation in nationalistic, military aims.

Psalm 47

In Ps 47, Wesley continues troubling the military, nationalistic narratives of soteriology present in Watts's translation of the Psalms. To recall, Watts turns Ps 47, a Psalm of universal sovereignty over all the nations, into a hymn that places Britain as the first of God's great works among the

32. Watts, "Psalm 20," 38.
33. Wesley, "Psalm XX," 42–43.
34. Wesley, "Psalm XX," 42–43.
35. Wesley, "Psalm XX," 43.

nations. Wesley reverses Watts's trajectory under a Christological interpretation of the Psalm. He writes, "Power is all to Jesus given, / Power o'er hell, and earth, and heaven! / Power he now to us imparts: / Praise him with believing hearts."[36] Power and authority are under Jesus's name. Jesus is the sovereign under which the nations are subject.

Wesley clarifies this lordship and sovereignty: "Peace to them and power he brings, / Makes his subjects priests and kings, / Guards, while in his worship joined, / Bids them cast the world behind. / On himself he takes their care, / Saves them not by sword or spear, / Safely to his house they go, / Fearless of th' invading foe."[37] Wesley draws a stark contrast between the means that Watts identifies as salvific and Jesus Christ. Christ saves, but Wesley stipulates Christ does not save by sword or spear. Furthermore, by Christ's saving work, all nations are numbered with Israel. All nations are chosen but chosen in Christ. This theology of election is a new theology of election not limited by nationalism.

In sum, Wesley offers a different read of key Psalms for the British people. Wesley critiques any nation's claim to divine privilege in his modern Britain. Wesley drives his interpretation of the Psalms by his brother's hermeneutical commitment. Much like Watts, Wesley offers various themes that form a political language for Wesleyans today.

The first theme is that of the unilateral activity of Christ in salvation. The Psalms offer a vision of participation distinct to the nation of Israel. Modern readers must not lapse into a supersessionist reading of the Psalms and acknowledge the unique place of Israel in redemptive history. For Wesley, Christ saves without spear or sword. Furthermore, Wesley shifts to a cosmic, spiritual definition of struggle and war in order to subvert the imperial interpretation of the Psalms.

Second, Wesley rejects the election of a particular nation that can serve as a parallel to Israel. Election, as Wesley shows, is in Christ. All the nations gather not according to the rule or privilege of a particular nation. Instead, Christ is a unique center of intimacy that redraws the boundaries of ancient kinship languages around his body. All tribes and people are his people and tribes. None can claim privilege, and none can erase a particular nation.

Third, Wesley's hymns move a faithful response to God away from violence toward faith. It is too much to claim that these hymns give a

36. Wesley, "Psalm 47," 78.

37. Wesley, "Psalm 47," 78.

thoroughgoing defense of non-violence. However, it is sufficient to say that the weapons and means of faith are not spears or swords, troops or navies, kings, or princes. Furthermore, Wesley's cosmic interpretation of conflict and his faint reference to martyrdom shift away from the militarization of the Psalms.

LOOPHOLE OF RETREAT

Wesley and Watts offer different yet compelling interpretations of the Psalter. Stated another way, Watts and Wesley offer differing accounts of the (*YHWH Malak*) Lord's Reign. Wesley's account is one that offers a unilateral reign of God despite the undertaking of the nations. The Lord reigns not by electing nations but by electing Christ.

Despite Wesley's compelling account of Psalms when compared with Watts, it does not erase Wesley's substantial compliance with imperialism. The question then becomes, how do Wesleyans locate a potential political theology from these texts as a possible tangential reading of Wesley's political theology? In short, they operate as a loophole of retreat.

A loophole of retreat comes from Harriet Jacobs's *Incidents in the Life of a Slave Girl.*[38] The danger Jacobs faced is evident in the slavery common to a woman trapped in slavery. As a slave, she was subject to forced servitude, bondage, and social death, but as a woman, she was subject to constant sexual advances. In order to escape this torment, Jacobs chooses various places of confinement such as broom closets, garrets, and eventually her loophole of retreat. This space measured three feet by nine feet by seven feet. It was in an attic of her slave masters house with a viewing hole from which she can see her family still in bondage. The loophole of retreat is an ambiguous title for this structure because it at once signals a place of withdrawal from her enslavement as well as a place of confinement. She is not free from her bondage, but she marks her liberation, starting from her time in the loophole.

All of these elements (confinement, retreat, freedom, and vision) form the hermeneutical posture Wesleyans must take when approaching Charles Wesley's political theology for today. The loophole is the hymns on the Psalms. From this place, Wesleyans are not free from the various narratives of imperialism, colonialism, and militarism in Wesley's other hymns and writings. However, we do find a place of retreat and

38. Jacobs, *Incidents in the Life of a Slave Girl.*

a perspective to look on the other material still caught in bondage. If we, like Jacobs, confine our interpretations of political theology to these hymns, we too might experience new freedom though still bound by Wesley's limitations.

The hymns, as loopholes of retreat, are also a place to envision freedom for a Wesleyan political theology because Wesleyan politics happens inside the *ordo salutis*. That the Lord reigns, according to Charles Wesley, means a radical redefinition of politics that embraces a variety of peoples and worships *with* them. It should not escape our attention that these hymns, like the Psalms, find their place in the communal worship of the people. These hymns are intended for worship in a variety of tongues in order to form a people of God. Worship as a form of life suggests that we do not come to our political commitments absent our ecclesial practices of the Lord's Table, the reading and proclaiming of Scripture, and also praise of God. Only in light of these practices can political commitments mature. Wesley's hymns, then, invite us to consider a politics arising from this praise: "Glorious is the Lord most high, / Terrible in majesty, He his sovereign sway maintains, / King o'er all the earth he reigns."[39] A practice that places this as the emerging politics of a people redraws the lines of peoplehood around the Lord who reigns and not around nationhood or boundary.

CONCLUSION

In conclusion, I recognize that Wesleyans may never get beyond the politics of the Wesley brothers. In truth, the Wesley brothers do not give their ecclesial descendants a robust common political language. I hope that this loophole of retreat in the hymns on the Psalms of David will provide a much-needed liberation akin to Weber's liberation of John. Finally, we live in difficult political times. The thesis in this chapter is confessional not just as Wesleyan but a person who lives in such a time as our own. Praise and worship have never been so crucial as they are today. As the opening of the 1933 Hymnbook of the Methodist Church states, "Methodism was born in song."[40] Might our politics be born in song as well.

39. Wesley, "Psalm 47," 77.

40. *Hymnbook of the Methodist Church*, "Preface," 1.

CHAPTER 9

Empire, Evil, Eschaton, and Location

Forgiveness as a Political/Apocalyptic Act

Henry Walter Spaulding III

INTRODUCTION

POLITICAL PHILOSOPHER HANNAH ARENDT proclaims that our ambivalence with politics arises out both hope and fear. She writes that there is "fear that humanity could destroy itself through politics and through the means of force at its disposal, and . . . the hope that humanity will come to its senses and rid the world . . . of politics."[1] Politics often oscillates between these two verities. Politics may protect us from evil and from ourselves. Yet a calculation of fear exists, suggesting that without politics we will be subject to the evils we fear. Arendt argues an uncertainty arises in these calculations because with all the newfound "force" at our disposal we are yet to rid ourselves from evil. Politics play some role in the very evil we wish to abolish. The problem lies in what the center of evil entails, namely death. Even the strongest political force, Empire, is not strong enough to end human dying. Thus, while proclaiming the hope to overcome death, Empire and its violent ways cannot ultimately deliver on the promised end. Rather, Empire as a political reality can only continue the cycle of violence evil enacts and must use fear to maintain sovereignty.

1. Arendt, *Promise of Politics*, 97.

My argument is that Empire cannot provide an appropriate deliverance from evil and death. Rather evil and death can only be overcome by the Triune God and by embodying the apocalyptic-political act of forgiveness. I will show this by first defining evil and the ways in which Empire deals with the problems. Secondly, I will critique the position of Empire's claim over death with the apocalyptic drama of the Triune God. Lastly, I will show the appropriate Christian political act is an embodied practice of apocalyptic forgiveness.

Empire suffers just at the point where, by whatever evil death enters the picture. Empire seeks to provide for the populace it governs a hope against death and evil causing it. Empire produces significance by promising protection from evil that claims life. Empire thus establishes itself as a "savior-like" structure opposed to that of the Christian narrative. We turn now to an examination of philosophy of empire.

This chapter must be read as an expression of holiness theology insofar as it situates sanctification as a form of resistance to empire. Rather than framing holiness as individual moral striving, this chapter emphasizes the communal and political dimensions of sanctified life, particularly in its refusal to accommodate the powers and principalities that shape modern empires. In doing so, it retrieves the Wesleyan conviction that holiness is not merely personal piety but a social and prophetic witness. The chapter critiques Empire's capacity to mimic sacred authority, co-opt moral language, and deform human desire, thereby calling the church to a holiness that refuses such compromises. Holiness, then, is not withdrawal from political realities but a Spirit-empowered disentanglement from the idolatry of imperial power—a participation in God's redemptive work that reorients allegiances and exposes the false ultimacies of empire. This broadens the conversation around Wesleyan-Holiness theology by recovering sanctification as a public, disruptive, and deeply theological act.

EMPIRE

Empires are a unique political reality. It is worth noting the distinction between empire and its counterpart, kingdom. Empire differs from kingdom by seeking the interests locally but more importantly it seeks interests abroad. Kingdoms do seek to protect themselves against foreign rule, but Empire seeks to advance its influence on other social and geographic areas. Kingdoms possess borders, but empires do not.

Empires understood in this way break down into two main categories: 1) State and 2) Economic. These two are both political realities at their most basic level because, as political theorist Carl Schmitt writes, they both (state and economic entities) can "group human beings effectively according to friend and enemy."[2] Empire, both economic and state, seeks to group people to these categories. The grouping is a part of the sequence whereby Empire orders a populace or demographic according to its interests. The "friends" are all those interests that further the empire. Friends also are associated with giving life, but "enemies" do just the opposite. The enemy takes life and seeks to limit the influence and power of Empire. Grouping provides the legitimization Empire needs for its rule and programs. As Michael Hardt and Antonio Negri write in their book titled *Empire*,

> Empire sets in motion an ethico-political dynamic that lies at the heart of its juridical concept . . . Empire exhausts historical time, suspends history, and summons the past and future within its own ethical order. In other words, Empire presents its order as permanent, eternal, and necessary.[3]

Hardt and Negri portray the actions of Empire as legitimate by upholding justice and achieving its own objectives. The justice and ethical actions meted out by the empire are according to the above friend/enemy distinction. The empire may justify its actions by claiming to transcend time and space in its fight against evil and death, even if these distinctions are false. Empire provides the populace with the means to understand how the "empire" provides the only avenue for safety and security. Thus, the ethico-political dynamic set up by the empire should be permanent, eternal, and necessary. Niccolo Machiavelli and Thomas Hobbes illuminate the means that Empire uses to overturn death and evil.

Machiavelli

Niccolo Machiavelli (1469–1527) stands in history as a unique political philosopher. Machiavelli is understood as a political realist and shows the strongest example of this philosophy. His publication, *The Prince*,

2. Schmitt, *Concept of the Political*, 37.
3. Hardt and Negri, *Empire*, 11.

seeks to depict the role of the prince as savior yet also shows some of the consequences of this philosophy. Machiavelli writes, "it is much safer to be feared than to be loved when one of those two must be lacking."[4] Fear is necessary for Machiavelli as a mechanism to maintain the rule of the prince. The people should fear the prince for his capabilities for violence on his people, but also fear the prince if he were ever not to rule. Deep to the philosophical realism of Machiavelli is the notion that the prince must maintain his rule against foreign entities at all costs. Machiavelli understood the rule of the prince to be one that was more prosperous for the common populace than the rule of exterior government. Machiavelli writes, "The common people . . . give their support to one man and make him prince in order to have protection of his authority."[5] This points to the statement by Hannah Arendt where there exists tension between the fear of violence from exterior means and the violence caused by the prince or political entity. For Machiavelli virtue is a secondary pursuit to maintaining rule. Accordingly, he writes, "any harm done to a man must be the kind that removes any fear of revenge."[6] Machiavelli suggests that if a prince wants to maintain his order, he must respond in order to simultaneously destroy the immediate threat, yet also deter any future dissension.

Machiavelli provides a basic logic for developing a philosophical method for understanding the mechanisms of Empire. Holding to our definition of Empire set out by Hardt and Negri, Machiavelli presents violence as the means that Empire uses to achieve an order of necessity. Violence both achieves the internal order for the prince and the external security for the common people. Machiavelli presents a chilling realism to his readers and yet fuels the ideological development of the liberal tradition. The tradition seeks to make animosity the chief component between people, thus enabling government to provide "savior-like protection." Thomas Hobbes represents the next stage of the rise of liberal tradition.

4. Machiavelli, *Prince*, 56.
5. Machiavelli, *Prince*, 34.
6. Machiavelli, *Prince*, 11.

Thomas Hobbes

The most striking notion in Thomas Hobbes's (1588–1679) work *Leviathan* is his understanding of human nature. For Hobbes, human beings are a combination of moving particles heading towards objects. Humans are only truly free when they become unconstrained and are allowed to move towards objects. Desire is the motion of a man towards an object. Thus, freedom is understood, for Hobbes, as the ability to move to one's desires. As Hobbes writes, "a freeman, is, that in those things, which by his strength and wit he is able to do, is not hindered to do what he has a will to."[7] The state (the great Leviathan), according to Hobbes, is the giver of this freedom. Humans are not capable of moral choice in the work of Hobbes, they are rational but only rational according to their own self-preservation.[8] Thus, each human is set against each human in a war to secure objects according to each human's capacity to desire. Humans would continue in this motion unless they were constrained by some outside force, namely the Leviathan.[9] The Leviathan is the "artificial man" who secures peace among the people and keeps them from destroying themselves.

Hobbes lays out a political philosophy where sovereignty is necessary for peace and the end of violence. Much like in Machiavelli, the means of the Leviathan are violent to secure this peace. One of the reasons the many pledge allegiance to the sovereign is because of their fear of death.[10] The Leviathan implicitly promises freedom from the fear of death by in turn threatening death. This is how the imperial philosophy crosses over into the eternal. If an empire can promise freedom from the fear of death it begins to be an entity that offers salvation; yet we must ask about the means of this political salvation and if it needs not be questioned. Evil and death are confronted in Empire with different forms of evil and death, thus making the salvific process of Empire an inherently violent one. We are then left to conclude Empire is a form of a different kind of evil, a systemic evil.

This system of evil deploys different techniques to maintain sovereignty. It should be noted that Empire is not a new political concept.

7. Hobbes, *Leviathan*, 139.

8. For a developed contemporary working of this idea see Fukuyama, *End of History*, 149–51.

9. Hobbes, *Leviathan*, 123–31.

10. Hobbes, *Leviathan*, 132.

However, the form that Empire has taken in recent years reveals a variety of new mechanisms. These techniques closely relate to the rise of postmodernism and globalization. The main mechanisms, as stated above, Empire deploys are violence and fear. However, Machiavelli understood fear to be an inadequate motivator to maintain sovereignty.[11] Rather, as Daniel Bell writes, it takes a thinker like Hobbes to notice "what was needed was a way for citizens to participate in, and a reason for them to collaborate with, this induction of fear."[12] Postmodernization and globalization contribute to this move to participation and even continuation of fear and violence. The methods laid out by Machiavelli and Hobbes, enhanced towards postmodernization and globalization, achieve a "therapy of violence." This therapy offered by Empire, or any systemic evil, in globalization and postmodernization enable the monarch to redefine evil and goods in order to name good globally according to what is done domestically.

With regards to how these two contemporary mechanisms (postmodernism and globalization) work towards the enhancement of sovereignty and even participation on behalf of the citizens we turn to media relations in the new century and our advancing practices of violence. Edward Herman and Noam Chomsky write in opening chapter of their book *Manufacturing Consent,*

> The mass media serve as a system for communicating messages and symbols to the general populace. It is their function to amuse, entertain, and inform, and inculcate individuals with the values, beliefs, and codes of behavior that will integrate them into the institutional structures of the larger society.[13]

Herman and Chomsky are arguing for an understanding of media that assists a political entity with how to train the populace in a specific social ethic. The media is a relatively new phenomenon in the political order, at least on the scale of what is present in the modern-day mass media. The domination of the media is a symptom of the postmodern. Before the postmodern era, the economic-political landscape was dominated by the manipulation and production of goods (raw and durable). Now it is dominated by the manipulation and manufacturing of information.[14]

11. See Bell, "Politics of Fear," 429–33.
12. Bell, "Politics of Fear," 432.
13. Herman and Chomsky, *Manufacturing Consent*, 1.
14. This thesis is explicit in Hardt and Negri, *Empire,* 280–303.

With the gift of postmodernism, the mass media is able to produce truth. An example is the manufactured anti-Semitism in Nazi Germany at the beginning of the twentieth century. Adolf Hitler, from the beginning of his fürhership, would stock local bookstores with not only *Mein Kampf* but also several autobiographies of Hitler, collections of Hitler's speeches, and other anti-Semitic pamphlets. In addition to this, with the help of notable German intellectuals, Hitler, through speeches and newsreels, cast the question of anti-Semitism as an issue of pride in the *Volk*, or race. Historically this is a move for Hitler to seize control of power. Coming out of the crushing blow to German identity in World War I, the political landscape was awaiting a figure to restore pride in the German people. Thus, pride in the Aryan race was one of the main platforms Hitler used to become Fürher, and he even promoted himself as the *Volkskanzler*, race/people's chancellor. This method is just an example of how postmodernization of media can work. Hitler manufactured his virtue to achieve the felt need of the German identity in the early twentieth century. Yet, history will remember his rule as a systemic evil. Tactics this blatant are not normative for all situations, but imperial ideology can lead to such tragic results. The main aspect that is constant is the ability to redefine significance to events or people. This means that Empire can define evil as any opposition to its sovereignty.

The second contemporary phenomenon, globalization, also plays a crucial role in the violence of Empire. Meaning, now the world can witness the violence, be it linguistic or physical, of Empire no matter their location. The lack of constraint on geographic borders enables Empire to make claims on sovereignty in a variety of locations. Globalization is an excuse to be violent wherever and whenever it chooses. We can understand this concept based on what Jeremy Betham, and later Michel Foucault, calls "Panopticism." This is based on a French prison design where a single guard tower suspends down the center of a spiral cellblock. The purpose of the tower is not to strictly monitor the prisoners, but to provide the illusion to the prisoners that they were being watched. Foucault comments,

> The Panopticon functions as a kind of laboratory of power. Thanks to its mechanisms of observation, it gains in efficiency and in the ability to penetrate into men's behavior; the

> knowledge follows the advances of power, discovering new objects of knowledge over all the surfaces on which power is exercised.[15]

Panopticism, especially understood with an element of globalization, describes the process whereby Empire penetrates every life on a global level and systematizes power to every individual. Empire's use of Panopticism serves two purposes. The first advances the definition of Empire laid out at the outset by Hardt and Negri. Namely, if Empire can appear to police the world evils[16] then the populace will verify practices of Empire as true practices of the elimination of evil. The second is far more devious. Foucault shows, "The Panopticism is the general principle of a new political anatomy whose object and end are not the relations of sovereignty but the relations of discipline."[17] Discipline, here, is a matter of dealing with the issues that cause us to turn to Empire's salvation, the evils that cause death. They do so by establishing a pseudo-surveillance meant to watch those we fear. Yet at the same time, Panopticism seeks to also remind us of our place as fellows among the monitored. Foucault reveals the "relations of discipline" as a means to train citizens that the rule of Empire is necessary for justice, nevertheless there is an element of fear of the very same mechanisms used in imperial justice that are meant for citizens to view their place as well.

Accordingly, because Empire cannot "deliver us from evil" we must recognize, as William Cavanaugh illuminates, the "transfer of ultimate loyalty to the nation-state [or Empire] has only increased the scope of modern warfare."[18] The violence we thought we could rid ourselves of by paying allegiance to the Leviathan has only led to the increase of this violence. Citizens, and Christian citizens especially, should re-think the ways we have dealt with violence and pledged allegiance to Empire.

Isaac Watts (1674–1748) a well-known English hymn-writer published a series of hymns called *The Psalms of David* (1719) where Watts, taking the book of Psalms, replaced Israel with the British Empire. The result was a transfer of significance from the Psalter's emphasis on Israel and its priority to the British Empire. Watts is not necessarily in these hymns trying to articulate a political theology, yet as John Hull writes,

15. Foucault, *Discipline and Punish*, 204.

16. Evil in this instance is whatever Empire teaches to be evil and also whatever fulfills the basic criteria for moral, natural, and systemic evils.

17. Foucault, *Discipline and Punish*, 208.

18. Cavanaugh, *Theopolitical Imagination*, 43.

one can see that "in Isaac Watts' collection, the powers of the Hebrew monarch are transferred to Jesus Christ, and by implication if not always directly to the British King."[19] For example, in Watts's hymn based on Psalm 60, he writes "Sing to the Lord, ye distant lands. / Sing Loud with solemn voice. / While British tongues exalt his praise. / And British hearts rejoice."[20] Here Watts goes on to make the point that the British Isle is the chosen land of God. Watts draws out these implications to include the British Army to be an agent. As he writes in Psalm 20,

> In his salvation is our Hope,
> And in the name of Israel's God
> Our Troops shall lift their Banners up,
> Our navys spread their Flags abroad.
> O may the Memory of thy Name
> Inspire our Armies for the Fight!
> Our Foes shall fall and die with Shame,
> Or quit the Field with shameful Flight.[21]

The salvation of God here is linked by Watts to the actions of the British Army. Though Watts suggests that the salvation of Great Britain lies in part to the British military, he still maintains a divine role in war. Thus, Watts also aligns himself, at least in part, with the attractiveness of imperial violence; yet, lacking a clearer distinction, also suggests God's actions are simultaneous with of imperial violence.

Watts was not the only one to write a collection of hymns based off the book of Psalms. Charles Wesley (1707–1788), another British hymnist, wrote on several of the same Psalms as Isaac Watts, yet with a different purpose. Charles Wesley was operating under an understanding of the Psalms handed down to him from his older brother Samuel Wesley Jr. (1691–1739). Samuel's understanding is summed up best in his poem called "Upon altering the Psalms, to apply them to a Christian State." In this poem Samuel Wesley writes,

> His Psalms unchang'd the Saints employ,
> Unchang'd our God applies;
> They fuit th' Apostles in their Joy,
> The Savior when he dies.
> Let David's pure unalter'd lays

19. Hull, "From Experiential Educator to Nationalist Theologian," 99.

20. Hull, "From Experiential Educator to Nationalist Theologian," 98.

21. Hull, "Isaac Watts and the Origins of British Imperial Theology," 65, verses 4 and 6.

Transmit through Ages down,
To Thee, O David Lord, our Praife
To Thee, O David's Son![22]

Samuel Wesley Jr. was very influential in the rearing of Charles, so one could imagine that this poetic proverb played a role when Charles wrote his hymns. In fact, it is most clear when comparing them to the hymns of Isaac Watts. For example, in Watts's hymns (such as Pss 20 and 60) he sings the praises of the British army and the British Empire as the chosen nation. These same two hymns, Pss 20 and 60, Charles Wesley took a different stance on their adaptation. Wesley writes in the fourth verse of Ps 20,

Some in Chariots put their trust,
In Horses some confide,
We of GOD will make our boast,
And in his Word abide:
Him we ever bear in mind,
All his faithful Mercies claim,
Life, and Strength, and Succour find
In Jesus conquering Name.[23]

Charles Wesley here does what Isaac Watts does not. In Watts's hymn on Ps 20 he writes, "Our Troops shall lift their Banners up, / Our navy spread their Flags abroad."[24] For Watts, his hymns were a chance to educate the populace on the glory of the British army, navy, and chariots as well as God. However, Wesley, developing from his brother's teaching, shows that the hymns and Psalms are only a chance to show where our trust should be. It is not in chariots, horses, or the British Empire that we boast, but in God and his mercy we claim. The political critique of the Wesleys is that we cannot begin to hand over our understanding of salvation to political regimes and Empires. The question we are left with next is: Does a narration of the Christian faith provide a better way of salvation?

TRINITARIAN APOCALYPTICISM

Thus far we have explored the logic of Empire and its violent means defeating evil. We have also seen the logic of Empire and its techniques of

22. Wesley, "Upon Altering the Psalms."
23. Wesley, "Psalm XX," 17–19.
24. Watts, "Psalm 20," 70.

violence to overcome evil. These techniques have failed to achieve the affect and have only enhanced the evils we wish to overcome. Yet, as the Wesleys have suggested, our confession as Christians commends us to put salvation and trust in God who overcomes evil and death. Thus, with the Wesley brothers, we can begin to see rather a Trinitarian Apocalyptic alternative to Empire's violence. This alternative begins to take shape when we first acknowledge God's invasion of our present deathly situation with the life of God's Son.

LOCATING FORGIVENESS AS A POLITICO-APOCALYPTIC ACT

The work of God in Christ suggests an embodied set of practices that evacuate violence. For these practices to be uniquely a Christian apocalyptic-political act they must meet two criteria. First, according to theologian Robert W. Jenson, we must have a "hope . . . immune to death and everything else."[25] A Christian apocalyptic-political act "is hope rising again."[26] Second, according to Jürgen Moltmann, the Christian faith must provide a means for Christians to live in a world amidst terrible suffering. Christ's work of reconciliation and forgiveness on the cross meets these two requirements. This work presents an alternative to Christians in the wake of Empire.

There are some difficulties in applying this on a political level. One difficulty certainly lies in the logic laid out by Machiavelli and Hobbes. The significant force between two people in Christian forgiveness transcends what is found in either Hobbes or Machiavelli. If we understand Christian forgiveness as the only response to wrongs done, as Machiavelli suggests, it "must be the kind that removes any fear of revenge."[27] Forgiveness presents difficulty for Empire because it precisely undoes this cycle of violence, which is one of its central mechanisms.

Another difficulty lies in a critique of forgiveness laid out by Jacques Derrida. He writes, "when the crime is too serious, when it crosses the line of radical evil, or of the human, when it becomes monstrous, it can no longer be a question of forgiveness; forgiveness must remain, between

25. Jenson, "Eschatological Politics," 20.
26. Jenson, "Eschatological Politics," 21.
27. Machiavelli, *Prince*, 11.

men."[28] Therefore, Derrida suggests that forgiveness must transcend the routine, "forgiveness only aquire[s] its meaning and its possibility of forgiveness where it is called on to do the im-possible and to forgive the un-forgivable."[29] The impossible can be done on a human scale, but the monstrous exceeds mere human capabilities according to Derrida. Derrida maintains certain events are too monstrously significant to be forgiven.

Forgiveness is an apocalyptic political act precisely because it achieves a common practice that restores community between estranged individuals. It is apocalyptic because it involves the Christian, with Christ, facing violence of the evils of the world and, rather than acting out in violence, forgiving as Christ forgave those who persecuted him. It is political precisely because it transcends the political, by redefining the friend/enemy distinction. As Balthasar writes,

> since we are part of the body of Christ, also, in a sense, inside one another; and indeed, not only with a group, not only with a communion or church, but with all those for whom Christ surrendered himself, in expiation, for the forgiveness of sins. No one is excepted from this. Therefore, a Christian does not know the word "enemy."[30]

Christian forgiving makes death the only enemy and instead reaches for reconciliation between individuals. This can only be possible because forgiveness is, again, apocalyptic. For if death were the true end for the Christian, forgiveness would be a mere gesture in the face of the monstrous. As it is, all Christians can hope for the eschaton when all will finally be put right. Forgiveness suspends the present situation until that time when death will be no more. Forgiveness is an apocalyptic-political act precisely because it gives hope ultimately immune to death and a way to exist amid suffering. This practice of forgiveness allows Christians not to slip into patterns of violence amid the monotony of coercion. However, we are posed with the question of realism in so much political rhetoric that fuels the mechanisms of Empire. Can this method of apocalyptic-political forgiveness work in a concrete situation?

Consider one such example: on October 6, 2006, Charles Roberts entered an Amish school in Nickel Mines, Pennsylvania, with the intent

28. Derrida, "To Forgive," 27.

29. Derrida, "To Forgive," 29.

30. Balthasar, *Credo*, 92.

to bind, sexually assault, and ultimately murder ten girls. Roberts succeeded in killing five, but it was clear what he intended. Many commentators on this event described Roberts's intentions as monstrous. But in a strange turn of events, the Amish forgave Roberts and his family. Yet as David C. Steinmetz writes,

> And so the Amish forgave Roberts for imprisoning their children, for maiming and murdering them, and even for intending to molest them while they were helplessly in his power. They forgave him, not because he had been driven by private demons or because his act was anything but heinous. They forgave him because they thought Jesus had told them to and they were not clever enough to think he didn't mean it.[31]

Derrida might have disagreed with the methods that the Amish came by forgiveness. For example, Roberts was already dead, and one could argue it is easy to forgive the deceased. Yet there is something pure in the actions of the Amish of Pennsylvania. Steinmetz continues, "But the Amish matched their words with deeds. They invited Roberts' widow to the funerals of their children, insisted that some of the money raised to help them be used to help her, and even attended the graveside service of the man who has so cruelly wrested their children from them."[32] These actions may not be satisfactory according to Derrida's analysis of what forgiveness must entail, but it certainly meets the requirements of Christian reconciliation. As Steinmetz concludes,

> the unworldly but morally substantial Amish gave their worldly but morally less substantial fellow citizens a brief glimpse of a peaceable kingdom, where the lion lies down with the lamb, where swords will be beaten into plowshares, where violence ceases and a gentle magnanimity reigns. You can't say it is impossible or hopelessly utopian, because you have just seen it done.[33]

This forgiveness meets the requirements of an apocalyptic-political act set forth by Jenson and Moltmann. Accordingly, for the Amish, forgiveness proclaims a hope that their children's lives may be taken but that they too will rise again. Also, it provides a way to exist amid suffering by allowing reconciliation and God's forgiveness to be the designation

31. Steinmetz, "Forgiveness Springs From Their Faith."

32. Steinmetz, "Forgiveness Springs From Their Faith."

33. Steinmetz, "Forgiveness Springs From Their Faith."

between people. It can do this because, as Samuel Wells shows, "To forgive, one must let go of the ways one gives significance to one's life, of the impulse to control the world to make it right, of the power gained by forgiving without receiving forgiveness."[34] As Wells shows, our lives are not supposed to be defined by the cycles of violence that we constantly throw ourselves into, or even the need to try and overcome death. Balthasar shows there is a procession and return in the Trinitarian life, and so are we meant to define our lives. We forgive because, as the Amish understood, Christ told us to (Matt 18) and somehow in forgiving we reenact Christ as he forgives those who do the monstrous to Christ. By forgiving we re-enact Christ overcoming death on the cross. L. Gregory Jones writes, "forgiveness is costly, since it involves acknowledging and experiencing the painful truth of human sin and evil at its worst."[35] Further, "In the midst of such brokenness, God's forgiveness aims at healing people's lives and re-creating communion in God's eschatological Kingdom."[36] Forgiveness is thus a Trinitarian apocalyptic-political act precisely because it performs the function that Empire seeks to achieve with its mechanisms of violence. It denies the inherent need for animosity between humanity, or that a Leviathan has the means to solve it, all the while by announcing God's breaking in "to set us free from the present evil age" (Gal 1:4 NRSV) It suspends and goes beyond the standard definition of justice as rendering what is due and locates all of humanity as "forgiven sinners." Thus, it is a therapy of forgiveness rather than a therapy of violence that seeks to overcome evil.

CONCLUSION: AT THE END OF HISTORY

Francis Fukuyama presents the chilling realism of Machiavelli and Hobbes in his publication *The End of History and the Last Man.* In this work, Fukuyama details how the end of history comes. He is referring to the end in a Hegelian sense, claiming that history by means of progress and movement of time comes to a consummate end. This end represents the best possible of worlds. Fukuyama believes this to be the triumph of capitalism and liberal democracy. The methods he describes name the methods of Empire. He writes, "The end of history would mean the end

34. Wells, *Transforming Fate Into Destiny*, 145.
35. Jones, *Embodying Forgiveness*, 163.
36. Jones, *Embodying Forgiveness*, 163.

of wars and bloody revolutions . . . Human life, then, involves a curious paradox: it seems to require injustice, for the struggle against injustice is what calls forth what is highest in man."[37] This is the false eschatology that Empire claims to enact, and the wars and blood of history all are towards an end to all wars. That the mechanisms of violence are working because the injustices Empire uses to face injustice are the "highest" in man. Thus, history's winners are the ones who maintain the capitalistic liberal democracy. The losers are the ones not violent enough to achieve this.

In response to Fukuyama, Daniel M. Bell Jr. writes that as Christians we confess that the end of history has already come. The cross and resurrection, as Balthasar has shown, pronounces the end to history's violence. In fact, when understood by the means of the Empire, the cross is an impossibility.[38] We must find ourselves aligned on one side or another in this war of how evil will be overcome. If Empire says that we will be seen as history's losers if we do not turn over to the side of violence, then we will be on the side of Christ, where history's violence finds example and defeat. Then it will be as Daniel M. Bell Jr. writes at the conclusion of his response to Fukuyama

> When history's losers, the crucified people, follow in the steps of Jesus and forgive their enemies, they are wagering on God. They are wagering that God is who the Gospel proclaims God to be, the one who defeats sin and wipes away every tear, not with the sword of justice that upholds rights but with the gift of forgiveness in Christ. Fukuyama and his neoconservative cohorts can declare that history has attained its end with the triumph of capitalism because the true end of history remains momentarily fugitive. Although the tomb is empty, the Lamb who is slain has yet to return in final victory. In the meantime, the crucified people, awaiting his return and the consummation of the judgment of grace, refuse to cease suffering.[39]

In essence, the end of history will not come through technology's progression or Empire's violence. The wars of history and of Empire may rage around, but Christians are called to forgive as Christians are themselves forgiven. Christians can do this because the significance of our lives is not in what anyone can do to them, for their lives cannot be taken

37. Fukuyama, *End of History*, 311.

38. von Balthasar, "Liberation Theology," 143.

39. Bell, *Liberation Theology After the End of History*, 195.

from them. Rather, the tears of history shall be brought to confession of all that we have been forgiven and all that has been done on our behalf. Humanity was not made for strife, but to be caught up in the mutuality of God's Triune life and accordingly in one another. Until that time, we shed tears and bury our dead, but only in the apocalyptic hope of God's continual breaking in.

CHAPTER 10

Embodied Holiness

A Global Wesleyan Theology

Henry Walter Spaulding III

INTRODUCTION

THE WESLEYAN-HOLINESS TRADITION HAS long claimed a global mission, yet its theological center of gravity remains Western mainly and Eurocentric. In our present age, shaped by the legacies of colonialism and the ongoing pressures of globalization, this centering creates a distorted moral vision. What is needed now is not simply a re-articulation of old truths, but a reframing of holiness theology through the lived experiences of the oppressed. Drawing on Pierre Bourdieu, we must resist the "scholastic disposition" that abstracts theology from the world of suffering, sustaining instead what he calls "a theodicy of one's own privilege."[1]

This chapter argues that the way forward for Wesleyan theology lies in a preferential option for the poor—not only as a sociopolitical commitment, but as a theological necessity. The roots of such an approach already exist in our tradition. Phineas F. Bresee's founding vision for the Church of the Nazarene in Los Angeles, for example, was explicitly formed around solidarity with the poor and marginalized. Naming the church after Jesus of Nazareth—who came from a place of contempt ("Can anything good come out of Nazareth?")—was a deliberate identification

1. Bourdieu, *Pascalian Meditations*, 15.

with those whom society disregards.[2] Holiness, in Bresee's vision, was not abstract perfectionism but embodied compassion, lived in the streets, among the poor, and with those cast aside by economic systems.

To reclaim this vision today, we must re-evaluate Wesley's theology of experience not only in personal but also in communal and global terms. Global bodies—especially those under the weight of colonialism and neoliberal exploitation—must be re-centered in our theological method. Chela Sandoval's theory of love as a decolonial force offers a constructive lens here, and when placed in dialogue with Wesley's call to perfect love, reveals a path toward a holiness theology fit for a fractured world.

Ultimately, a Wesleyan-Holiness theology for the next fifty years must name the global structures of sin that entangle our neighbors and us. To be faithful to our tradition, we must also be loyal to the Spirit's liberating work, which calls us not merely to personal sanctification but to structural transformation—a holiness made visible in solidarity with Nazareth.

THE HISTORY OF LIBERATION THEOLOGY AND THE PREFERENTIAL OPTION FOR THE POOR

Liberation theology emerged in Latin America as a "drastic epistemological rupture, a radical change in paradigm, and a significant shift in both the ecclesial and social roles of theology."[2] Born in the sociopolitical tumult of the 1960s and early 1970s, it drew intellectual and spiritual energy from anti-colonial liberation movements, Marxist critique, and a renewed reading of Scripture from the underside of history. Rivera-Pagán identifies this diverse origin, noting how "many agents of social protest adopted the title of 'liberation movement' as a means of public self-presentation."[3]

A significant ecclesial turning point occurred with the 1968 Conference of Latin American Bishops in Medellín, Colombia. While Vatican II had opened theological dialogue with modernity, Medellín turned decisively toward a prophetic commitment to social justice. The bishops declared:

2. Rivera-Pagán, "Karl Barth and the Origins of Liberation Theology," 15.
3. Rivera-Pagán, "Karl Barth and the Origins of Liberation Theology," 16.

> A deafening cry pours from the throats of millions of men and women asking their pastors for a liberation that reaches them from nowhere else . . . Christ, our savior, not only loved the poor . . . he centered his mission in announcing liberation to the poor.[4]

This statement offered theological permission and pastoral urgency for theologians like Gustavo Gutiérrez to reimagine the task of theology. Just a month before Medellín, in July 1968, Gutiérrez had already laid the groundwork in his lecture "Toward a Theology of Liberation," where he linked spiritual salvation to human liberation.[5]

The publication of *Teología de la liberación: perspectivas* in 1971 established Gutiérrez as a foundational figure. In it, he articulated a "triadic understanding of human liberation—liberation from social and economic oppression, history as a process of self-determined humanization, and redemption from sinfulness."[6] His vision was soon joined by theologians such as Hugo Assmann, who insisted, "The contextual starting point of a 'theology of liberation' is the historical situation of domination experienced by the peoples of the Third World."[7]

At the heart of this theological project was a deep, scriptural commitment to what would become known as the preferential option for the poor. Rivera-Pagán identifies this as one of the five central tenets of liberation theology, describing it as: "The divine preferential option for the poor, the excluded, and the destitute of this world. The church must become the church of the poor by sharing the poor's sorrows, hopes, and struggles."[8] Though initially centered on socioeconomic exclusion, the preferential option widened to encompass "indigenous communities, racial and ethnic minorities, women, and sexual orientation."[8] It was both a theological affirmation and a practical mandate: God sides with the poor, and so must the church.

Theologians like Jon Sobrino and Leonardo Boff offered Christologies that emphasized Jesus as Liberator, showing solidarity with the "wretched of the earth" and reclaiming "the semantic roots of the term 'redemption' (the deliverance of a captive or slave)."[9] Their vision

4. Rivera-Pagán, "Karl Barth and the Origins of Liberation Theology," 18.
5. Rivera-Pagán, "Karl Barth and the Origins of Liberation Theology," 18–19.
6. Rivera-Pagán, "Karl Barth and the Origins of Liberation Theology," 19.
7. Rivera-Pagán, "Karl Barth and the Origins of Liberation Theology," 19.
8. Rivera-Pagán, "Karl Barth and the Origins of Liberation Theology," 20.
9. Rivera-Pagán, "Karl Barth and the Origins of Liberation Theology," 20.

of the kingdom of God was not otherworldly, but historical: "a social configuration characterized by justice, solidarity, and freedom."[10]

Base ecclesial communities became a new ecclesial form that embodied this vision, functioning as "seeds for reconfiguring the church as 'the people of God.'"[11] They generated theological, liturgical, and political resources for the flourishing of the oppressed, rooted in their key theme: historical transformation.[12]

Despite its growing influence, liberation theology met fierce opposition from the Vatican. The Sacred Congregation for the Doctrine of the Faith, led by Cardinal Joseph Ratzinger, criticized it for "emphasizing historical and social liberation to the detriment of spiritual salvation" and for "politicizing biblical hermeneutics, Christology, and the church."[13] Yet the movement persisted. As Rivera-Pagán notes, "Rome had lost the capability to repress this new theological movement."[14] In summary, Latin American theologians did not merely analyze injustice—they heard its "deafening cry" and constructed a theology rooted in the liberating praxis of the Gospel. The *preferential option for the poor* became not only a theological principle but a revolutionary lens through which Scripture, Christ, and the church were reread and reformed.

THE FOUNDING OF THE CHURCH OF THE NAZARENE: A MISSION TO THE POOR

Phineas F. Bresee, originally a Methodist minister, became increasingly concerned with the spiritual and material needs of the urban poor in Los Angeles. In 1894, he withdrew from the Methodist Episcopal Church to serve as pastor at the Peniel Mission, an independent ministry to the homeless. However, differences in vision led Bresee to part ways with the mission's founders. He believed that "the best ministry for the urban poor was to create strong churches that ministered to entire families," whereas the Fergusons, the mission's founders, focused on transient populations.

In October 1895, Bresee, along with Dr. Joseph Pomeroy Widney, a prominent Los Angeles physician and former president of the University

10. Rivera-Pagán, "Karl Barth and the Origins of Liberation Theology," 20.
11. Rivera-Pagán, "Karl Barth and the Origins of Liberation Theology," 21.
12. Rivera-Pagán, "Karl Barth and the Origins of Liberation Theology," 21.
13. Rivera-Pagán, "Karl Barth and the Origins of Liberation Theology," 22.
14. Rivera-Pagán, "Karl Barth and the Origins of Liberation Theology," 23.

of Southern California, established a new church. Widney suggested the name "Church of the Nazarene," emphasizing identification with the toiling masses of ordinary people for whom Jesus lived and died. Bresee articulated his vision succinctly: "It has been my long-cherished desire to have a place in the heart of the city, which could be made a center of Holy Fire, and where the gospel could be preached to the poor."[15] This commitment to serving the marginalized was foundational to the church's identity.

The first congregation met in downtown Los Angeles, including at the "Glory Barn" located at 526 S. Los Angeles Street from 1896 to 1903. A focus on holiness and compassionate outreach characterized the church's early ministry. Bresee emphasized that the church should be accessible to all. The mission was essentially planned so that every board would welcome the poorest. This approach was not merely symbolic. The church actively engaged with the community's needs, addressing issues such as poverty, addiction, and despair. The minutes of an early meeting declared that the church was called to minister to "the neglected quarters of the city," reflecting a theology that demanded engagement rather than distance.[16]

As the church grew, it maintained its commitment to the poor and marginalized. The Los Angeles First Church of the Nazarene, established in 1895, became a model for this mission. Over time, the church expanded to include congregations serving Spanish, Korean, and Filipino communities, reflecting its dedication to diverse urban populations. Additionally, the Bresee Foundation was established as a non-profit organization committed to addressing the social needs of the community. Bresee's influence extended beyond Los Angeles. In 1907, he led the Church of the Nazarene into a union with other Wesleyan-holiness denominations, forming a broader movement that retained its focus on holiness and service to the poor. '

The choice to name the movement the *Church of the Nazarene* was deeply symbolic. It intentionally invoked the scornful biblical phrase, "Can anything good come out of Nazareth?" (John 1:46), identifying the church not with prestige or power but with the margins. In the eyes of empire and polite society, Nazareth was a place of insignificance, its people unworthy of honor. Yet this is where Jesus was raised, and from

15. LA First Church of the Nazarene, "About Us,"

16. Nazarene Compassionate Ministries, "Compassion Is in Our DNA."

where God chose to begin the public ministry of redemption. Bresee and Widney understood the power of this theological identification. They chose the name "Church of the Nazarene" to align the church with the toiling masses of common people for whom Jesus lived and died. This was not merely symbolic; it was a practical theological commitment—a *preferential option for the poor* long before that language became widely used in global theological discourse.

To be a Nazarene was to cast one's lot with the places and people the world dismisses. It was to insist that holiness must be lived and embodied among the poor, the addicted, the broken, and the left-behind. Bresee embodied this vision when he declared, "We want places so plain that every board will say welcome to the poorest," linking the church's very architecture to its mission of radical hospitality and incarnational solidarity. In this way, the Church of the Nazarene was founded not simply as a denomination, but as a movement to be the church *with* and *for* the poor. Just as Latin American liberation theologians would later speak of God's special nearness to the oppressed, Bresee envisioned a holiness church that bore witness to that same nearness by standing where Jesus stood—in Nazareth, not Jerusalem; among the overlooked, not the exalted.

WESLEY'S THEOLOGY OF EXPERIENCE AND THE GLOBAL TURN

John Wesley's theology of experience offers a vital resource for reimagining holiness in a world shaped by globalization and colonization. While Wesley did not invent the theological category of experience, he uniquely emphasized it within his understanding of salvation and sanctification. Importantly, Wesley did not treat experience as isolated or individualistic, but as something that emerged within shared human realities. Wesley's conception of experience is primarily public and external. It is aimed precisely at providing objective standards for reference. Experience, then, was for Wesley a site where the reality of sin, grace, and transformation could be observed—personally felt, but socially verifiable.

At the same time, Wesley's own context was relatively bounded: many of his appeals to experience occurred in communities that shared a relatively uniform social world. This presents a challenge when applying Wesley's theology of experience across global contexts shaped by structural inequality, cultural diversity, and the enduring scars of colonialism.

But this challenge is also an opportunity. The very forces of globalization that expose us to suffering beyond our borders also make visible the urgency of a global theology of holiness. Engaging Wesley's theology of experience in this expanded horizon does not mean universalizing one culture's perceptions but rather recovering experience as a theological category capable of naming both sin's systemic dimensions and the Spirit's liberative presence.

Wesley's treatment of experience was most fully expressed in his soteriology. Unlike many of his Anglican contemporaries who focused on Scripture, reason, and tradition (or "antiquity"), Wesley made experience a fourth source of theological reflection—especially as it pertained to assurance of salvation and sanctification. As Randy Maddox observes, Wesley's appeals to experience varied by purpose: sometimes he appealed to experience to verify doctrinal claims, but more often he employed it to describe the experiential confirmation of God's saving work.[17] Experience, then, was never the foundation of doctrine, but often its proving ground.

Experience as proving ground is evident in Wesley's depiction of original sin, where he examines the collective experience of humanity—from Noah to his own age—to demonstrate sin's corruptive force. Sin is the corruption of human nature, which brings forth all the miseries of life. It is not only individual acts, but a deep disordering of the human condition—a habitual bent toward self and against others. Sin, for Wesley, deforms our tempers and inclines our actions toward enmity, injustice, and estrangement. Wesley's framing offers a powerful theological bridge to understanding systemic sin as experienced in colonization, economic domination, and racialized exploitation.

Wesley's description of sin as a shared and observable affliction opens a path to expanding holiness theology to account for collective wounds. If holiness is the transformation of the self and society into love, then liberation from structural sin must be central to any faithful Wesleyan theology today. The global pressures of colonization and globalization—seen most acutely in the experiences of the poor and marginalized—reveal the very kind of "bent tempers" Wesley spoke of, now writ large in systems and histories.

Thus, recovering Wesley's theology of experience in our current context allows us to see sin not merely as personal failing but as structural

17. Maddox, *Responsible Grace*, 46–48.

estrangement—and to see sanctification not only as inward renewal but as outward, liberative action. This reframing is not a departure from Wesley but a rediscovery of his method through the lens of global suffering and Spirit-empowered resistance. Experience, rightly understood, becomes the crucible in which holiness is tested and lived. It allows theology to remain faithful both to Scripture and to the lived reality of those crying out for liberation. To do so, theology must also interrogate the systems that deform human lives and identities on a global scale. This leads us to one of the most pressing yet often unspoken concerns in theological discourse today: the structural sins of globalization and colonization.

SIN, IDENTITY, AND THE GLOBAL IMAGINATION

One of the silent spaces in Scripture—and a necessary site for contemporary theological reflection—is the systemic reality of globalization and colonization. While not explicitly named in biblical texts, these forces shape the lived experience of millions today and must be addressed if holiness theology is to speak truthfully and liberatively in our time. Appropriating Wesley's theology of experience into this context requires us to take seriously the way global bodies experience sin, not only as moral failure but as structural affliction that shapes identity and imagination.

Wesley understood sin as a corruption of the human condition—a disease that distorts both personal desires and social relations. When brought into conversation with globalization and colonization, Wesley's insights open a way to theologize about identity as something wounded by systemic sin. As Owen Thomas argues, theology must address "authentic character transformation" and provide "answers to existential questions."[18] Wesley's theology of experience, while context-specific and often emerging in shared cultural settings, nevertheless contains the seeds for a broader, objective theological anthropology. It allows us to ask how distorted experiences of identity, shaped by historical trauma, exclusion, and exploitation, might be transformed by the Spirit.

This is where theologian Willie Jennings's theological diagnosis becomes indispensable. Jennings critiques the linguistic and symbolic constructions—"developed" vs. "undeveloped," "faithful" vs. "apostate," "believer" vs. "heretic"—that colonization has used to remake the world. He writes:

18. Thomas, "Theology and Experience," 193.

> Like the designations of sinner and saint, convert and heretic, believer and unbeliever, faithful and apostate, this linguistic deployment alters reality, blowing by and through the specifics of identity bound to land, space, and place and narrating a new world that binds bodies to unrelenting aesthetic judgments.[19]

Such language is not neutral. It reshapes imagination, enacts domination, and turns theology into an aesthetic regime that judges value based on nearness to Eurocentric norms. The result is what Jennings calls a "diseased social imagination," one that holiness theology must confront if it is to be faithful to the gospel.

Here, Wesley and Jennings converge. Both name the corruption at the level of human identity: Wesley through the lens of original sin; Jennings through the lens of racialized, colonial power. Both implicitly call for a theological vision that heals this brokenness—not by retreating into abstract spirituality, but by recovering holiness and love as practices of resistance and renewal. Wesley's call to perfect love becomes, in this context, a summons not only to personal sanctification but to communal liberation. The Spirit's work of transformation must include deliverance from the structures that deform human identity and imagination.

Therefore, holiness in a global Wesleyan tradition must deconstruct the logics of colonization and globalization by reimagining identity through the Spirit's liberating presence. It is not enough to declare "all are welcome"; we must also dismantle the linguistic and political structures that presume some identities are more human—or more holy—than others. The way forward, as both Wesley and Jennings show, is love: not as sentimentalism, but as theological resistance. Holiness is not purity from the world, but faithful participation in God's healing of it.

HOLY LOVE: A POST-COLONIAL PERSPECTIVE

Chela Sandoval offers an understanding of love for those under the weight of globalization and colonization. For her, much like Wesley, love is the way out, but she provides a nuanced account of it for a new time. The benefit of love, according to Sandoval, creates with in the individual experiencing the weight of globalizing, colonizing powers an "oppositional consciousness" that allows for a different mode of being

19. Jennings, *Christian Imagination*, 31.

in the world unfettered by these realities.[20] In her understanding, "'love' as a hermeneutic, as a set of practices and procedures . . . can transit all citizen-subjects, regardless of social class, toward a differential mode of consciousness and its accompanying technologies of method and social movement."[21] In this sense love is a practice of sociality that cuts or, in Sandoval's words, "punctures" through the ways narratives locate bodies among a variety of corrupted modifiers tied to power and free of place and time.[22] This is because love requires of our humanity a particular kind of submission to what is, in her words, "intractable."[23] In short, love ties us to a reality that is "not subject to control or governance."[24] Sandoval understands this movement of love through the lens of becoming a lover. This allows for the creation of identity in proximity to another in a relationship not ruled by power.[25] Therefore, love, as oppositional consciousness, creates a world where the binaries in place that define the world (i.e., colonized/colonizers, third world/first world, etc.) are undermined.[26] This is because the one who loves, rather than choosing between binaries, "drifts."[27] This drifting allows for the lover to slip through structures of knowing and being tied to globalization and colonization. Therefore, love in the key of differential consciousness serves as a middle voice intended to transform those subjected to globalizing and colonizing realities.[28] Love then has a disruptive potential that provides survival despite the ideological interventions made into their social location because it weaves through the ambiguities of place and power, leading towards a liberation of the way these realities come to define subjected people.[29]

Sandoval's oppositional consciousness of love arises not from intentional theological reflection but from thinkers, including herself, who have experienced these pressures and reflected on a way out. These thinkers include Guevara, Fanon, Anzaldua, Perez, Minh-ha, and Cherrie

20. See Davis, "Preface," xii–xiii.
21. Sandoval, *Methodology of the Oppressed,* 140.
22. Sandoval, *Methodology of the Oppressed,* 140–41.
23. Sandoval, *Methodology of the Oppressed,* 142.
24. Sandoval, *Methodology of the Oppressed,* 142.
25. Sandoval, *Methodology of the Oppressed,* 140–43.
26. Sandoval, *Methodology of the Oppressed,* 151.
27. Sandoval, *Methodology of the Oppressed,* 146–47.
28. Sandoval, *Methodology of the Oppressed,* 156.
29. Sandoval, *Methodology of the Oppressed,* 157.

Moraga.[30] Sandoval's work represents the experience of how liberation is possible. It also provides a foundational understanding of love not wed to Western metaphysics that tied together colonization and the colonized. As theologians of the Wesleyan-Holiness tradition, we can recognize this type of liberation. For it resembles the same liberation of addicts from addiction and other forms of sin that held captive individuals witnessed to and through the work of the various Wesleyan-Holiness traditions. Therefore, Sandoval assists holiness theologians to see the proximity of their work for a tangential identity to globalization and colonization as systemic orders of sin. This identity can be nothing other than sanctification. Furthermore, Sandoval gifts Wesleyan-Holiness theology the language of experience of those subjugated as a new avenue for articulating it. This area has been largely overlooked in our tradition so far. Therefore, this language of love will inform, yet remind the Wesleyan-Holiness tradition that it's theology is centered on love, namely "love shed abroad in our hearts" as an essential element of understanding holiness, identity, and salvation.[31]

The love of God shed abroad in our hearts is essential for Wesley because one cannot do what one has not experienced; in short, one cannot love unless God first loves us.[32] In Sandoval's terms, this would be the submission to that which is "intractable." Wesley writes in a letter to John Smith,

> I believe firmly, and that in the most literal sense, that "'without God we can do nothing . . ." What do I mean by saying that faith, hope, and love are not the effect of any, or all, of our natural faculties? I mean this: That supposing a man to be now void of faith, hope, and love, he cannot effect any degree of them in himself by any possible exertion of his understanding, and of any or all his other natural faculties, though he should enjoy them in the utmost perfection. A distinct power from God, not implied in any of these, is indispensably necessary, before it is possible he should arrive at the very lowest degree of Christian faith, or hope, or love . . . he must be created anew, thoroughly and inwardly changed by the operation of the Spirit of God; by a

30. Sandoval, *Methodology of the Oppressed*, 140.

31. Quoted from Wesley, "On Love," and Wesley, *Explanatory Notes*, 1 John 4:7.

32. Much of the following has been repurposed from a previous article written by the author. Though a lot of the material is similar, the language has been refocused around the topic of globalization and colonization. See Spaulding, "Sanctifying Atonement."

> power equivalent to that which raises the dead, and which calls the things which are not as though they were.[33]

This quote illustrates Wesley's understanding of "Spiritual Senses." The believer *senses* the love of God "shed abroad in our hearts" experiencing the inward power to love in a way distinctly Christian.[34] This experience calls a distinctly new mode of being in and from our lives despite orders that would affect us to the contrary. In short, we come to know ourselves out of this experience of the love of God rather than outside it. Thus, the love of God experienced in the heart of believers initiates a process of transformation in them. This is what Wesleyans should understand as the beginning of Wesley's view of holiness.

The work of the love of God shed abroad in our hearts achieves the forming of holy tempers from unholy tempers. With reference to Sandoval, this would include sinful binaries that affect consciousness as a bent temper. Wesley theologically extends for Sandoval the condition of systemic sin to include those who have been defined by and act out of sinful systems (i.e., colonization, globalization, etc.). In other words, Wesley helps readers see that globalization and colonization is nothing short of a theological rendering of the world in that it creates within the life of people a bent temper, namely a habit of subjugation to something else (i.e., sin). Furthermore, Wesley also narrates "how" an oppositional consciousness is created. The Holy Spirit, through grace, works persuasively to shape *bent* tempers and redirect them to holy ones. As Wesley writes,

> We are inwardly renewed by the power of God. We feel the "love God shed abroad in our heart by the Holy Ghost which is given unto us," producing love to all mankind, and more especially to the children of God; expelling the love of the world, the love of pleasure, of ease, of honour, of money; together with pride, anger, self-will, and every other evil temper—in a word, changing the; "earthly, sensual, devilish" mind into "the mind which was in Christ Jesus."[35]

This is a work of God and of grace in the heart of the believer. It is a work of the Holy Spirit that regenerates the believer. This grace is not

33. Wesley, "Letter to John Smith," 12:75.

34. *NT Notes*, 1 John 4:7.

35. Wesley, "Scripture Way of Salvation," 373.

unilateral; it is responsive. Thus, grace is responsible in the sense that we are encouraged to cultivate and respond to the work of God in us. The combination of our response and God's grace leads to the creation of holy tempers (i.e., virtues) and perfect love in the life of the believer.

The work of the Holy Spirit in forming holy tempers may seem distinct or different from oppositional consciousness. Still, they achieve similar ends, namely as an expression of freedom from sin (both propensity to sin and defining, systemic orders of sin). The creation of holy tempers is akin to Sandoval's "drifting" because it means passing through love of the world in its sinful sense toward the mind of Christ. What Sandoval calls prophetic love, yielding oppositional consciousness, can be translated into Wesleyan terms as love of God yielding Christian Perfection. As Wesley writes, "By perfection I mean the humble, gentle, patient love of God, and our neighbor, ruling our tempers, words and actions."[36] Sandoval's prophetic love would not disagree because Wesley's understanding of love of God is "not subject to control or governance."[37] The only way to be freed from systemic sin, ideology, and colonization is to realize an identity in the love of One who is unconditioned by systemic sin, ideology, and colonization, therefore, can condition our existence in such a way as to have "oppositional consciousness." Sandoval helps us see this new path to holiness through the experience of sin inherent to globalization and colonization because she sees that love is the way out. Therefore, it is only such a prophetic love, such an oppositional consciousness that can be called holiness in a world of globalization and colonization.

To sum up, the embodied holiness available through such an engagement outlined above means looking at the possibilities of holiness specific to the environment one inhabits. It means that holiness is no longer the struggle against abstract orders of sin, but specific sin that attempts to define an existence from the places above the ground. Furthermore, it means for a community the ability to recognize how these pressures affect others and our implication in those orders and our calling to help subvert them. Therefore, the future of holiness theology means once again looking at bodies and how they are influenced to give a coordinate sanctification that provides a way out.

36. "Brief Thoughts on Christian Perfection," January 27, 1767.

37. "Brief Thoughts on Christian Perfection," January 27, 1767.

A GLOBAL WESLEYAN THEOLOGY

The convergence of Sandoval and Wesley around love as a transformative force draws our attention to a deeper theological truth: the preferential option for the poor is not simply a political posture or ethical imperative—it is the material outworking of holiness in a globalized world marred by systems of domination. For Sandoval, the experience of oppression catalyzes a form of consciousness that resists the binaries imposed by globalizing and colonizing forces. For Wesley, the love of God initiates a sanctifying process that redirects bent tempers and forms a life marked by holy love. In both thinkers, love is not sentiment but revolution—an internal revolution that manifests externally as solidarity, liberation, and the redefinition of value and identity.

The preferential option for the poor, then, is not a theological addendum to the doctrine of holiness, but it's necessary extension. If holiness is, as Wesley affirms, "perfect love ruling the heart," then it must necessarily express itself in concrete love for those most afflicted by the structures of sin. Holiness without attention to the poor would be, in Wesley's terms, a form of perfection devoid of love—an impossibility. Holiness is always love enacted, and in a world shaped by colonization and economic stratification, love enacted is preferential love. It is love that hears the cry of the oppressed, that drifts toward those marginalized by dominant systems, and that seeks their flourishing as the concrete manifestation of sanctification.

Thus, a global holiness theology is not one that transcends culture or ignores political and economic realities, but one that attends to the wounds inflicted by them. Sandoval offers language and experience for those wounds; Wesley offers a theological grammar to name the healing process. Together, they reveal that sanctification is not merely the individual's moral betterment, but the reconstitution of the human person—and the community—in love that resists dehumanization. The preferential option for the poor, in this light, is not a concession to social concerns, but the clearest evidence of the Spirit's sanctifying work in the world. It is holiness made visible in the face of suffering, and love made incarnate in resistance to Empire.

CONCLUSION

If the Wesleyan-Holiness tradition is to remain faithful to its roots and relevant in a globalized world, it must embrace the theological demands placed upon it by the poor, the colonized, and the oppressed. This chapter has argued that holiness cannot be abstracted from lived experience, nor can it be confined to personal piety alone. Rather, holiness—true sanctification—is love made manifest amid the concrete realities of systemic sin, social exclusion, and global injustice.

By placing John Wesley's theology of experience in conversation with Chela Sandoval's theory of oppositional consciousness and prophetic love, we discover a shared insistence on transformation through love that resists domination. Sandoval helps us see the structural, epistemic, and affective dimensions of oppression. Wesley provides a pneumatological account of how divine love transforms bent tempers and calls forth new ways of being. Together, they reveal a dynamic vision of sanctification that is at once spiritual and political, personal and systemic.

The preferential option for the poor is not merely a social ethic that can be bolted onto holiness theology—it is its most faithful outworking in a colonized world. Wesleyan theology must therefore learn to speak not only with the language of revival and renewal, but with the language of resistance, solidarity, and liberation. The future of holiness is not in preserving its Western legacy, but in surrendering to the Spirit's work among those who cry out for justice, healing, and belonging.

To be holy in this age means to be present in Nazareth, not Jerusalem—to attend to the margins, not the center. It means that our churches, like Bresee's vision, must be places where every board welcomes the poor. And it means that our theology must be capacious enough to reckon with histories of violence, courageous enough to name the systems that deform human identity, and tender enough to hold space for the experience of love that drifts beyond binaries and leads into sanctifying liberation. This is the shape of global holiness to come—a holiness not of retreat, but of embrace; not of escape, but of redemption.

PART IV:

Wesleyan Theology as Public Theology

THIS FINAL SECTION INVITES readers to consider how Wesleyan theology lives, breathes, and responds within contemporary academic, ecclesial, and cultural contexts. Far from treating theology as an abstract discipline or the church as a static institution, these chapters stretch the Wesleyan-Holiness tradition into critical engagement with questions of education, power, identity, and fidelity.

Chapters 11 through 16 form a compelling conclusion by weaving together a Wesleyan theology of formation that integrates intellectual, spiritual, and moral dimensions. Chapter 11 reimagines Christian higher education as the convergence of Aldersgate and Athens, embracing the full humanity of students beyond the false binaries of head and heart. Chapter 12 continues this vision with a lyrical meditation on grace as the sustaining rhythm of academic vocation and spiritual life. Chapter 13 warns against the rise of fundamentalism in Wesleyan institutions, calling for a return to Wesley's generous orthodoxy and rejection of fear-based theological closures. Chapter 14 offers a reframing of Christian sexual ethics through the lens of sanctification, proposing "gracious longing" as a way to affirm desire without succumbing to repression or excess. Finally, chapter 15 delivers a prophetic witness from ecclesial exile, reclaiming the Nazarene identity as a cruciform solidarity with the poor, a resistance to power, and a return to the scandalous grace of Nazareth. Chapter 16 presents the culmination of the work that directs Wesleyan-Holiness to the work of the church. Together, these chapters present holiness not as an abstract doctrine but as a living, breathing witness—deeply Wesleyan, profoundly gracious, and fiercely attentive to the cries of a wounded world.

CHAPTER 11

What Has Aldersgate to Do with Athens?

Preliminary Thoughts on the Task of Wesleyan-Holiness Higher Education

Henry Walter Spaulding II

INTRODUCTION

LET ME BEGIN WITH a question: What does Aldersgate have to do with Athens? Those familiar with early Christian thought will recognize that I am paraphrasing a famous line penned by Tertullian from the second century. He was an essential voice from Carthage in North Africa, the first significant theologian of the church to write in Latin, and a vigilant defender of the faith against heresy. Therefore, he asked, "What has Jerusalem to do with Athens [or] the Church with the Academy?" These days, we might replace Athens with Berlin, Paris, New York, Los Angeles, Moscow, Tokyo, Cairo, Peking, or El Salvador. The concern expressed by Tertullian has increased in complexity over the centuries since his probing question. It is certainly an issue requiring the attention of Mount Vernon Nazarene University as we continue our journey into the twenty-first century.

WHY ALDERSGATE?

Those who live and work in the shadow of the Methodist family will immediately understand the reference to Aldersgate. John Wesley, an eighteenth-century Anglican, had a life-transforming experience at a Moravian gathering on Aldersgate Street; he observed,

> In the evening I went very unwillingly to a society in Aldersgate Street, where one was reading Luther's Preface to the Epistle to the Romans. About a quarter before nine, while he was describing the change which God works in the heart through faith in Christ, I felt my heart strangely warmed. I felt I did trust in Christ, Christ alone, for salvation; and an assurance was given me that He had taken away my sins, even mine, and saved me from the law of sin and death.[1]

While there is some debate regarding what this means and its possible significance for understanding Wesley, no one doubts the power of this moment for those who work in conscious debt to Wesley. This leads me back to my question: What has Aldersgate to do with Athens? How can we reconcile the life of holiness with the life of the mind? Should our faculty who teach chemistry, literature, accounting, mathematics, nursing, and so on be concerned about such things as Wesleyan-Holiness? Is it even possible for the streams of wisdom flowing from Sinai and Calvary to share anything with those sources of wisdom flowing from Athens? What difference do we bring to our learning community's intellectual and spiritual formation?

In this stream of questions, I have asked more than I should try to answer. You can relax. I will only make a few preliminary comments on the significant questions raised thus far. Let me begin with my answer to the question: What does Aldersgate have to do with Athens? I will assume that this University's work is where Aldersgate and Athens converge. No conflict exists between a "strangely warmed heart" and a disciplined, discerning mind. We do not turn our minds off on Sunday or our hearts the rest of the week. We bring our questions to this place in the full expectation that we will find disciplined and informed intellectual mentors on this campus. No question is off limits here. There is no need to limit our work because we are Christians. We are committed to critical thinking, academic rigor, and professional excellence in Wesley's *warm-hearted* faith. Toward this end, I want to make three relatively straightforward

1. Wesley, *Journal*, May 24, 1738.

observations regarding the significance of the convergence of Aldersgate and Athens for Wesleyan-Holiness Higher Education.

Wisdom

First, Aldersgate reminds us of the deep wells of wisdom. I understand that we live in a made-simple, formula-oriented, and historically-illiterate culture. These days, there is far too little tolerance for nuance, complexity, and critical reflection. We know how to do things, but we do not understand why. We live at the place where the rivers of Aldersgate and Athens intersect. The waters run deep, the resources are rich, and good work exists here. Perhaps, we resonate with the words of Job, "I have uttered what I did not understand, things too wonderful for me, which I do not know" (42:3b NRSV). Wisdom pushes the artificial, arbitrary, and rootless nature of much knowledge toward the deep wells of faith and understanding. According to the writer of Proverbs, "I, wisdom, live with prudence, and I attain knowledge and discretion" (8:12 NRSV). Aldersgate should remind us that humility is the greater part of understanding. The depths of wisdom challenge much of education's intellectual, spiritual, and moral pride. It is foolish for anyone to believe that the journey to understanding could truly end or be the basis for dismissing others. Depth leads to the capacity to appreciate life's mysteries and the intellect's joys. Depth leads to mature patience in the face of the vexing issues often confronting our investigations. Aldersgate and Athens frame harmony as possible through a mind saturated with truth.

I will never forget the utter joy and terror I experienced when I looked into the eyes of our first child. She was a beautiful, wide-eyed girl who simultaneously brought excitement and pride. A child is never an abstraction or an idle pleasure. A child calls us to develop the capacity to use what we know, celebrate the moments of insight, and ponder the complexities of life. Knowledge is of little significance apart from the capacity to practice understanding, that is, to govern our lives through reason. Alasdair MacIntyre writes,

> We cannot have any of the moral virtues adequately unless we also learn to have prudence, the only virtue that is both moral and intellectual. Without prudence we lack the capacity for right judgment, rightly directed prudence, and right action without which dispositions to act temperately, courageously,

> and justly will not issue in genuinely temperate, courageous, and just action.[2]

While I am sure that MacIntyre is not writing about my children, he could be. My daughters and son have required the capacity not only to say, but to do. Knowing apart from doing loses the harmony associated with the convergence of Aldersgate and Athens. Prudence is required to act rightly and justly and thus to chart a path forward. Aldersgate and Athens lead us along the still waters of prudence. Socrates considered himself a midwife because he understood wisdom requires more than IQ. Perhaps, we know that the task to which God calls us will require the tenacity of a midwife, the patience of a parent, and the prudence to discern, if we are to integrate our understanding with the profundity and depths of wisdom.

Once we have been to Aldersgate, a glimpse of a new land full of wisdom comes clearly into view. The refusal of the shallow and simplistic arises in the wake of Aldersgate. We who gather on this campus understand that eternity presents itself to us wrapped in swaddling clothes. Once we visited Bethlehem, we understood that even a keen intellect cannot reveal some things to us. Sometimes we find ourselves on the sure path to Damascus, only to learn a more excellent way. The serendipitous nature of our journey comes into full view in moments like this. John Milbank writes about the mind as an event of divine kenotic descent and an event of eschatological ascent. In this way, "The mind is the continuing event of this orientation, suspended between the already of a prediscursive glimpse of the final vision of God, and the note of the full realization."[3] The sort of education we have embarked upon understands the inherent risk, but we move forward in the confidence of a mind set ablaze by the truth and warmed through the Spirit. Richard John Neuhaus adds "If Christian truth does not illuminate and undergird every quest for truth, it is questionable that Christianity is true."[4] We stand amazed in the presence of the deep wells of wisdom brought in view at the place where Aldersgate and Athens converge.

2. MacIntyre, *God, Philosophy, Universities*, 88.
3. Milbank and Pickstock, *Truth in Aquinas*, 38.
4. Neuhaus, "Public Square," 63.

Intellectual Discovery

Second, Aldersgate helps us be attentive to the unexpected pleasures of intellectual discovery. Our work on this campus leads us to anticipate with joy the intellectual discovery among our faculty and students. When Aldersgate and Athens converge it is dangerous to have your mind made up. Wesley found a whole new world post-Aldersgate. Peter had his mind made up about Gentiles until he saw a sheet full of all kinds of four-footed creatures and reptiles and birds of the air (Acts 10:11). Jeremiah and Ezekiel were forced to re-think the meaning of the covenant, to look to a time when it would be written on the heart and mind. Job was forced to consider the collapse of a certain kind of faith in the shadow of the exile. The history of Christianity is filled with men and women who were forced toward what Mildred Bangs Wynkoop once referred to as "intellectual sweat."[5] We greet each freshman class with the hope that when Aldersgate and Athens converge there just might be a surprise along the way. We hope that the joys of Shakespeare or Augustine will be the occasion for pleasure. Maybe Einstein or Kepler will speak through the ages to those who have eyes and ears set upon the truth. Sometimes the class or the professor or the text becomes the occasion for unexpected insight and new direction. When Aldersgate and Athens converge we might well pray with Paul, "that the God of our Lord Jesus Christ, the Father of glory, may give you a spirit of wisdom and revelation as you come to know him, so that, with the eyes of your heart enlightened, you may know what is the hope to which he has called you" (Eph 1:17–18 NRSV). All of this leads us to be attentive to our task.

We cannot afford to coast along preoccupied with insignificance when around the next corner we might find a new thing. When Aldersgate and Athens converge, we move with the keen anticipation of what lies beyond our current knowledge. After all, according to Denis Robinson, "We do not go to university for answers, but to be inspired."[6] I might add that the point of the inspiration is to begin the path toward conclusions that will define our lives. Because we do not work in the fear of knowledge, we can say with Elmer John Thiessen, "Open-mindedness is not the same as empty-mindedness."[7] Here, the words of Saint John Chrysostom make a great deal of sense: "When you pray, always keep

5. Mildred Bangs Wynkoop, comment during theology lecture, n.d.

6. Robinson, "Sedes Sapientiae," 93.

7. Thiessen, *In Defence of Religious Schools and Colleges*, 40.

your mind in your heart."[8] The genius of an education informed by Aldersgate and Athens is that there will always be a place for imagination. Here we come to see what the mind is capable of when the fearlessness of a mind guided by the truth and in the power of the Spirit is enlivened by the grand horizon of our faith and intellectual traditions.

When you stand in a classroom and look into the faces of students who can hear the waters of Aldersgate and Athens, it is difficult not to be excited. It is an utter joy to look into the eyes of an eighteen-year-old or any person of any age and know that the journey ahead will inspire the imagination toward disciplined creativity heretofore unimagined. This means a thorough understanding of history must discipline that imagination. It also suggests that there is no conflict between discipline and imagination. Perhaps, the imagination can point us toward something more wonderful than logic can provide. It is our task and joy to walk this way together on this journey with all its amazing surprises.

My son decided in seventh grade and into eighth grade that he wanted to play football, but due to a series of unfortunate circumstances, he ended up with a fractured wrist. He turned in his pads and uniform with more than a bit of sadness. Yet, as this door closed, his band director asked him to march in the high school band carrying a saxophone. He was not allowed to play, but he learned to march. He went with the band to away games and marched for home games. The marching band was a great surprise for him. He expected football, but the band enriched him. He was the field commander for his last two years of high school. These were some of the best days of his life, but as he remained attentive, what was truly important came into view.

Transformation

Third, Aldersgate engenders the disciplines of transformation, that is, the practices of the Christian university. There are many rich practices on this campus. We are called to prayer, disciplined reading, accountability, gratitude, intellectual hospitality, and discernment. We often talk about the *Idea* of a Christian University, but Aldersgate calls upon us to talk more about the *Practice* of the Christian University. We are called to these transformation disciplines in the grand hope that real change might occur. MacIntyre writes, "What God's grace summons and enables those

8. Quoted in Walker and Wright, "Christian University Imagined," 69.

who receive it to achieve is a redirection of the whole human being, so that the exercise of our bodily powers, as well as our powers of mind and spirit, give expression to the will's transformation, a transformation that always remains incomplete in this present life."[9] The theoretical finds its rightful place here, but it is not until we find a practice that knowing meets wisdom. The sort of education toward which we reach repairs the ruin of humanity's sinful fall from grace by helping individuals regain a proper knowledge of God. This does not happen by a sheer act of will, it arises in the face of disciplined practices. Such an education engenders a restored rational nature, wrong passions are subdued, self-discipline emerges, and our needs become more important than our wants. All of this is a practical orientation for education.

Essentially, the practices envisioned here must be coherent and capable of addressing the capacity to embrace complexity. Practice does not make perfect. Instead, practice makes it permanent. The university at the convergence of Aldersgate and Athens works with socially established and cooperative activities that can render a whole life for its community and its graduates. Mount Vernon Nazarene University will be transformed into an agent of transformation by the coherence, complexity, and cooperative practices we embody. The narratives we believe about ourselves and the world we are called to serve become practices of discernment, memory, and graciousness in our community. We learn, extend, and pass on these noble truths to each succeeding generation.

This is where the faculty becomes essential as the practices of the Christian university are modeled. The faculty determines the character of the university. Our faculty will undoubtedly remember the many times I have said: *As the faculty goes, so goes the university*. The faculty must do more than talk about the direction; they must walk toward where Aldersgate and Athens converge. The imagination and discipline of the faculty will provide the substance of a Christian education. When this happens, students see the virtues enfleshed. The story will be told by a faculty member who drinks from the deep wells of Aldersgate and Athens. These truths and these narratives need to live in the imagination of the faculty, and they need to be rendered to this community in an act of intellectual generosity.

Growing up in a Christian home with my parents and two sisters was my privilege. My father did not complete a college degree but worked

9. MacIntyre, *God, Philosophy, Universities*, 25.

hard as an accountant for Chevron Oil Company. He surrounded himself with books; it was not unusual to see him spend hours reading. One of my first memories is of my mother studying algebra, so she could go back to college. She wanted to make sure that her children could go to college. I was in third grade when she started college. Before it was over, she had earned an undergraduate degree and four master's degrees. Her labor will forever be a symbol for me, depicting the convergence of Aldersgate and Athens. She and my father wanted a better life for the children, but my mother ensured it in a way she never imagined. She showed me that education matters because of her work, the books she surrounded us with, and the grand hope that an education is about a world far grander than words can fully describe. She was of faith and intelligence and never let me think a conflict was necessary. Deep faith and intellectual passion converged in her life. I stand here today because I saw that dream and practice in the eyes of my mother and father. Her life has flourished into her children and her grandchildren. My own children have all earned graduate degrees, but this began with a mother wanting a better life for her children. After everything has been said and done, the deep wells of wisdom, the unexpected pleasures of intellectual discovery, and the disciplines of transformation express the hope of Mount Vernon Nazarene University that all who come to this place in search of an education at the point where Aldersgate and Athens converge will find sufficient resources for the journey. I saw that first in my parents' eyes, but I have seen it in the disciplined practices of professors and colleagues. I stand here in a position and place that I could not have anticipated as a debtor of the wisdom of the cross, the love of my wife and family, the graciousness of the Church of the Nazarene, the trust of the Board of Trustees, and the partnership of this community. This day, let me say—I will stand with you at the place where Aldersgate and Athens converge. I intend to work with you so that a new generation of men and women will find a warm-hearted community at this University devoted to exploring the depths and heights of intellectual discourse in the shadow of the Cross.

May God grant us the courage to live where Aldersgate and Athens converge in the hope that understanding will be deepened, spiritual insights preserved, and a community gathered around the true, noble, holy, and virtuous.

CHAPTER 12

The Rhythm of Grace

Henry Walter Spaulding II

INTRODUCTION

THE RHYTHM OF GRACE characterizes the Christian faith. This comes into clear focus early in the *Gospel of Luke*. We see it in Mary's words: "My soul magnifies the Lord, and my spirit rejoices in God my Savior" (1:46–47 NRSV). We can hear the rhythm in Zechariah's words: "He has raised up a mighty savior for us in the house of his child David" (1:69). The angels reflect the same rhythm a little later, "Glory to God in the highest heaven, and on earth peace among those whom he favors (2:14 NRSV)!" The same chorus can be detected at the baptism of Jesus, "and the Holy Spirit descended upon him in bodily form like a dove. And a voice came from heaven, 'You are my Son, the Beloved; with you I am pleased'"(3:22b). *Luke* joins the rhythm of grace to tell the story of a pattern of movement in time or what moves music through time. Rhythm not only moves music along, but it stands under and behind God's unfolding grace.

Luke teaches us that without rhythm, there is no real life either. Discord and confusion may surround us, but for God's people, there is also a subtle rhythm supporting our faith. The degree to which we can hear that rhythm, we begin to understand the degree to which the kingdom has already dawned as we wait expectantly for the kingdom, this kingdom's dawning.

Luke overflows with the rhythm of grace. We can hear and see this rhythm in the birth narratives and the joyous response of Elizabeth and Mary. We can observe it as the young boy Jesus astounds the expert teachers. The voice that cries in the wilderness also testifies to this rhythm. Jesus is tempted, but we know that his life is entirely wrapped up in the rhythm of grace. The Spirit of the Lord is upon him. Therefore, nothing can distract him. His life is his mission. This Jesus teaches and heals, walks and waits, comforts and challenges, because it is in his life that we see the rhythm of grace unfolding for our salvation and that of the entire world. The leper is healed, and sins are forgiven. A Centurion's slave is healed, and Jesus says, "I tell you, not even in Israel have I found such faith" (7:9). *Luke* tells us about a woman lost in sin. She is so far away that she does not hear the rhythm of grace anymore, and maybe she never did. By the grace of God, she somehow hears Jesus. She anoints his feet with the contents of an alabaster jar, and she weeps. He also dries his feet with her hair. By any account, this is a strange story, that is, unless you hear the rhythm of grace.

There are more stories in this grand gospel than we have time to tell. We could talk about people possessed by demons, a little girl who died, five thousand who are fed, and a prayer that tells of a Father who is in heaven. And when we are done, we could start all over again and would never exhaust the riches and beauty of this rhythm of grace. We know that this rhythm finds its true end and its beginning in the sweet music of the Triune God. And it is just because that music overflows into the world that we can hear together a rhythm that speaks of the grace of God.

I am reminded of the summer when I was going home in my Tahoe. I pulled off the exit, stopped at the end of the ramp, and as I pulled onto the road, I felt a jolt. Since driving requires rhythm, I stopped at the visible stop sign. This rhythm escaped the driver behind me because he was going to the "dog track." This fact did not take the sting from my life that my bumper now had a dent. When I pulled over, he rolled out of his truck with one question: Why did you stop? Looking at him, I knew he had never heard the rhythm. The song he could listen to came from the "dog track." I think that until you hear the rhythm of grace, it is not easy to explain the utter joy of grace.

THE RHYTHM OF GRACE IS ALWAYS PARTICULAR

Sometimes, we get so accustomed to the horizon that we forget where our feet are planted. If we neglect this, we may overlook where our feet are positioned. We walk among little ones who depend upon us without noticing. Sometimes, we are the little ones, and we depend upon others. And I believe the "big picture" often keeps us straight in times of despair and confusion. But in the same measure, we must be reminded that the purpose of staying straight is to know the grace of God.

I have learned this lesson with our children. During their high school years, it was necessary to set the expectation that they would return home at a reasonable time. I soon learned that reasonable is far too general to communicate my genuine desire. So, I would say "Be home at 11:00 p.m". That is more than fair, but the tragedy that befalls when children attempt to get home always amazes me. After all, watch batteries are likely to fail between 10:45 and 11:00 p.m. And if you lose your keys, it will usually be on your way home and not out the door. Getting caught up in a meaningful conversation after 10:45 is easier than before. But I even noticed that the concept of home is up for interpretation. Let me be clear, I always thought of home as being on my side of the front door. Therefore, I expected my children to be on my side of the door by the appointed time. For my children, home meant being on some part of the driveway by 11:00 p.m. Now I understand how to give directions. Once my children understood, life has been an ongoing doxology.

Luke 17 is a testimony to the seemingly small things that are important. This could be understood as tyranny. It could suggest a God who applies a magnifying glass to our lives. And if this is the image, we will know that no passing grades could ever be earned. But the glory of it all is that the hand does not so much point to sin and failure as it opens in gracious gift. And if we look very closely, the hand that reaches us has a nail scar. Those scars should be on our hands, but He has borne our iniquities. It is the grace of God that meets our needs. It is the grace of God that heals our brokenness and opens our defensiveness toward wholeness and holiness. This is the rhythm of grace.

The Rhythm of Grace Is a Gift

Jesus puts it this way. Suppose you were a slave to a fair-minded master. Would this master invite you to his table after a long workday? He might or not, but it would not be our decision. And if, after a long workday, you were told to prepare supper, and maybe you could eat, that would be fair. There would be no factual basis for a complaint. We could well respond, "We are worthless slaves; we have done only what we ought to have done!" While this may strike you as a strange saying, it is a profound truth.

It has taken me most of my life to grasp this truth: all I am in Christ is a gift of grace. We do not climb up the ladder by our good work. We are never going to deserve a place at the table. We can never look toward God and say, "I have done my part," not "I have done yours." Life's plain and simple fact is that we live in the rhythm of grace and must be willing to accept the gift. God loves us first, last, and everywhere in between. Learning to live this rhythm is the essence of Christian life.

Many years ago, my son was interested in college football, especially the Florida State University Seminoles. Over the years, this became a rather painful journey as winning gave way to losing on many occasions. Yet, he remained true to his team. One year, we went to Tallahassee to see a game. It sounded good in theory, but I began to see a negative cash flow. I remember sitting in the game and not enjoying it as much as I expected because my wallet was thick with receipts. At the end of the game, as we were leaving, my son looked up at me and said, "Dad, this is the best day of my life." For a minute, I thought I was in a Mastercard commercial. But then it dawned on me he knows how to accept a gift, and I am beginning to forget. And it was my son who enjoyed that game the way it is supposed to be enjoyed as a gift.

God calls us to enjoy life that way. It is the very rhythm of grace that plays out as gift.

The Rhythm of Grace Is Now

Jesus says it this way, "For, in fact, the kingdom of God is among us" (21b)! What is the kingdom? It is Jesus who is the union of being and speech. It is the reign of God. He does not so much speak the kingdom as he is the kingdom. And as often as we do this, remember the sacrifice as we anticipate the fullness of the kingdom. In other words, practice the kingdom now as you wait for the return of Christ.

The power of sin has been defeated. Its power and sting are gone. We do not have to sin, and we do not have to live in bondage to sin. We can undoubtedly say with Paul, "There is therefore now no condemnation for those who are in Christ Jesus. For the law of the Spirit in Christ Jesus has set you free from the law of sin and death" (Rom 8:1–2 NRSV). The rhythm of grace is a song of freedom.

The Rhythm of Grace Is Seeing the End in the Beginning

We read, "Then he said to the disciples, 'The days are coming when you will long to see one of the days of the Son of Man, and you will not see it. They will say to you, 'Look there!' or 'Look here!' Do not go; do not set off in pursuit" (17:22–23 NRSV). Too often, the church comprises those locked in the past and those fixated on the future. For the first group, there is little more than the memory of better days. That was when the church was on fire, and everyone loved one another. It is all over for the second group, and things are so bad that we might as well dress in choir robes and find a tree to climb to wait for deliverance. In both cases, the first casualty is the rhythm of grace. We do not have to look back on the past or forward to the future when we live in the rhythm of grace.

Jesus says that while life is going on, its anticipation can only be understood initially. The rhythm of grace is the curious way in which the God who is Father, Son, and Spirit, and the beginning of all things, calls us into God's future, which is also our glory. Let me put it another way: we are what we are by the gracious love of God, and we will never be able to escape that love. The only thing we can do is turn inside out and convince ourselves that it is not grace. But it is grace, and is the rhythm that we cannot escape. We can only pervert it.

Luke 17 is about how the rhythm of grace can serve to interpret life. It is the lens through which I can live carefully, triumphantly, thankfully, presently, and hopefully. We have heard the rhythm of grace all along the way, and it is how we can live between Advent and Pentecost or Creation and Parousia.

During the summer of 1996, it became apparent that my mother-in-law was becoming too forgetful. First, there were little things like the difference between a fork and a spoon or where to sign a check. Then it was the big things, and finally the essential stuff. She had the slow, but at the same time, all too rapid descent into the fog of Alzheimer's. There are no words to describe the sorrow between 1996 and 2003 fully. Toward the end, she fell off the cliff. She had to be admitted to the lockdown unit of a local hospital. When my wife and I arrived at the hospital, she did not know who we were. It was a sad day, especially for my wife. The next day was Sunday, and we visited her. A church group had come to the unit to sing songs in the large room down the hall. They began to sing "Amazing Grace". Her mother immediately perked up. She sang every word as the piano played. As long as the piano played, she sang. It was as if the Lord was sending the family a message. She may have forgotten her name, but deeper still, there is a rhythm of grace. She has forgotten most everything, but the Lord has not forgotten her. The rhythm goes deeper than you will ever know. Two days later, she followed the rhythm of grace in the arms of her Lord and Savior.

CHAPTER 13

The Unexpected Challenge of Fundamentalism for Wesleyanism

Henry Walter Spaulding II

INTRODUCTION

TWENTY YEARS AGO, WHILE teaching theology in a Wesleyan university, fundamentalism was a hot topic among my students. While faculty in other universities were losing their positions due to their view of Scripture and doctrine, I confidently stated that Wesley's theological project was relatively immune to fundamentalism. This was my considered judgment based on my theological training with H. Ray Dunning, who on many occasions offered a stringent critique of fundamentalism. Now that I have retired, my sad duty is to revise my original optimism regarding Wesleyanism's capacity to bend its knee to fundamentalism. It is becoming an unexpected challenge for those thinking theologically in Wesleyan churches and universities.

THE EMERGENCE OF FUNDAMENTALISM

While fundamentalism extends beyond the West, specific forces have combined to create fertile soil for fundamentalism. I will consider its trajectory in the West. The emphasis on human subjectivity, the scientific revolution, and the instability of authority combined to create intellectual uncertainty. Descartes aimed to establish a new physics grounded in a philosophical foundation. Continental Rationalists pushed Descartes's philosophy to its proper logical conclusion. The issue revolved around using mathematical knowledge as an ideal. They did not fully understand that rationalism cannot finally obtain a matter of fact. Locke, on the other hand, took a different path. He was most interested in the actual world. The central idea here was that the outside world causes perception. Hume pointed out that if we start from the assumption of people's mental states, we will generally stop there. We would not know anything about the outer world. We would only know about our mental state. Descartes had failed, and Kant considered precisely where the problem resided. He unleashed his considerable analytical skills to attempt a resolution to this problem. Kant noted that if the test of truth is agreement of the mind with an external object, only a particular truth can be known. Scientific knowledge shows that knowledge is much larger than the agreement of the mind with synthetic a priori objects of the world. Yet, if this were the case, we would never arrive at scientific knowledge. The hypothesis became that the mind's object must agree with the mind. We must distinguish between form/a priori and content/a posteriori. Kant worked on the assumption that the mind's power of sense perception and understanding/a posteriori, along with reason/transcendental. This begins to organize knowledge according to the mind's capacity. This led to several conclusions:

- If transcendentalism can be called metaphysics, objective experience can be treated as a science.
- The synthetic a priori can assist with constructing a metaphysics of nature.
- These assumptions can be helpful with a metaphysics of psychology and the categorical system.
- If the categorical system extends beyond the norms of the field of knowledge it is not useful for knowledge.
- Principles cannot legitimate the existence of God or any supersensible being.

One way to think of this is to do metaphysics if you must. Pure reason, using categories, can organize our thoughts and propositions, but it does not equate to traditional metaphysics. This places significant doubt regarding the stability of knowledge. Hegel casts a version of this idea onto the flow of history. Marx used this to place dialectical material on top of this to erase any metaphysical elements effectively. Nietzsche understands this as providing the basis for the claim that we have killed God.

A THEOLOGICAL INVESTIGATION

Fundamentalism is a symptom of the uncertainty born in the wake of modernity. One might say it is the wrong answer to the right question. Living and thinking in a post-Enlightenment world will require a courageous faith and unflinching commitment to truth. This begins with the capacity to trust in the Scripture Paul writes about in 2 Tim 3:16–17, "All scripture is inspired by God and is useful for teaching, for reproof, for correction, and for training in righteousness, so that the person of God may be proficient, equipped for every good work" (NRSV). Fundamentalism's penchant for "inerrancy" is unnecessary to establish the authority of Scripture, which demonstrates some certainty.

Perhaps, the authority fundamentalists seek is more about tradition or nostalgia for a simpler time. One that is free of the epistemological challenges of our time, but faith demands that we proclaim the good news. Wesley believes Scripture should be interpreted in its plain sense. He did his theological work, seeking the whole tenor of Scripture as the bedrock for the place where we make theological judgments. James Smart's works apply to the question of authority and the use of Scripture, "The voice of the Scripture is falling silent in the preaching and teaching of the church and in the consciousness of the Christian people, a silence that is perceptible even among those who are most insistent upon devotion to the scriptures."[1] There is no need for inerrancy to establish a firm basis for theological reflection in the spirit of Wesleyanism. This text demonstrates that God inspires Scripture. Therefore, the authority of Scripture arises from God alone. It is the basis for teaching, reproof, correction, and training in righteousness. There is little need to add anything to this to honor the Scripture and the quality of a righteous life. We should defend the Scripture by letting it lose in communities of faith and the world. While the fundamentalists choose to defend the Bible with the exhaustive defense of the idea of total inerrancy, the true power of the Scripture is found in the proclamation of Jesus Christ. Fundamentalism exists to defend the authority of the Scripture in a world where the pillars

1. Smart, *Strange Silence*, 15–16.

of authority are crumbling. Therefore, as we have already observed, fundamentalism asks the right question but provides the wrong answer.

Fundamentalism began in England before moving to Princeton Theological Seminary and then to Westminster Theological Seminary, and it has flourished mainly in the Southern Baptist tradition. This is not to say that all Baptist churches have affirmed either the ethos or the theology of fundamentalism. The same can be said of many other traditions because of the simplicity of conservative denominations' hermeneutics, including the Wesleyan family. Much of the style and theology of fundamentalism is located within the horizon of a book where the so-called fundamentals are located:

- Inerrancy and verbal inspiration of the Scripture
- Trinity
- The virgin birth and incarnation of Christ
- Original sin
- Atonement of Christ
- Resurrection of Christ
- Premillennial return of Christ
- Spiritual rebirth
- Bodily resurrection and eternal damnation

Add to this a dogged affirmation of young-earth creationism, and much of the trajectory of fundamentalism comes clearly into view. When I first read this list, my first thought was, "I think I agree with all of these statements, but further reflection revealed my central problem. For example, I affirm total inerrancy on all matters pertaining to the faith. The fundamentalists affirm a view of Scripture that wants what 2 Timothy refuses. Verbal inspiration is required for this view of Scripture to work. I see no reason to affirm a premillennial return of Christ. A much stronger view from my perspective is the simple affirmation that Jesus is coming again. It is not the fundamentals that frustrate me as much as the extreme defensiveness and the reactiveness. I have named the latter as Pharisaical Fundamentalism. This represents an aggressive nature that personalizes theological convictions, damaging universities, seminaries, and churches. Wesley held a high view of Scripture in concert with a catholic spirit.

THE WESLEYAN HERITAGE AND FUNDAMENTALISM

The Wesleyan tradition should not be fundamentalism's native home. We must address the changing face of fundamentalism as we examine the complex relationship between fundamentalism and the Wesleyan tradition. R. T. Williamson, a General Superintendent, said at the Seventh General Assembly (1928) that every delegate in the assembly is a fundamentalist, and so far as we know, there is not a modernist in the ranks of the Church of the Nazarene. Setting aside the theological acumen of the General Assembly, his statement requires more nuance to provide guiding principles for the debate. Much of the most dangerous aspects of fundamentalism are extra-biblical. For example, inerrancy or any possible cognates can be found in the Scripture. Inerrancy was added to Article IV in 1928, effectively yielding to ecclesial forces and cultural currents. J. Kenneth Grider, a thirty-plus-year theology professor at Nazarene Theological Seminary, wrote in *A Wesleyan-Holiness Theology*, "Most of us Wesleyan-Holiness scholars are hunters after the Bible's soteriological message and do not like to engage ourselves with such matters as to whether it errs on non-faith and non-practice matters."[2] Grider was committed to the authority of Scripture but had little interest in punishing those who disagreed with him. While his actual practice became retributive, he did so by abandoning the teaching of Wesley. Paul Bassett concludes in his article on fundamentalism in the *Wesleyan Theological Journal*,

> Fundamentalism could not leaven the whole lump. However, it has continued to affect the Church of the Nazarene, especially as it has become increasingly clear that she has inherited two fundamentally incompatible points of view; not on some peripheral issues, but about the central nature of spiritual-theological authority.[3]

The fact that Wesleyan theology and fundamentalism are theologically incompatible has made little difference for the Church of the Nazarene.

2. Grider, *Wesleyan-Holiness Theology*, 75.

3. Bassett, "Fundamentalist Leavening," 83.

FUNDAMENTALISM COMPARED TO WESLEYANISM

As I conclude my reflections, I would like to contrast Fundamentalism succinctly and Wesleyan for clarity, and with the understanding that these are general statements.

- Fundamentalism curses the dark, while Wesleyanism names the light.
- Fundamentalism nervously reduces faith and grace as it looks toward the future, while Wesleyanism boldly and courageously proclaims the new reality in Christ as it joyfully anticipates the future.
- Fundamentalism is happiest about what it can conserve and protect.
- Wesleyanism is happiest about what it has freed by preaching the word, celebrating the sacraments, and uniting the Christian community.
- Fundamentalism must be clear, even at the risk of being wrong. Wesleyanism is willing to embrace faith and grace amid life's tensions and ambiguities.

Wesley writes,

> The thing which I was greatly afraid of all this time and which I resolved to use very possible method of preventing was a narrowness of spirit and party zeal, a being straightened in our bowels, that miserable bigotry which makes many unready to believe that there is any work of God bur among themselves.[4]

I served as president of a Nazarene university for almost eleven years in a part of the country and in the Church of the Nazarene, where fundamentalism seems to have won, even at a Nazarene school. I have been engaged by many trustees, parents, and pastors who have mistaken Wesleyanism for liberalism. Because they were fed fundamentalism, they reject Wesleyanism. No amount of conversation could move the needle with these individuals. People have lost their jobs and reputation in the church. This was unnecessary, as it was mean-spirited and fell well below the threshold of theological and academic integrity. I lamented then and now at the damage created by individuals held captive by fundamentalism. The inability of Wesleyanism to capture the imagination of this generation is

4. Wesley, *Works*, 8:257.

partly due to the dullness of its opponents and the inherent risk posed by even entertaining the conversation.

Paul does not address fundamentalism in the passage but does address how people are excluded for frivolous reasons. Discernment will be required because doctrinal issues matter, but so do people. This essay is a call for charitable, non-coercive discourse.

CHAPTER 14

Gracious Longing

A Wesleyan Moral Theology of Sexual Desire

Henry Walter Spaulding III

INTRODUCTION

SEXUALITY IS A CHIEF concern for the church today. Many churches and denominations find themselves split down the middle of a deep divide using specific orthodox pictures of sexual relationships to test their fellow members of the Body of Christ. The result is a zero-sum game, much like the trinitarian and Christological heresies of the early church, where sexuality serves as the barrier to community. Today the discussion of Christian sexuality relies heavily on the *kinds* of relationships that are appropriate to the point that it cannot reason about the *meaning* of sexuality at all. In short, a theology of sexuality consists, as philosopher Ludwig Wittgenstein writes about modernity, of a "*picture* [that] held us captive. And we could not get outside it, for it lay in our language and language seemed to repeat it to us inexorably."[1] Wittgenstein's statement does not charge that Scripture and theologians speak about sex or sexual relationships, but that our discourse is so monotonous, we lack the moral reasoning to understand why we adopt it in the first place.

Wesleyan theologians are ideally placed to answer this conundrum. Wesley does not offer much in the way of explicit sexual ethics, but I

1. Wittgenstein, *Philosophical Investigations*, 41e (§115).

believe his theology of grace offers guidance for moral discernment. Wesley's theology of grace and subsequent sanctification offers believers a guide to the sanctification of their desires through the shedding of grace abroad in their hearts. Grace shapes sexual desires, along with all desires, according to the rhythm of God's healing desire for all humanity. As such, sexual desire should be bound to the formation of a sexual ethic that affirms the created goodness of every creature. This holy sexual ethic should be the standard by which one judges sexual relationships rather than the opposite. Therefore, I argue Wesley's theology of grace aids the formation of a sexual ethic that encourages the creation of bodily affirmation of creaturely goodness.

INNOCENT SEX

Though I argue Wesley's account of grace offers the most robust, theologically informed sexual ethic, I do admit that an Augustinian perspective helpfully clarifies the gridlock already expressed. One such example is *The Romance of Innocent Sexuality* by Geoffrey Rees.[2] The book attempts to dislocate privileged sexual relationships in a world of original sin. When one considers the captivating picture that focuses on the *kinds* of sexual relationships, such an insight begins to clear the way for a different conversation. Rees argues, utilizing St. Augustine's theology of lust, that every human participates in the original sin of our ancestors. Thus, no sexual relationship or desire is freer of the impact of original sin than others.[3] Though this seems strict, Rees persuasively argues this not as an act of shame but rather presents as "charitable solidarity" with fellow sinners.[4] He writes, "A literal interpretation of the doctrine of original sin thereby weakens the hold of the fantasy that human beings through particular forms of sexual relationships—usually, but not necessarily, marriage—can create for themselves privileged spaces of redemptive divine encounter."[5] This elimination of what Rees terms "innocent sex" is equitable. As Rees continues that eliminating innocent sex "renders cognizable as fantasy all claims that the shame of sin can be proportioned differentially, that any such thing as a person exists who hasn't already

2. Rees, *Romance of Innocent Sexuality*.
3. Rees, *Romance of Innocent Sexuality*, 6–8.
4. Rees, *Romance of Innocent Sexuality*, 11.
5. Rees, *Romance of Innocent Sexuality*, 12.

sinned and suffered the shame of its consequences."[6] This emphasis does not shame individuals but instead dismantles the idols of innocent sex that either side attempts to hold beyond critique. Dismantling privileged places of innocent sex allows the moral space to critique those activities typically defended carte blanche. Furthermore, rather than relying on the crutch of a specific picture, Rees breaks open the image one privileges to provide an account of sex that *guides* relationships. In short, Rees challenges Christians to do the theological work of locating a moral theology of sexual desires that fit within our humanity as created by God and not just fixing sexual desire on specific images that hold us captive.

SINFUL DESIRE OR UNHOLY TEMPERS

Rees presents a unique opportunity to Wesleyans to think through this same challenge with their unique Wesleyan grammar. As theologians and church historians can attest, Wesley did not share Augustine's account of original sin. Wesley believed humans possessed "in-being sin," which means, as theologian Randy Maddox summarizes, that humans "only become guilty when we reject the offered grace of God, *like* Adam and Eve did."[7] Though Wesley and Augustine offer a complimentary account of grace and sin, Wesleyans take a point of departure with Wesley because his theology of grace allows space for the goodness of sexual desire itself while also critiquing spaces of privilege. Rees's use of Augustine on original sin, while making an important point about the safety of preferred relationships, does not attend to the goodness of sexual desire itself as a part of our graced, created being. On the other hand, Wesley understands the created goodness of human beings while also recognizing that they are prone to misuse their good created being for sin and maintaining original sin. Wesley's account of sanctification through grace offers an essential model within which sexual desire itself can be understood as good and leading to holy sexual practice.

Before directly engaging the question of sexual desire, one must first explain Wesley's theology of in-being sin, the *imago Dei*, and responsible grace that forms a Wesleyan grammar of the creature that will then lend itself to a Wesleyan grammar of sexual desire. Unlike most Western theologians of his time, Wesley presents a unique perspective on original

6. Rees, *Romance of Innocent Sexuality*, 12.

7. Maddox, *Responsible Grace*, 74.

sin.[8] For Wesley, the original state of humanity was one of love, which mirrored the love of God.[9] As such, the first humans enjoyed the liberty of affection in which they were able to attach themselves correctly to proper objects of love.[10] The consequences of the Fall were such that when the "taste of the fruit" occurred, these natural abilities became corrupted.[11] To be clear, Wesley's emphasis on the Fall, inherited from Eastern Christianity, is on the severed relationship between the creature and God, which severely impacts human faculties.[12] Humans do not naturally "delight" in God or love God by our natural faculties.[13] Instead, humans become "sunk partly into the image of the devil, in pride, malice, and all other diabolical tempers . . being fallen under the dominion of brutal passions and grovelling [*sic*] appetites."[14] Being separated from God in this way deprives humanity of the essential relationship needed for holiness and inevitably leads to debilitation and moral depravity.[15] To clarify, this merely impacts our affections, compromising our ability to act, but it is not impossible. Thus, the malformed tempers impacted by the severed relationships are the seedbed from which actual sins arise.[16]

HOLY DESIRE: SEXUAL APPETITES IN THE ORDO SALUTIS

In Wesley's theology, like in Augustine's theology, the fallen state of humanity confronts the transforming grace of God. Sin impacts these capacities by the severing of this relationship.[17] However, God's grace begins to transform humanity "prior to justification" as God initiating the work of salvation.[18] It is this grace that moves the believer to love God and, thus, the renewing of this gracious capacity to correct relationships

8. Maddox, *Responsible Grace*, 75.
9. Wesley, "Image of God," 15.
10. Wesley, "Image of God," 15–16.
11. Wesley, "Image of God," 17.
12. Maddox, *Responsible Grace*, 81.
13. Wesley, "Original Sin," 330.
14. Wesley, "God's Love to Fallen Man," 476.
15. Maddox, *Responsible Grace*, 81.
16. Maddox, *Responsible Grace*, 82.
17. Maddox, *Responsible Grace*, 70.
18. Maddox, *Responsible Grace*, 84.

with God, self, world, and others.[19] There is an intimate connection, but not equivocation, between creatures in their original capacities and the one restored in grace. As such, God's saving grace restores the relationship with God and regenerates the capabilities of believers by enabling them to love not only God but also their neighbor. Therefore, it is not the desires themselves but the tendency to misuse and abuse creation, including humanity, after the Fall. In short, fallen proclivity to sin mimics the Fall in loving fellow human creatures and all creation away from their created goodness in the image of God.

In Wesley's account of salvation, desires themselves are not the issue but rather the ends of desires. In short, grace working through salvation impacts how humans desire to treat one another. The love of God kindles the love in our hearts that produces love for one another. As Wesley states, "We feel the 'love of God shed abroad in our heart by the Holy Ghost which is given unto us,' producing love to all mankind . . . expelling the love of the world, the love of pleasure, of ease, of honour, of money; together with price, anger, self-will, and every other evil temper."[20] The love of God shed abroad in our hearts is the "very moment, *sanctification* begins," which includes transforming evil tempers into holy ones.[21] The creation of holy tempers out of evil tempers arises from restoring a relationship with God wherein desire finds appropriate ends in God.

The sanctification of the human through the transformation of holy tempers has ramifications for one's relationship to God and non-human creation, other humans, and self. The sanctification of the believer includes one's desires, which leads to appropriate passions for others. Humans move from evil tempers (characterized by pride, anger, self-will, love of money) to holy tempers that honor others according to their created goodness. As already mentioned, Wesley's vision of sanctification is a fulfillment of the goodness already embedded in humanity as creatures of God. The desires that one has for another creature must also affirm this goodness. Sanctification, then, is an affirmation and perfecting of the creature as it recovers its *imago Dei*. Therefore, the solidarity that Wesley envisions for each creature is gracious solidarity with each other's goodness, not sinfulness.

The implications of Wesley's account of sanctification give a theological grammar in which to understand sexual desire. Wesley's theology

19. Wesley, "Witness of Our Own Spirit," §15–16, pp. 1:309–10.

20. Wesley, "Scripture Way of Salvation," 373.

21. Wesley, "Scripture Way of Salvation," 373. Emphasis original.

would not argue that every desire is sinful. Instead, desires are prone to seek the other outside God's ends for them. For example, a desire to objectify or seek harm is a manifestation of a desire to seek sinful ends. However, a sanctified, holy temper desires to affirm creaturely goodness already present in the *imago Dei sincerely.* The grace of God transforms the heart of the believer through the revelation that God deeply loves them and makes them capable of loving God and creation, including fellow humans. There is no place to retreat that does not seek the person's twofold sanctification of desires.

Furthermore, this rubric does not first proceed from the place of *a priori* relationships. Instead, this solidarity in goodness seeks uplifting, holy desires that affirm and honor the goodness of our neighbor within the relational community Wesley envisions. Instead of a critique that removes the innocence of sex to allow critique where it previously was not allowed, a Wesleyan theology preserves the innocence of sexual desire. It positively presents the goodness one's desires toward which one must move.

The journey of sanctification that transforms the directionality of desire requires further clarity. In short, what is the entire grammar of a Wesleyan moral theology of sexual desire? In order to distinguish holy tempers from unholy, evil tempers in sexual desire, one must rely on the grace that transforms tempers in the first place. It is grace that initiates humanity into the love of God and one that transforms the heart of the believer and affirms the believer has intended created goodness. Grace, then, gives humanity the grammar necessary to understand the tempers from which moral sexual desires emerge. However, grace does not naturally translate into sexual desire.

THE BODY'S GRACE

Using grace as a grammar appears foreign to the world of sexual desire. However, Rowan Williams suggests that it is not. He writes, "Grace, for the Christian believer, is a transformation that depends in large part on knowing yourself to be seen in a certain way: as significant, as wanted."[22] This affirmation of the quality of grace is naturally compatible with sexual desire. God's grace sheds the love of God abroad in our hearts, which enables humans to know that they are loved and wanted by God. Such

22. Williams, "Body's Grace," 59.

relationality inspires humanity to love God and grow in grace through love to non-human creatures, themselves, and their neighbors. Grace encourages this resounding affirmation of the relational *imago Dei* in each human. The entire drama of grace, as Williams continues, is that "God desires us, *as if we were God,* as if we were that unconditional response to God's giving that God's self makes in the life of the Trinity."[23] The agent responds to grace in love that affirms and enkindles love for God, self, and others. A gracious desire is one in which the agent knows they are wanted and desired in a way comparable to God's love. This is holy love. It is not objectifying or violent but seeks the gracious affirmation of the other. Furthermore, this grace also elicits a response, namely the loving, gracious desire of the other in return—this is for God, themselves, and the beloved. Much like responsible grace to God's love, gracious longing enkindles this loving affection for self and others that also elicits a loving response for self and others. Relationally it must affirm the other, not destroy or objectify. Gracious desiring means that one's desire for another must treat the other as an "occasion of joy."[24] Sexual desire, then, in the order of sanctification, requires an ordering of desire according to shared solidarity with the neighbor in their goodness.

Like Rees, this grammar of grace illustrates that privileged relationships are not the place to begin. Gracious longing is not first about the *kinds* of relationships often cited as the consummate end of sexual ethics, but neither is it primarily about sex acts. As Williams continues, "sexual union is not delivered from mortal danger and ambiguity by satisfying a formal socioreligious criterion. Decisions about sexual lifestyle, to repeat, are about how much we want our bodily selves to mean, rather than what emotional needs we're meeting or what laws we're satisfying."[25] Gracious longing is about the bodily meaning that God desires for humanity. It is a longing that finds fulfillment in seeking the neighbor not as a sexual object but as one created *imago Dei.* It does not deny that we have sexual attractions and drives, but neither does it condemn them. To believe in the sanctifying work of the Holy Spirit means that our full humanity, desires and all, find restoration in the relational creation that God intends. Gracious longing recognizes that our desires for sex can only be an affirmation already present in creatures who themselves are deeply loved by God. Therefore, one can learn about sexual desire for the committed

23. Williams, "Body's Grace," 59.

24. Williams, "Body's Grace," 59.

25. Williams, "Body's Grace," 64.

and the celibate because it does not make sex acts the fulfillment of one's created goodness. This longing, then, is not predicated on evil tempers that establish hierarchies of violence that serve to destroy the body but rather grow from holy tempers that desire to affirm the creature's place among the economy of God's love.

CONCLUSION

In conclusion, the future of sexuality in the church is unclear. Christian fellowship has suffered division and loss due to the lack of a shared grammar and a loss of theological concepts. It is in these moments that traditions must turn to their theological grammar. Wesley's grammar of sanctification is a great place to begin this conversation in traditions that share his influence. Wesleyans should discuss the relationships in which sex occurs, but the relationships one blesses must fit the grammar rather than making the grammar fit the relationships. Only this way can we be free of our idols and participate in God's gracious call to beloved community.

CHAPTER 15

What Is a Nazarene?

A Witness from Exile[1]

Henry Walter Spaulding III

FRIENDS, SIBLINGS IN CHRIST, colleagues and companions in the faith, I come before you not simply as a theologian or church historian, but as one who has walked the dusty roads of denominational life, tasted its graces, and now speaks from a peculiar kind of exile. I am a Nazarene. And I carry the weight and joy of that identity not as a badge of tribalism, but as a testimony to a theological and ethical vision that once named the poor as its first interlocutors and built its sanctuaries beside the forgotten. The question I am tasked with today is simple and searching: *What is a Nazarene?*

To answer that, we must first look backward to a time when Nazareth was not a denomination but a punchline. "Can anything good come out of Nazareth?" (John 1:46) Nathanael's question wasn't just geographical snobbery—it was theological. It was a confrontation with the logic of divine humility. To be Nazarene, then, is to be identified with the unlikely, the overlooked, the poor. It is to belong to the people and places the world forgets. The earliest followers of Jesus bore that name with the scandal of solidarity. They were called Nazarenes because their Lord was Jesus of Nazareth—a man from nowhere who spoke as if he owned everything and emptied himself as if he had nothing to lose.

1. Originally given June 30, 2025 as a brief lecture on the definition of a Nazarene to a group of non-Nazarenes gathered together.

The Church of the Nazarene—founded in the crucible of early twentieth-century revivalism, urban poverty, and social holiness—embraced that same identification. Its founders did not merely preach holiness of heart and life; they located it among the laboring classes, the immigrants, the illiterate, and the addicted. To be a Nazarene was not simply to affirm a doctrine of entire sanctification. It was to claim a preferential option for the poor before the phrase was coined.

Phineas F. Bresee, a key founder of the Church of the Nazarene, famously insisted that the church was to be "a church of the poor." He did not say this as a romantic gesture or marketing slogan. He said it as a theological conviction: the holiness of God cannot be proclaimed apart from the presence of the poor. He and others planted churches in neglected urban neighborhoods. They preached sanctification in mission halls and storefronts. They did not build cathedrals; they built rescue missions.

In those early days, to be a Nazarene was to echo that first skeptical question: Can anything good come from Nazareth? And to answer with your life: Yes, because grace is born in strange places.

But like all ecclesial movements, the Church of the Nazarene has changed. Growth brought respectability. Respectability brought buildings, institutions, pensions, and power. And power always tempts us to forget our beginnings. I do not speak this in bitterness—I have been nourished by this tradition. But I now live in exile from its center. Not by choice, but by conviction. Because when the church ceases to be a church for the poor, those who remember must remain with the poor.

What is a Nazarene? A Nazarene is someone who remembers where Jesus is from. To be Nazarene is not merely to affirm a list of Articles of Faith or to maintain denominational loyalty. It is to embody the rhythm of grace in places of rupture. It is to preach holiness not as moral achievement, but as the miracle of God's hospitality breaking into fractured lives. It is to see sanctification not only in personal purity but in social solidarity.

The preferential option for the poor is not an ecclesial add-on; it is the pulse of holiness theology. Holiness is always relational—it draws us into deeper communion with God and with neighbor. And if our neighbor is poor, holiness must bend in that direction. Wesley taught that there is no holiness but social holiness. The Nazarenes, at their best, translated this into concrete acts of mercy: shelters, food pantries, orphanages, schools for the underserved.

But there is more to be said. Holiness, rightly understood, is an identification with the crucified Nazarene—the one who was condemned by the religious and political powers of his day. He did not die as an outsider to the system of goodness; he died within it. Jesus was executed by the very mechanisms that claimed to uphold righteousness, order, and truth. In this light, holiness cannot be reduced to moral cleanliness or doctrinal precision. It is the costly identification with the crucified one, whose death exposes the violent underpinnings of all coercive systems disguised as good.

To be holy is to stand where Christ stands—in solidarity with the excluded, the judged, the scapegoated. It is to see the cross not simply as a place of substitution, but as a site of revelation: here is where false righteousness dies, and divine grace rises. To be Nazarene, then, is to confess that sanctification will always pull us toward those crushed under the weight of systems that claim moral superiority. It is to recognize that the holiness movement is cruciform—or it is nothing.

To be Nazarene, then, is to have one's imagination shaped by Nazareth. It is to believe that the incarnation always happens in the margins. That redemption walks with dusty feet. That the Spirit blows not through boardrooms but through back alleys and battered homes.

I speak now as one whose ecclesial belonging has become complicated. I no longer find myself at home in the institutional spaces that once gave me language and liturgy. Yet I remain Nazarene in exile. I remain because I still believe holiness is good news for the poor. I remain because I believe Jesus still shows up in Nazareth.

And let me be clear: exile is not abandonment. It may feel like shame or embarrassment to leave or be forced to leave. It may feel like failure. But true exile is a form of witness. When the church forgets its poor, it is not the poor who have moved. It is the church. And those who remember must choose—to go with the institution or to stay with the poor. My conviction is that fidelity to the gospel means staying.

To be Nazarene is to say with Mary, "He has lifted up the lowly; he has filled the hungry with good things, and sent the rich away empty" (Luke 1:52–53). It is to build communities where the hungry are fed, where the addict finds recovery, where the immigrant finds welcome, where the forgotten find family. It is to hold the hand of the dying in underfunded hospitals and to sit with the incarcerated as if they were Jesus himself.

This is not merely activism. It is a sacrament. The Church of the Nazarene must reclaim its roots not for the sake of nostalgia, but for the sake of its future. If we forget Nazareth, we lose the Gospel. If we ignore the poor, we lose our holiness.

So, what is a Nazarene?

A Nazarene remembers that the word became flesh—not in Rome or Jerusalem—but in Nazareth. A Nazarene believes that sanctification is not a status but a summons to love God with heart, soul, mind, and strength, and to love neighbor with open hands. A Nazarene believes that grace flows downward, that glory is hidden in weakness, and that the church is never more holy than when it kneels.

In a time when the church is tempted to seek relevance through power, professionalism, and prestige, we must remember that the One we follow came not to be served, but to serve. He lived in Nazareth. He died outside the city. He rose in hiddenness. And he still walks among the poor.

If the Church of the Nazarene is to be what its name proclaims, it must return again and again to the margins. It must learn to hear the music of grace not in the halls of influence but in the quiet cries of those the world overlooks. And if it will not go, then let us remain—there, in Nazareth—with the poor, with the crucified, with Christ.

This, my friends, is what it means to be Nazarene.

Amen.

CHAPTER 16

Sanctified Imagination

Holiness Theology and the Trajectories of Wesleyan Ecclesiology

Henry Walter Spaulding II and Henry Walter Spaulding III

INTRODUCTION

THIS CHAPTER INVITES READERS to consider the enduring theological significance of ecclesiology within the Wesleyan tradition. We argue that serious theological reflection must attend not only to individual holiness but to the communal nature of salvation and the church's formative role in shaping Christian imagination. The apostle Paul addresses the church in Corinth as "those who are sanctified in Christ Jesus, called to be saints, together with all those who in every place call on the name of our Lord Jesus Christ, both their Lord and ours" (1 Cor 1:2 NRSV). He later adds, "For in every way you have been enriched in him, in speech and knowledge of every kind" (1:5), underscoring the richness of the church's spiritual and intellectual life. Such language gestures toward a sanctified imagination—one cultivated within and through the life of the church.

The church fosters a sanctified imagination through its worship and practices: the proclamation of the gospel, the celebration of the sacraments, the ordination of ministers, the commissioning of missionaries, the exercise of discipline, and the transmission of doctrine. As the community of the Incarnate One, the church becomes a living history—a people who articulate, preserve, and extend this imagination across time and space. Rowan Williams captures this when he writes, "The Church, therefore, is not a 'special' system of human relations, but the place where the rationale of all other relations is made plain and their deepening and securing made possible."[1] Accordingly, the church is not merely a sociological category, but a theological reality grounded in the narrative of God's self-giving love. This chapter aims to initiate a conversation about the nature, meaning, and eschatological hope of the church, particularly about Wesleyan notions of heart holiness. We propose that holiness, rightly understood, is inseparable from ecclesiology. While our reflections are necessarily limited in scope, we aim to offer a glimpse into a deeper understanding of how the church's origins and vocation shape what it means to be a saint in the twenty-first century.[2]

THE PROBLEM OF THE CHURCH AND HOLINESS THEOLOGY

The fact that Article XI, "The Church," is the last article added to the sixteen articles of faith contained in the Manual of the Church of the Nazarene complicates the association between Sanctification and ecclesiology. There are several interrelated historical and theological reasons for the underdevelopment of ecclesiology within the Church of the Nazarene and the broader American Holiness Movement. First, the roots of the movement lie in revivalism and the camp meeting tradition, which often operated in parallel with, rather than within, the established structures of the institutional church. This emphasis on personal conversion and spiritual experience sometimes came at the expense of sustained reflection on the nature and function of the church itself. Second, in its formative years, the Church of the Nazarene was often portrayed as a reforming movement—an effort to "save" or renew the church rather than to replicate existing ecclesial models. This reformist posture contributed to a practical ecclesiology but did not always produce a robust theological articulation of the church.

Third, the denomination's near-exclusive focus on the doctrine of holiness—particularly entire Sanctification—further shaped its self-understanding. William Greathouse, a leading theologian, pastor, seminary and college president, and general superintendent, once proposed that the Church of the Nazarene might be best understood not merely as a

1. Williams, *On Christian Theology*, 226.

2. Grenz, "Ecclesiology," 252–68.

denomination but as a kind of ecclesial order within the one, holy, catholic, and apostolic church. He compared it to the Franciscans or Benedictines, suggesting that its vocation was to preserve and proclaim the doctrine of entire Sanctification as a gift to the wider church. This idea finds resonance in early editions of the Nazarene Manual, which suggest an implicit ecclesiological vision shaped by a commitment to holiness as the church's defining mark and mission.

The enormous energy spent on Article X: Christian Holiness and Entire Sanctification provides some justification for believing that the church understood itself early on as a movement, but the issue lies much deeper. Mark Quanstrom writes, "The church refused to forsake the distinctive doctrine of entire Sanctification. If the church was not going to be used by God to help usher in the millennial kingdom, then the church was going to be used by God to preserve and defend the holiness doctrine."[3] The language of holiness in the Church of the Nazarene has been predicated almost exclusively in terms of personal experience if not individualistic experience

According to Article X, "sanctification is the work of God which transforms believers into the likeness of Christ." The entire article is framed as an "experience." Article X acknowledges the importance of the church nurturing holiness: "Without such purposeful endeavor, one's witness may be impaired, and the graces itself frustrated and ultimately lost. Participating in the means of grace especially the fellowship, disciplines, and sacraments of the church, believers grow in grace and in wholehearted love to God and neighbor."[4] The major themes of holiness theology are focused primarily upon an experience with minor reference to the importance of the church. There can be little doubt that heart holiness is an experience that frees believers from the *necessity* of sin. However, the challenge has always been to comprehend the sanctified imagination in and through the church. For example, J. Kenneth Grider, the late professor emeritus of theology at Nazarene Theological Seminary, develops his theology of holiness without meaningful reflection upon ecclesiology. H. Ray Dunning, professor emeritus of theology at Trevecca Nazarene University, appears equally uninterested in theologizing about holiness in relation to ecclesiology. In fact, the doctrine of the church functions much more like an addendum to theology in both

3. Quanstrom, *Century of Holiness*, 23.

4. *Manual*, 9–10.

Grider and Dunning. This lack of interest has had profoundly negative implications for understanding the sanctified imagination. We contend that this theological problem has hindered a proper understanding of both Article X and XI.

The essence of the problem presents itself as a false choice between experience (personal) and the history of sanctity (ecclesiology). Article XI affirms the church as "the covenant people of God," that the church is expressed "by obedience to Christ, holy living, and mutual accountability," and that "the Church fulfills its mission by making disciples."[5] There can be little doubt that the articulation, preservation, and transmission of the holiness message are inseparable from the life and witness of the church. Any sustained holiness movement—or even a holiness order—only makes sense within the broader ecclesial context. It is the church that canonizes Scripture, formulates doctrine, ordains ministers, administers the sacraments, and proclaims the gospel. The apostle Paul's missionary strategy reflects this ecclesial impulse: he begins in synagogues but ultimately organizes communities of faith—churches—that become the loci of Christian formation and mission. His letters are directed not to individuals in isolation but to churches whom he exhorts, teaches, and corrects. The church cannot be reduced to a voluntary association of like-minded believers. It is instead a theological reality with sacramental, historical, and communal dimensions—one that participates in the ongoing work of Sanctification. As such, the task of cultivating a sanctified imagination—a way of seeing and inhabiting the world through the lens of God's holiness—requires the church in all its fullness: its history, its liturgical and communal habits, and its embodied practices. In short, the church is not merely the container of the holiness message; it is how saints are formed. Robert Jenson writes, "A body that is a polity is a communion. Only as a shared body could a body be a plurality and so, perhaps, a polity. Or conversely: a polity that is also a personal body must be a communion."[6] The problem emerges with equal clarity—our attempts to promote holiness are made more difficult considering our failure to think ecclesiologically. Therefore, if Wesleyans continue to participate in communities that promote holiness, then their ability to think ecclesiologically must advance.

5. *Manual*, 9–10.

6. Jenson, *Systematic Theology*, 2:220.

Several theological implications emerge when holiness forms an ecclesiology. First, the church is not merely a gathering of individuals, but a community constituted by the cultivation and naming of a particular kind of character—namely, the character of Christ. The epistemological claims of the church, therefore, are grounded not in abstract reasoning or mere institutional authority but in the sanctified lives of its members. The gospel is authenticated when it takes root in persons whose lives are visibly shaped by Christ's holiness. Second, the church exposes the inadequacy of experientialism as the sole foundation for Christian holiness. While emotional responses to divine grace are not insignificant, the sanctified imagination is not fully expressed in a moment of ecstasy or revival. Rather, it emerges through the slow, communal, and embodied journey of discipleship. Holiness is not a private event but a public and shared way of life. Third, the church embodies the new society envisioned in the New Testament—a community of mutual accountability that nurtures holiness through practices of encouragement, correction, and prayer. John Wesley's emphasis on class meetings and small groups was precisely an effort to foster such accountability. The early holiness movement also reflected this ecclesial instinct, emphasizing testimony, shared prayer, and mutual admonition as essential to spiritual growth and Sanctification. Fourth, the church is the polity—a spiritual and social body—capable of imagining and enacting life "in Christ Jesus, who became for us wisdom from God, and righteousness and sanctification and redemption" (1 Cor 1:30b–31). In this way, the church not only proclaims holiness but becomes the context in which it is both discerned and made manifest, offering a counter-witness to the wisdom of the world by boasting only in the Lord.

The plea for a sanctified imagination and its material association with an ecclesiological imagination must not intend to diminish the personal nature of holiness or its experiential reality. Rather, the argument made in this chapter intends to comprehend holiness, Sanctification, and Christian perfection in a manner that admits to the spiritual power of a history of sanctity. Sanctification depends upon the imagination created in the history, habits, and practices of the church. We are the body of Christ and the Temple of the Holy Spirit together. Our lives are bound together in the practice of the faith as a community of incarnation. We gather to hear the word proclaimed so that nonbelievers may be invited to salvation and believers might be equipped to live out the gospel in a broken world. Possessive individualism is the bane not only of the church but also of a life of holiness. We are persons in a community or covenant who bear one another's burdens and encourage one another to press on toward the high calling of full salvation. Therefore, the juxtaposition of person and church is not only unhealthy but also theologically and pastorally unwarranted.

THEOLOGICAL IMAGINATION AND HOLINESS THEOLOGY

Embedded deep within the theological grammar of the Church of the Nazarene lies the presupposition summed up by William Willimon: "Nazarenes are the most radical people I know because they believe that one can be free from their sins."[7] Willimon's acknowledgment already positions the church of the Nazarene's approach to theology, ministry, and ecclesiology in a distinct register from many contemporary ecclesiological frameworks. The task before us, therefore, is not to adopt a ready-made ecclesiology but to engage in one shaped by a particular set of theological presuppositions—presuppositions that demand a robust and sanctified theological imagination.

By "imagination," we do not mean inventing a theology ex nihilo or crafting an abstract ecclesiology disconnected from history. Rather, we speak of imagination as a creative and constructive engagement with our tradition—drawing on the Church of the Nazarene's past, critically engaging present ecclesiologies across Christian traditions, and receiving the broader history of Christian thought. This kind of theological imagination is both playful and profound, grounded in the conviction that the church must discern and articulate its identity within the contested spiritual and cultural terrain shaped by the "principalities and powers" (Eph 6:12). Thus, our ecclesiological work is not merely descriptive but transformational—it aims at the conversion of the imagination.

In this context, imagination refers to the way Christians perceive and interpret the world. It is not a neutral faculty but one formed by what it consumes—liturgies, practices, stories, and theological convictions. The imagination, therefore, is central to how the church and its members come to understand themselves as living on "borrowed time," participants in God's unfolding reign. To speak of the sanctified imagination as the ecclesial pulse of the Church of the Nazarene is to recognize

7. Willimon, unpublished lecture, Conference at Trevecca Nazarene University.

that the church plays a vital role in shaping how we envision the kingdom of God and our place within it. The task of ecclesiology, then, is not only to describe the church but to nurture an imagination capable of embodying holiness in context—to envision and enact the kingdom of God here and now in concrete, communal ways. Willie Jennings, professor of theology at Yale Divinity School, writes, "Imagine forming Christians who can look out on their worlds and see beginnings where others only see the end."[8] The forming takes place in the context of holiness. What feeds the imagination is the vision of the kingdom of God, and being attuned to the works of the Holy Spirit in our context, or as Article XI states, "The mission of the church in the world is to share in the redemptive and reconciling ministry of Christ in the power of the Spirit."[9] This is the context of what it means to have imagination and to be the church.

To begin, one must acknowledge the process by which individuals in the church possess the imagination that they do versus the sanctified imagination. As Rowan Williams writes, "Christianity was always a religion of conversion, and that means that it has always proposed to human beings that what has been taken for granted about their identity, their relationships, isn't necessarily fixed and final. Conversion is choosing to be different; it is a step out of the culture you once belonged in."[10] Rowan Williams identifies imagination as a fundamental faculty of human beings—one that enables the envisioning of hope, the orientation toward the future, and the shaping of communal life, both within one's tradition and broader communities. In this sense, true conversion is never merely cognitive or moral; it is a conversion of the imagination. Such conversion entails the adoption of a new set of theological and existential presuppositions about the nature of hope, the shape of the future, and the meaning of community. The church, then, serves as the eschatological horizon where this reorientation of imagination is cultivated. It is within the liturgical, communal, and theological practices of the church that the imagination is re-scripted, reformed, and sanctified.

A sanctified imagination must be decisively distinguished from imaginations shaped by the disordered desires and narratives of a sinful world. Whereas the dominant cultural imagination may be formed by consumption, individualism, fear, or domination, the sanctified imagination is shaped by communion, self-giving love, eschatological hope,

8. Jennings, "Healthy Scriptural Imagination."

9. *Manual*, 35.

10. Williams, *Faith in the Public Square*, 66. Emphasis original.

and the redemptive story of Christ. It envisions life not according to the logic of the present age but according to the coming kingdom of God—a vision that is nurtured, enacted, and embodied in the life of the church. Its difference lies in the coming of Christ, which, as Karl Barth writes, "defines a historical occurrence and marks the point where the unknown world cuts the known world."[11] The revelation of Christ cuts into historical time; the Word became flesh and dwelt among us and disrupted the previous modes of being in the world. Thus, our imagination—both church and humanity—is fundamentally transformed by the historical event of Christ's incarnation, life, death, and resurrection. In the advent of Christ, the very ground beneath our feet is reconstituted. His life is not merely an intervention into history but a redefinition of reality itself. The revelation of Christ unveils a world in which the old order persists but only on borrowed time. Reality, as it was previously understood, now coexists with a new creation that has begun to dawn in Christ. As the apostle Paul suggests, we live in the tension between "what is passing away" and "what is coming to pass" (cf. 1 Cor 7:31; 2 Cor 3:11). This apocalyptic shift demands not only a change in moral disposition but a radical reorientation of the imagination—one that sees the world, the church, and the human person in light of the new creation already inaugurated in Christ. As theologian Garrett Green writes, "For God has chosen to reveal himself in the world in a manner accessible only to the imagination."[12] This does not suggest that revelation is a form of esoteric or specialized knowledge accessible only to a select few. Instead, it demands that the church cultivate the capacity to see beyond the limitations of its own historically embedded and systemically distorted contexts—contexts that often render the reality of revelation implausible or inaccessible. Revelation calls the church not to retreat into abstraction but to orient itself toward eschatological horizons, where the fullness of God's self-disclosure in Christ reshapes its vision, imagination, and mission.

This reorientation is not merely theoretical—it was embodied from the beginning in a concrete community. The Way was the name given to the New Testament community that first encountered this revelation and began living in this new way of being in the world. It was the church in its primordial form. This way represented a whole new reality breaking into the world and acknowledged that to see it, one must look through

11. Barth, *Epistle to the Romans*, 29.

12. Green, *Theology, Hermeneutics, and Imagination*, 206.

a set of bifocal lenses.[13] These lenses, like bifocals, allow one to see the world passing away and the coming to pass of the kingdom of God simultaneously. This type of vision is fostered as it is imparted and takes a community to train and teach the imagination. For it is in teaching, as J. Louis Martyn writes, "that [we] see the cosmos that God is bringing into existence as his new creation."[14] Thus, the ecclesial, sanctified imagination consists of seeing the difference between that which is passing away and that which is coming to pass. The confession that most closely aligns with the Wesleyan ecclesial imagination is rooted in the theology of holiness. Sanctification fosters ecclesial imagination because, as David Kelsey writes, Sanctification consists in the "full disclosure and judgment of who we are."[15] Kelsey alludes that Sanctification consists of the ways imagination comes under the judgment imparted to us by God.

This aligns with the Church of the Nazarene's confession in Article X: "We believe that sanctification is the work of God which transforms believers into the likeness of Christ." The church is the image of Christ, just as Christ is the image of God. The judgment of the identity of individual believers within the church, as well as the corporate church, consists of its Sanctification, or rather, as the article continues, the "infilling of the Holy Spirit," where the church and the individual are affirmed in their identity as Christians. Article XI affirms just this sentiment.[16] There, it is written, "God calls the Church to express its life in the unity and fellowship of the Spirit."[17] Furthermore, in the church's Sanctification, the imagination, too, becomes sanctified. As Paul writes, "Be transformed by the renewing of your mind" (Rom 12:2). The mind, being the housing place of the imagination, becomes transformed in its Sanctification to see what has been missed. Thus, the sanctified imagination disrupts the sinful order's possession of the imagination.

The church must serve as the locus where the imagination is reclaimed from the forces that hold it captive. The logic of consumer capitalism shapes one of the most pervasive forms of captivity in the modern West. Within this framework, the imagination is constrained by an economic rationality in which human freedom is equated with the unimpeded ability to purchase, accumulate, and pursue capital. The Western

13. Martyn, *Galatians*, 103–4.

14. Martyn, *Galatians*, 23.

15. Kelsey, *Imagining*, 82.

16. *Manual*, 33.

17. *Manual*, 33.

subject, thus formed, comes to understand autonomy not in moral or relational terms but as the freedom to consume without coercion. In this context, the church is called to resist such ideological formation by cultivating an alternative imagination—one grounded in communion, generosity, and the economy of grace. William Cavanaugh defines this freedom as "freedom from the interference of others, especially of the state. Freedom is what exists spontaneously in the absence of coercion . . . To be free, it suffices that there be no external interference."[18] Furthermore, this mode of freedom captivates the imagination of the church. The individual assumes the role of the sole beneficiary of grace, transforming the church into a collection of individual proprietors rather than a unified body. Furthermore, his insight into the economic imagination of the twentieth-century economic and marketing world is evident in the very structure of the articles themselves. Namely, the articles of faith on Sanctification come before the church. Therefore, indirectly and confessionally, one's salvation and Sanctification remain expected before one comes to the church.[19] If our ecclesial imagination remains in the economic worldview, then the parallels between the ecclesial and economic imagination become clear. The church must imagine beyond the parameters of the sinful submission of the Christian imagination. For example, the economy is generally not questioned but presupposed as an entity unto itself, possessing a unique personality. Thus, we do not question why the housing market is down, why joblessness increases, or why the price of gas climbs; these are seen as givens. This worldview, i.e., the worldview of the market, only sees attempts to imagine beyond its parameters as idealistic. The church must challenge these very presuppositions.

The task of the church is to be more imaginative than the culture that produces such patterns. For example, Cavanaugh draws on the example of Rosa Martinez. He writes, "'Rosa Martinez produces apparel for US markets on her sowing machine in El Salvador. You can hire her for 33 cents an hour.' So goes an advertisement paid for by the [USAID] . . . Why do companies pay such wages? Again, because they can. Transnational corporations are able to shop around the globe for the most advantageous wage environments, that is, those places where people are so desperate that they must take jobs that pay extremely low wages, in many cases wages insufficient to feed and house themselves and their dependents."[20]

18. Cavanaugh, *Being Consumed*, 3.

19. Events took place at the 1989 General Assembly.

20. Cavanaugh, *Being Consumed*, 21–22.

Cavanaugh will continue with questions such as, "Is this transaction truly free?" Yes, Martinez chooses to lower her wages to thirty cents an hour. Furthermore, the company can choose to open factories that pay living wages rather than a lower rate to Rosa, thereby increasing its profit. However, as mentioned above, although this economic decision is considered free, it possesses an underlying logic that the process of transaction cannot be isolated from such a violent cycle. Cavanaugh writes that the parties involved "feel as if they have no choice in the matter because they assume that, given the prevailing logic of free exchange, consumers will want to maximize their gain in any transaction by paying the lowest price possible for a product."[21] Therefore, by exploiting the entire world, companies can pay extremely low costs to service consumer needs. Thus, the producers of goods and services are caught in a vicious cycle of logic consumed in sinful imagination wherein a solution beyond the parameters appears impossible.

At this point, what does any of this have to do with ecclesiology? More specifically, what bearing does it have on the Church of the Nazarene and the future of its ecclesial identity and mission? In short, everything. The distorted relationship between the dominant economic order and the moral imagination of parishioners is neither incidental nor peripheral to ecclesiological reflection—it is central. Too often, ecclesiology is reduced to a pragmatic exercise in church growth, driven by strategies to attract larger congregations through ministries, programs, and sermon series designed to appeal to consumer sensibilities. In such a framework, the church comes to resemble a transnational corporation, marketing religious goods and services to individuals conditioned to maximize personal gain.

This framework represents not only a theological misstep but a profound captivity of the ecclesial imagination. When churches attempt to "out-imagine" the prevailing economic order using their tools—adopting business models, demographic analysis, and market-based language—they do not subvert the logic of consumerism; they reinforce it. In such cases, the imagination becomes colonized by external systemic forces, rendering it incapable of envisioning alternative modes of life.

However, within the Nazarene tradition lies a latent ecclesiological potential—namely, the articulation of a sanctified imagination. This is an imagination shaped not by metrics of growth or efficiency but by the

21. Cavanaugh, *Being Consumed*, 21–22.

inbreaking of the kingdom of God. It recognizes and names the world that is passing away while bearing witness to the new world breaking in from above. Such an imagination refuses to conform to this age but is transformed by the renewing of the mind (Rom 12:2), enabling the church to envision and embody holiness in the community. Thus, as Cavanaugh writes, "Humans need a community of virtue [or sanctification] in which to learn to desire rightly."[22] This means that a community, to desire rightly, must foster its imagination to see beyond the sinful structures that hold imagination captive and dictate the parameters of appropriate responses. As stated above, the Nazarene Church community values Sanctification, and Sanctification requires "Participating in the means of grace, especially the fellowship, disciplines, and sacraments of the Church, believers grow in grace and in wholehearted love to God and neighbor."[23] The church's emphasis on Sanctification expressed through the means of grace (i.e., fasting, communion, baptism, and tithing) names its sanctified imagination. These disciplines, unintelligible to prevailing economic logic in themselves, provide an alternative to the imagination of economic imagination. In other words, economic imagination asks: why would an individual choose to abstain from a meal when it can be easily provided? Why would one give away 10% of a salary when jobs remain scarce and the economic situation desperate? What difference does taking the Eucharist make?

The Means of Grace as the fostering of the sanctified imagination yields practical results in loving those run over by the sinful economic imagination. Practicing the means of grace, as encouraged by the Manual and explained by Cavanaugh, fosters the sanctified imagination as church practice. The way the church understands itself is caught up in the lives of those it pours its life into and not caught in ways of doing its mission inside of sinful economic language. The sanctified imagination lies at the heart of what Nazarene ecclesiology must accomplish for its unfolding mission to the world.

To return to an earlier theme, Sanctification, as David Kelsey writes, is the "full disclosure and judgment of who we are."[24] Furthermore, since this is the reality against which the church and Christians are judged, it also proves to be a judgment of the structures (i.e., economic, political, etc.) passing away. As Rowan Williams writes, "The ordinary Christian,

22. Cavanaugh, *Being Consumed*, 9.

23. *Manual*, 34.

24. Kelsey, *Imagining Redemption*, 82.

living in this rather precarious setting, would have a sort of double vision—the world, the prevailing culture as it was, and the Kingdom of God by which the current order was judged."[25] As a result, the sanctified imagination yields an ecclesiology centered on being in history, constantly renewed and transformed by the Spirit's work. The church leads the community to foster the sanctified imagination, namely an enfleshed life of holiness. Once this community is set apart, the sanctified imagination judges reality based on this revelation of God and is the ecclesiological imagination of the Church of the Nazarene.

So what? Why all this talk of imagination and ecclesiology? Is this a rupture with the past? Where has this imagination been seen in our holiness tradition? Professor of Church History at Trevecca Nazarene University, Steve Hoskins, recounts such an incident in our tradition: "It was an unseasonably warm fall season when the fourth annual Pentecostal Mission Convention convened in the movement's headquarters located at the corner of Summer and Jo Johnson Avenues on October 21 1902."[26] Furthermore, this convention featured "nearly 400 delegate members of the Mission, whose addresses stretched from Kentucky to Texas to Florida, covering the entirety of the Southeastern U.S."[27] The delegates represented a significant presence of holiness across the Southeast and would comprise a substantial portion of what would become the Church of the Nazarene in the South. The delegation took place in the headquarters of the Pentecostal Mission (PM), which would become Nashville First Church of the Nazarene and was under the direction of J. O. McClurkan, who would go on to found Trevecca College (now Nazarene University). During the lifetime of the individuals present at the conference, those directly associated with the Pentecostal Mission became architects and leaders in the Church of the Nazarene.

The conference provides a case study due to the actions taken at this conference and its location against the background of its cultural climate. This year (1902) lands in the middle of Jim Crow's rise to influence in Nashville, Tennessee, and the height of the lynching period in the South (1882–1915). It is estimated that some 204 African Americans were lynched in Tennessee during this period. In addition, since this

25. Williams, *Faith in the Public Square*, 66.

26. Hoskins, "Black and White in Jim Crow Nashvegas."

27. Hoskins, "Black and White in Jim Crow Nashvegas."

conference was made up of mostly southeasterners, it was also estimated that an additional 2,532 African Americans were lynched in the areas represented by the delegates.[28] The silence of the church on this matter betrays an imagination largely uninformed by holiness.

However, the stigmas that gripped the social imagination of the South were not present in the Pentecostal Mission and this 1902 conference. As Hoskins notes,

> The building also stood in the middle of a district that was dubbed "Hell's Half Acre," at the foot of the Tennessee State Capitol and was home to several brothels, gambling dens, and the city's first government-funded housing projects for African Americans under the managerial efforts of J. C. Napier, Nashville's first African American councilman, the president of the one-cent savings Bank catering to "colored" clientele.[29]

Its location is not uncommon for what the Nazarene churches would be associated with (e.g., Breese's Church of the Nazarene on Skid Row, Nashville First's current location, etc.). However, what was most shocking was not the location but the speaker who took the pulpit at the convention on October 23, 1902, a noted black evangelist, Charles Price Jones. He preached a sermon about his own Sanctification and life as an African American boy growing up in the South.[30] He preached so well that McClurkan would invite him to speak at the Pentecostal Mission service the next day. Hoskins continues, "While it is clear to the historical record that such inter-racial mixing and the combining of evangelistic efforts was certainly a hallmark of the Holiness Movement as it spread across America during the nineteenth century, the presence of Jones as a black man at a white religious convention in Nashville was something else."[31] As noted earlier, this congregation in Nashville, as well as congregations across the South, had to answer the questions of Jim Crow regulations, such as the one promulgated by Nashville officials in 1905 regulating African Americans to the rear of the bus, which shortly after suffered its first boycott.

28. UMKC School of Law, "Lynchings."
29. Hoskins, "Black and White in Jim Crow Nashvegas."
30. Hoskins, "Black and White in Jim Crow Nashvegas."
31. Hoskins, "Black and White in Jim Crow Nashvegas."

Jones marked a decisive moment in sanctified imagination. Hoskins writes, "While it was one thing to print encouragement, it was another thing altogether to mix black and white in the place of public worship in Jim Crow Nashvegas, especially with a black man preaching the holiness gospel to white people eager to hear it."[32] However, McClurkan would not stop there. Though the Pentecostal Mission faced criticism for mixing races in a place of worship, McClurkan would invite Edward F. Walker, who would become the fourth General Superintendent of the Church of the Nazarene, to the convention a year later. In his Thursday evening sermon, Walker said, "When the Holy Spirit comes as a comforter to his people, He comes as Reprover to the World . . . A blind man cannot see; a deaf man cannot hear. A man who is born blind cannot say anything about colors," or we might add, can imagine either.[33] Walker, McClurkan, Jones, and the other fledgling members of what would become the Nazarene Church knew what has been argued in this chapter thus far: the sanctified imagination gives one perspective on that which is passing away, namely the Jim Crow South and racism, and see that which is coming to pass, namely the kingdom of God where social bonds do not dictate interpersonal relations. This action aligns with the statement in Article XI of the current Manual.

Furthermore, McClurkan would follow Edward's sermon with an address. McClurkan states, referencing the Nashville regulations forcing African Americans to the rear of the bus,

> What we want to do in the South is to get enough religion to keep off other people's backs—to get enough religion to agree to disagree . . . When we begin to live as we preach, when we get so dead, we will always look at the other fellow's interests; when someone has to stand up in a crowded car, we will be found trying to do the standing, in fact when we begin to deliver the goods—leave people in every place we preach who will live all they profess—we are going to get up a big trade in this line.[34]

For McClurkan, as an influential figure in Nazarene holiness theology, it was a matter of the entire church being sanctified, working for justice, and bearing witness to the kingdom of God. Furthermore, this radical action of the Pentecostal Mission represents the church at its best. It is not merely

32. Hoskins, "Black and White in Jim Crow Nashvegas."

33. Hoskins, "Black and White in Jim Crow Nashvegas."

34. Hoskins, "Black and White in Jim Crow Nashvegas."

implied that McClurkan thinks the church in his time should stand up to racial injustice, but explicit in his referencing the bus segregation. Rowan Williams could be summing up the spirit of McClurkan when he writes, "The cultural and political climate in which the Christian lived might be the reality for the majority, completely taken for granted, even regarded as sacred—but the Christian would know that it was still under judgment and that what seemed natural and beyond question in this environment was still open to question by the standards of God."[35] Furthermore, the spirit of McClurkan and the holiness theology ask the tough questions of the guiding narratives it encounters. Sanctified imagination, informed by holiness theology, encourages discipleship, compassion, justice, and being set apart, all of which have become integral to our doctrinal stance as the church. The imagination of the Jim Crow–era South captivated Nashville, shaping it as a cultural norm. However, for those in the PM, McClurkan, Edwards, and those who would comprise the Church of the Nazarene, the Sanctification of believers led to an ecclesial imagination that transcended racial lines. Furthermore, the Nazarene Church's identity lies in its ability to transcend the reality of sin that passes away and imagine a new reality in which the church is born.

In conclusion, the ecclesiology of the church lies in this continual life in the Spirit, leading to Sanctification and the fostering of its imagination. Imagination possesses the ability to look past the trappings of sinful economic imagination and any one epoch. McClurkan demonstrates what Sanctification means for ecclesiology, not confined to any epoch. This is a practice of faith, as that which is passing away is consistently being revealed considering that which is to come, and it avoids sinful economic models of the church. The Wesleyan-Holiness Church must continue in the Spirit, as exemplified by founders like McClurkan, and identify with those individuals that the sinful economic imagination has overlooked. This is the heart of the word Nazarene, and this must again become its future. Fostering the imagination is a work of the Spirit embedded in the very life of holiness ecclesiology. Thus, the practice of the church looks different in each location and system it encounters as it attempts to preach and be about the diverse colors and sights it sees. The life of the sanctified imagination means to live as we preach. The Church of the Nazarene possesses a tremendous opportunity to be a church that lives, sees, and talks about the world in a new way. The church, through its preaching

35. Williams, *Faith in the Public Square*, 66–67.

of holiness theology, possesses the imagination to see through sin's false ways of seeing the world. Hopefully, this ecclesiology brings the world to a new picture of itself considering God's revelation. Alternatively, as Garrett Green writes, "The faithful imagination learns to hear the melody of revelation in the polyphony of Scripture. Proclamation can be thought of as singing the scriptural melody so that others may also learn to hear and enjoy it and to join in singing."[36] It turns out that we are called unto holiness. It is not just a song but also a concise statement of self-identity.

36. Green, *Imagining God*, 151.

Conclusion

The Wounds of Holiness and the Rhythm of Grace

Henry Walter Spaulding II and Henry Walter Spaulding III

At the center of the Christian story—and at the very heart of Wesleyan theology—stands a crucified Savior. Not a conquering warrior, not a distant moralist, but a wounded God whose holiness is marked not by distance from human pain but by His intimate solidarity with it. The holiness of Jesus is not a purity preserved from suffering, but one that is tested, pierced, and poured out. His is a holiness that embraces the world's brokenness, bears it in love, and transfigures it not by domination, but by divine mercy.

This vision of holiness—grace-drenched, cross-shaped, and incarnational—has been obscured in much of the Wesleyan-Holiness movement, especially where it has drifted toward fundamentalism. In the Church of the Nazarene, this drift is painfully visible in the move to include the *Covenant of Christian Conduct* among the *Articles of Faith*—a decision rooted not in the spirit of historic holiness, but in a fundamentalist fear of change. The justification that "our conduct has always been the same" ignores the very real and documented shifts in Christian ethical norms within the denomination itself over time. What was once shaped by a practical, pastoral holiness has hardened into an ideology of control and conformity.

Rather than addressing the profound complexity of Christian discipleship in today's world, these changes have often functioned as tools of exclusion and suppression. Trials, excommunications, and character assassinations now arise not primarily from heretical Christologies or denials of grace, but from political or ethical disagreement. Ironically, in a tradition birthed by a theology of sanctifying grace, ideological purity has become the new metric of faithfulness. In such a climate, mere disagreement on matters of justice, ecclesial practice, or even pastoral care results in being labeled "progressive," a term increasingly used not descriptively but pejoratively, as a mark of suspicion and threat.

This, more than debates about human sexuality, poses the greatest threat to the future of Wesleyan-Holiness theology: not that we might disagree, but that we have lost the ability to disagree without declaring war. What is missing is not moral clarity, but moral imagination—a practical holiness capacious enough to hold space for woundedness, complexity, and difference. A holiness that sees the other not first as a threat to order but as a bearer of God's image and a recipient of God's grace.

The way forward is not more boundary policing, nor a return to a mythologized past. What is needed is a new rhythm of grace—one that echoes the self-emptying love of the crucified Christ. It is a rhythm that listens before it judges, welcomes before it categorizes, and restores before it excludes. This rhythm has always been the hidden heart of Wesleyan theology, even when forgotten by its institutions. And it must be our heartbeat now.

To be holy, in the way of Christ, is to bleed with the world, not to stand above it. It is to see wounds not as disqualifying, but as sacred space where resurrection begins. In a time when the Church of the Nazarene—and the broader Holiness tradition—is tempted to trade grace for uniformity, and holiness for control, we must return to the One whose holiness was revealed not in a throne room, but on a cross.

Holiness that cannot suffer with, walk beside, and weep over is no holiness at all. The holiness of Jesus remains our only path—not to ideological victory, but to resurrection. And if Wesleyan theology is to live, it must again be cruciform.

Only then can it be holy.

Only then can it be grace.

Bibliography

Abraham, William J. "The End of Wesleyan Theology." *Wesleyan Theological Journal* 38 (2003) 7–25.

Anderson, E. Byron. "Trinitarian Grammar of the Liturgy and the Liturgical Practice of the Self." *Wesleyan Theological Journal* 34 (1999) 54–74.

Anselm of Canterbury. *Cur Deus Homo*. Translated by Sidney Norton Deane. Chicago: Open Court, 1903.

Alter, Robert, translator. *The Book of Psalms: A Translation with Commentary*. New York: Norton, 2007.

The Hebrew Bible: A Translation with Commentary. Volume 3. New York: Norton, 2019.

Aquinas, Thomas. *The Summa Theologica*. Translated by the Fathers of the English Dominican Province. The Great Books 19. Chicago: Encyclopedia Britannica, Inc., 1952.

Arendt, Hannah. *The Promise of Politics*. Edited by Jerome Kohn. New York: Schocken, 2005.

Aristotle. *Nicomachean Ethics*. Translated by Martin Ostwald. New York: Bobbs-Merrill, 1962.

Athanasius of Alexandria. *On the Incarnation*. Translated and edited by John Behr. Popular Patristics Series. Yonkers, NY: St. Vladimir's Seminary Press, 2011.

Augustine. *The Confessions of St. Augustine*. Translated by John K. Ryan. New York: Doubleday, 1960.

———. *The Trinity*. Translated by Edmund Hill. Brooklyn: New City, 1997.

Baker-Fletcher, Karen. *Dancing with God: The Trinity from a Womanist Perspective*. St. Louis: Chalice, 2006.

Baker-Fletcher, Karen, and Garth Kasimu Baker-Fletcher. *My Sister, My Brother: Womanist and Xodus God-Talk*. Eugene, OR: Wipf & Stock, 2002.

Balthasar, Hans Urs von. *Credo: Meditations on the Apostles' Creed*. Translated by David Kipp. San Francisco: Ignatius, 1990.

Barth, Karl. *Church Dogmatics, Volume 2: The Doctrine of God*. In *Theological Aesthetics: A Reader*, edited by Gesa Elsbeth Thiessen, 318. Grand Rapids: Eerdmans, 2004.

———. *Church Dogmatics IV/1: The Doctrine of Reconciliation*. Translated by G. W. Bromiley. Edinburgh: T. & T. Clark, 1956.

———. *Church Dogmatics I/1: The Doctrine of the Word of God*. Translated by G. T. Thomson. Edinburgh: T. & T. Clark, 1936.

———. *The Epistle to the Romans*. 6th ed. New York: Oxford University Press, 1968.

Bassett, Paul. "The Fundamentalist Leavening of the Holiness Movement, 1914–1940." *Wesleyan Theological Journal* 13 (1978) 65–92.

———. "The Interplay of Christology and Ecclesiology in the Theology of the Holiness Movement." *Wesleyan Theological Journal* 16 (1981) 79–92.

Bassett, Paul, and William Greathouse. *The Historical Development. Volume 2: Exploring Christian Holiness.* Kansas City, MO: Beacon Hill Press of Kansas City, 1985.

Bauerschmidt, Frederick Christian. "The Word Made Speculative? John Milbank's Christological Poetics." *Modern Theology* 15 (1999) 417–32.

Bell, Daniel M., Jr. *Liberation Theology After the End of History: The Refusal to Cease Suffering.* New York: Routledge, 2001.

———. "The Politics of Fear and the Gospel of Life." In *Belief and Metaphysics*, edited by Peter M. Candler Jr. and Conor Cunningham, 429–33. London: SCM, 2007.

Blondel, Maurice. *Action: Essay on a Critique of Life and a Science of Practice.* Translated by Oliva Blanchette. Repr. Notre Dame: University of Notre Dame Press, 1984.

Bonhoeffer, Dietrich. *Creation and Fall: A Theological Exposition of Genesis 1–3.* Translated by Douglas Stephen Bax. Minneapolis: Fortress, 2004.

Bourdieu, Pierre. *Pascalian Meditations.* Stanford: Stanford University Press, 1997.

Bowman, Shearer Davis. *Masters and Lords: Mid-Nineteenth-Century U.S. Planters and Prussian Junkers.* Oxford: Oxford University Press, 1993.

Bréhier, Émile. *The Philosophy of Plotinus.* Translated by Joseph Thomas. Chicago: University of Chicago Press, 1958.

Brockhaus, Richard. *Pulling Up the Ladder: The Metaphysical Roots of Wittgenstein's Tractatus Logico-Philosophicus.* La Salle, IL: Open Court, 1991.

Brock, Rita Nakashima, and Rebecca Ann Parker. *Saving Paradise: How Christianity Traded Love of This World for Crucifixion and Empire.* Boston: Beacon, 2008.

Browning, Robert L., and Roy A. Reed. *The Sacraments in Religious Education and Liturgy.* Birmingham, AL: Religious Education Press, 1985.

Bulgakov, Sergius. *On Dogma and Dogmatic Theology.* Translated by Peter Bouteneff. Paris: YMCA, 1937

Bultmann, Rudolf. "The Christian Hope and the Problem of Demythologizing." In *Essays Philosophical and Theological*, edited by James M. Robinson, translated by Schubert M. Ogden, 95–108. New York: Macmillan, 1955.

———. "Ist die Apokalyptik die Mutter der christlichen Theologie?" In *Gesammelte Aufsätze*, 1:1–20. Tübingen: Mohr Siebeck, 1954.

———. "New Testament and Mythology." In *Kerygma and Myth: A Theological Debate*, edited by Hans Werner Bartsch, translated by Reginald H. Fuller, 1–44. New York: Harper & Row, 1961.

———. *Theology of the New Testament.* Translated by Kendrick Grobel. 2 vols. New York: Charles Scribner's Sons, 1951–1955.

Bundy, David. "Christian Virtue: John Wesley and the Alexandrian Tradition." *Wesleyan Theological Journal* 26 (1991) 139–63.

Callen, Barry L. *God As Loving Grace.* Nappanee, IN: Evangel, 1996.

Cannon, Katie Geneva, et al., eds. *Womanist Theological Ethics: A Reader.* Louisville, KY: Westminster John Knox, 2011.

Carter, Charles. "God's Ethical Ideal for Humanity." In *A Contemporary Wesleyan Theology: Biblical, Systematic, and Practical*, edited by Charles Carter et al., 2:951–1006. Grand Rapids: Zondervan, 1983.

Carver, Frank. "Biblical Foundations for the 'Secondness' of Entire Sanctification." *Wesleyan Theological Journal* 22 (1987) 7–23.

Cavanaugh, William. *Being Consumed: Economics and Christian Desire*. Grand Rapids: Eerdmans, 2008.

———. "The City: Beyond Secular Parodies." In *Radical Orthodoxy: A New Theology*, edited by John Milbank et al., 182–200. New York: Routledge, 1999.

———. *Theopolitical Imagination: Discovering the Liturgy as a Political Act in an Age of Global Consumerism*. New York: T. & T. Clark, 2002.

Childs, Robert. *Theological Transition in American Methodism: 1790–1935*. Nashville: Abingdon, 1965.

Cobb, John B., Jr. *Grace and Responsibility: A Wesleyan Theology for Today*. Nashville: Abingdon, 1995.

Cone, James H. *The Cross and the Lynching Tree*. Maryknoll, NY: Orbis, 2011.

Congdon, David W. *The God Who Saves: A Dogmatic Sketch*. Eugene, OR: Cascade, 2016.

Crawford, Donald. "Kant." In *The Routledge Companion to Aesthetics*, edited by Berys Gaut and Dominic McIver Lopes, 63–75. New York: Routledge, 2002.

Cunningham, David. *These Three Are One: The Practice of Trinitarian Theology*. Malden, MA: Blackwell, 1998.

Davis, Angela. "Preface." In *Methodology of the Oppressed*, by Chela Sandoval, xii–xiii. Minneapolis: University of Minnesota Press, 2000.

Derrida, Jacques. "To Forgive: The Unforgivable and the Imprescriptible." In *Questioning God*, edited by John D. Caputo et al., 27–48. Bloomington: Indiana University Press, 2001.

Descartes, Rene. "Meditations on First Philosophy." In *From Plato to Derrida*, edited by Forrest E. Baird and Walter Kaufmann, 377–416. Upper Saddle, NJ : Prentice Hall, 2008.

Deschner, John. *Wesley's Christology: An Interpretation*. Grand Rapids: Zondervan, 1985.

Dunning, H. Ray. *Grace, Faith, and Holiness: A Wesleyan Systematic Theology*. Kansas City, MO: Beacon Hill, 1988.

———. *Reflecting the Divine Image: Christian Ethics in Wesleyan Perspective*. Downers Grove, IL: InterVarsity 1998.

Dykstra, Craig, and Dorothy C. Bass. "A Theological Understanding of Christian Practices." In *Practicing Theology: Beliefs and Practices in Christian Life*, edited by Miroslav Volf and Dorothy C. Bass, 13–32. Grand Rapids: Eerdmans, 2002.

Finch, H. L. *Wittgenstein*. Rockport, MA: Element, 1995.

Flew, Antony, and Alasdair MacIntyre, eds. *New Essays in Philosophical Theology*. New York: Macmillan, 1954.

Foucault, Michel. *Discipline and Punish: The Birth of the Prison*. Translated by Alan Sheridan. New York: Vintage, 1991.

Fukuyama, Francis. *The End of History and the Last Man*. 2nd ed. New York: Free, 2006.

Garver, Newton. "Philosophy as Grammar." In *The Cambridge Companion to Wittgenstein*, edited by Hans Sluga and David Stern, 139–70. Cambridge: Cambridge University Press, 1996.

Gaventa, Beverly Roberts. *Our Mother Saint Paul*. Louisville, KY: Westminster John Knox, 2007.

Glancy, Jennifer A. *Slavery in Early Christianity*. Minneapolis: Fortress, 2006.

Glock, Hans-Johann. *A Wittgenstein Dictionary*. Cambridge: Blackwell, 1996.

Green, Garrett. *Imagining God: Theology and the Religious Imagination*. Grand Rapids: Eerdmans, 1998.

———. *Theology, Hermeneutics, and Imagination: The Crisis of Interpretation at the End of Modernity*. New York: Cambridge University Press, 2000.

Greathouse, William M. *Wholeness in Christ: Toward a Biblical Theology of Holiness*. Kansas City, MO: Beacon Hill, 1998.

Grenz, Stanley. "Ecclesiology." In *The Cambridge Companion to Postmodern Theology*, edited by Kevin Vanhoozer, 252–71. New York: Cambridge University Press, 2003.

Grider, J. Kenneth. *A Wesleyan-Holiness Theology*. Kansas City, MO: Beacon Hill, 1994.

Hanby, Michael. "Desire: Augustine Beyond Western Subjectivity." In *Radical Orthodoxy: A New Theology*, edited by John Milbank et al., 102–17. New York: Routledge, 1999.

Hankey, Wayne. "Theoria Versus Poesis: Neoplatonism and Trinitarian Difference in Aquinas, John Milbank, Jean-Luc Marion, and John Zizioulas." *Modern Theology* 15 (1999) 387–415.

Hanson, Paul D. *The People Called: The Growth of Community in the Bible*. San Francisco: Harper and Row, 1986.

Hardt, Michael, and Antonio Negri. *Empire*. Cambridge, MA: Harvard University Press, 2000.

Hart, David Bentley. *The Beauty of the Infinite: The Aesthetics of Christian Truth*. Grand Rapids: Eerdmans, 2003.

———. *The New Testament: A Translation*. New Haven, CT: Yale University Press, 2017.

Harvey, Barry. *Another City: An Ecclesiological Primer for a Post-Christian World*. Harrisburg, PA: Trinity Press International, 1999.

Hastings, Adrian. *The Construction of Nationhood: Ethnicity, Religion and Nationalism*. Cambridge: Cambridge University Press, 1997.

Hauerwas, Stanley. *After Christendom? How the Church Is to Behave if Freedom, Justice, and a Christian Nation Are Bad Ideas*. Nashville: Abingdon, 1991.

———. *Character and the Christian Life: A Study in Theological Ethics*. Notre Dame: University of Notre Dame Press, 1975.

———. *Christian Existence Today: Essays on Church, World, and Living in Between*. Durham, NC: Labyrinth, 1988.

———. *A Community of Character: Toward a Constructive Christian Social Ethic*. Notre Dame, IN: University of Notre Dame Press, 1981.

———. *Dispatches from the Front: Theological Engagements with the Secular*. Durham, NC: Duke University Press, 1994.

———. *Sanctify Them in the Truth: Holiness Exemplified*. Nashville: Abingdon, 1998.

Hauerwas, Stanley, and David Burrell. "From System to Story: An Alternative Pattern for Rationality in Ethics." In *Why Narrative? Readings in Narrative Theology*, edited by Stanley Hauerwas and L. Gregory Jones, 157–75. Eugene, OR: Wipf & Stock, 1997.

Hays, Richard B. *The Moral Vision of the New Testament: A Contemporary Introduction to New Testament Ethics*. San Francisco: HarperSanFrancisco, 1996.

Heidegger, Martin. "Kant's Doctrine of the Beautiful: Its Misinterpretation by Schopenhauer and Nietzsche." In *Nietzsche: A Critical Reader*, edited by Peter R. Sedgwick, 105–6. Malden: Blackwell, 1995.

Hegel, G. W. F. *Aesthetics: Lectures on Fine Art*. Translated by A. V. Miller. Oxford: Oxford University Press, 1975.

———. *Introductory Lectures on Aesthetics.* Translated by Michael Inwood. New York: Penguin Group, 1993.

Herman, Edward, and Noam Chomsky. *Manufacturing Consent: The Political Economy of the Mass Media.* New York: Pantheon, 2002.

Hobbes, Thomas. *Leviathan.* Edited by J. C. A. Gaskin. New York: Oxford University Press, 1996.

Holmes, Arthur F. *The Idea of a Christian College.* Rev. ed. Grand Rapids: Eerdmans, 1987.

Hoskins, Steve. "Black and White in Jim Crow Nashvegas: J. O. McClurkan, Charles Price Jones, and the Pentecostal Mission Convention of 1902." Unpublished paper presented at the Wesleyan Theological Society, March 2011.

Hull, John. "From Experiential Educator to Nationalist Theologian: The Hymns of Isaac Watts." *Panorama: International Journal of Comparative Religious Education and Values* 14 (2002) 99.

———. "Isaac Watts and the Origins of British Imperial Theology." *International Congregational Journal* 4 (2005) 65.

Hymnbook of the Methodist Church. "Preface." Nashville: Methodist Publishing, 1933.

Inwood, Michael. "Hegel." In *The Routledge Companion to Aesthetics*, edited by Berys Gaut and Dominic McIver Lopes, 76. New York: Routledge, 2002.

Irenaeus. *Against the Heresies.* In *The Scandal of the Incarnation: Irenaeus Against the Heresies*, edited by Hans Urs von Balthasar, 58. San Francisco: Ignatius, 1990.

Jacobs, Harriet. *Incidents in the Life of a Slave Girl.* New York: Penguin, 2000.

Jennings, Willie James. *The Christian Imagination: Theology and the Origins of Race.* New Haven, CT: Yale University Press, 2010.

———. "A Healthy Scriptural Imagination: Learning to Read in the World." *Divinity Magazine*, Duke Divinity School. Spring 2013. http://divinity.duke.edu/community-student-life/divinity-magazine/spring-2013/healthy-scriptural-imagination.

Jenson, Robert. "The Doctrine of Justification and the Practice of Counseling." In *Essays in Theology of Culture*, 110. Grand Rapids: Eerdmans, 1995.

———. "Eschatological Politics and Political Eschatology." In *Essays in Theology of Culture*, 13–25. Grand Rapids: Eerdmans Press, 1995.

———. *Systematic Theology: Volume 2, The Works of God.* New York and Oxford: Oxford University Press, 1999.

Jones, L. Gregory. *Embodying Forgiveness: A Theological Analysis.* Grand Rapids: Eerdmans, 1995.

Jones, Serene. "Graced Practices: Excellence and Freedom in the Christ Life." In *Practicing Theology: Beliefs and Practices in Christian Life*, edited by Miroslav Volf and Dorothy C. Bass, 42–63. Grand Rapids: Eerdmans, 2002.

Kant, Immanuel. *Critique of Judgement.* Translated by J. H. Bernard. New York: Hafner, 1951.

———. *Critique of Judgment.* Translated by James Creed Meredith and edited by Nicholas Walker. New York: Oxford University Press, 2007.

———. *Fundamental Principles of the Metaphysics of Morals.* Translated by T. K. Abbot. Amherst, NY: Prometheus, 1988.

Käsemann, Ernst. "The Beginnings of Christian Theology." In *New Testament Questions of Today*, translated by W. J. Montague, 82–107. Philadelphia: Fortress, 1969.

———. "On the Subject of Primitive Christian Apocalyptic." In *New Testament Questions of Today*, translated by W. J. Montague, 108–37. Philadelphia: Fortress, 1969.

———. "'The Righteousness of God' in Paul." In *New Testament Questions of Today*, translated by W. J. Montague, 168–82. Philadelphia: Fortress, 1969.

Kelsey, David. *Imagining Redemption*. Louisville, KY: Westminster John Knox, 2000.

Kenny, Anthony. *The Legacy of Wittgenstein*. Oxford: Basil Blackwell, 1984.

King, Thomas, and Alexander Varughese. "Report of the Scripture Study Committee to the Twenty-Eighth General Assembly Church of the Nazarene." *Didache: Faithful Teaching* 13 (2013) 1–13.

Klaiber, Walter, and Manfred Marquardt. *Living Grace: An Outline of United Methodist Theology*. Translated by J. Steven O'Malley and Ulrike R. M. Guthrie. Nashville: Abingdon, 2001.

LA First Church of the Nazarene. "About Us." https://la1stnaz.org/about-us/.

Langford, Thomas. *Practical Divinity: Theology in the Wesleyan Tradition*. Nashville: Abingdon, 1983.

Long, D. Stephen. *The Goodness of God: Theology, The Church, and Social Order*. Grand Rapids: Baker, 2001.

———. *John Wesley's Moral Theology: The Quest for God and Goodness*. Nashville: Abingdon, 2005.

———. *Saving Karl Barth: Hans Urs von Balthasar's Preoccupation*. Minneapolis: Fortress, 2014.

Loughlin, Gerard. "The Basis and Authority of Doctrine." In *The Cambridge Companion to Christian Doctrine*, edited by Colin Gunton, 41–64. Cambridge: Cambridge University Press, 1997.

Lyons, George. "Modeling the Holiness Ethos: A Study Based on First Thessalonians." *Wesleyan Theological Journal* 30 (1995) 187–211.

Machiavelli, Niccolò. *The Prince*. Translated by Peter Bondanella. New York: Oxford University Press, 1998.

MacIntyre, Alasdair. *After Virtue: A Study in Moral Theory*. 2nd ed. Notre Dame: University of Notre Dame Press, 1981, 1984.

———. *God, Philosophy, Universities: A Selective History of the Catholic Philosophical Tradition*. Lanham, MD: Rowman & Littlefield, 2009.

Maddox, Randy L. "A Change of Affections: The Development, Dynamics, and Dethronement of John Wesley's 'Heart Religion.'" In *"Heart Religion" in the Methodist Tradition and Related Movements*, edited by Richard Steele, 3–31. Metuchen: Scarecrow, 2001.

———. "Reconnecting the Means to the End: A Wesleyan Prescription for the Holiness Movement." *Wesleyan Theological Journal* 33 (1998) 29–66.

———. *Responsible Grace: John Wesley's Practical Theology*. Nashville: Kingswood Books, 1994.

———. "Responsible Grace: The Systematic Perspective of Wesleyan Theology." *Asbury Theological Journal* 38 (1983) 7–22.

———. "Social Grace: The Eclipse of the Church as a Means of Grace in American Methodism." In *Methodism in Its Cultural Milieu*, edited by Tim Macquiban, 131–60. Cambridge: Applied Theology, 1994.

———. "Visit the Poor: Wesley, the Poor, and the Sanctification of Believers." *Theological Symposium Papers: Hope for a Hurting World. Fourth Quadrennial Nazarene Compassionate Ministry Conference*, October 29–November 1, 1998.

Manual, Church of the Nazarene. Kansas City: Nazarene Publishing, 1919.

Marquardt, Manfred. *John Wesley's Social Ethics: Praxis and Principles.* Translated by John E. Steely and W. Stephen Gunter. Nashville: Abingdon, 1992.

Martyn, J. Louis. *Galatians.* The Anchor Bible Commentary 33A. New York: Doubleday, 1997.

Mays, James L. *The Lord Reigns: A Theological Handbook to the Psalms.* Louisville, KY: Westminster John Knox, 1994.

McClendon, James William, Jr. *Biography as Theology: How Life Stories Can Remake Today's Theology.* Nashville and New York: Abingdon, 1974.

———. *Doctrine.* Vol. 2 of *Systematic Theology.* Nashville: Abingdon, 1994.

McGinn, Marie. *Wittgenstein and the Philosophical Investigations.* London and New York: Routledge, 1997.

Metz, Donald S. *Studies in Biblical Holiness.* Kansas City: Beacon Hill, 1971.

Milbank, John. "Can a Gift Be Given?: Prolegomena to a Future Trinitarian Metaphysic." *Modern Theology* 11 (1995) 119–61.

———. "Intensities." *Modern Theology* 15 (1999) 481–500.

———. "Postmodern Critical Augustinianism: A Short Summa in Forty-Two Responses to Unasked Questions." *Modern Theology* 7 (1991) 371–85.

———. *Theology and Social Theory: Beyond Secular Reason.* 2nd ed. Malden, MA: Blackwell, 2006.

———. *The Word Made Strange: Theology, Culture, Language.* Cambridge: Blackwell, 1997.

Milbank, John, and Catherine Pickstock. *Truth in Aquinas.* London: Routledge, 2001.

Milbank, John, et al. "Suspending the Material: The Turn of Radical Orthodoxy." In *Radical Orthodoxy: A New Theology,* edited by John Milbank et al., 1–20. London and New York: Routledge, 1999.

Moltmann, Jürgen. "Political Theology." In *The Experiment Hope,* edited by M. Douglas Meeks, 101. Eugene, OR: Wipf & Stock, 2003.

Nazarene Compassionate Ministries. "Compassion Is in Our DNA." https://ncm.org/blog/inourdna.

Neuhaus, Richard John. "Counting by Race." *First Things,* February 1996. Accessed December 24, 2025. https://firstthings.com/counting-by-race/.

Nietzsche, Friedrich. *Genealogy of Morals.* Translated by Francis Golffing. Garden City, NY: Anchor, 1956.

———. "Thus Spake Zarathustra." In *The Portable Nietzsche,* translated by Walter Kaufmann, 103–439. New York: Penguin, 1954.

———. *The Will to Power.* Translated by Walter Kaufmann and R. J. Hollingdale. New York: Random, 1967.

Outler, Albert. *Evangelism and Theology in the Wesleyan Spirit.* Nashville: Abingdon, 1996.

Outler, Albert C., and Richard P. Heitzenrater. *John Wesley's Sermons: An Anthology.* Nashville: Abingdon, 1991.

Passmore, John. *A Hundred Years of Philosophy.* Middlesex, England: Penguin, 1957.

Patterson, Orlando. *Slavery and Social Death: A Comparative Study.* Boston: Harvard University Press, 1982.

Pickstock, Catherine. *After Writing: On the Liturgical Consummation of Philosophy.* Maiden, MA: Blackwell, 1998.

Plato. *The Republic*. In *The Collected Dialogues of Plato*, edited by Edith Hamilton and Huntington Cairns, translated by Paul Shorey, 575–844. Princeton: Princeton University Press, 1961.

Plotinus. *The Enneads*. Translated by Stephen MacKenna and edited by John Dillon. New York: Penguin, 1991.

———. *The Enneads*. Translated by A. H. Armstrong. 7 vols. Loeb Classical Library. Cambridge, MA: Harvard University Press, 1966–1988.

Powell, Sam. "The Doctrine of the Trinity in 19th Century American Wesleyanism 1850–1900." *Wesleyan Theological Journal* 18 (1983) 33–48.

Quanstrom, Mark. *A Century of Holiness: The Doctrine of Entire Sanctification in the Church of the Nazarene, 1905–2004*. Kansas City: Beacon Hill, 2004.

Rae, Murray. "Learning the Truth in a Christian University." In *Knowing and Doing: The Academic Study of Religion and Theology*, edited by John Stackhouse, 99–114. Oxford: Oxford University Press, 2000.

Rees, Geoffrey. *The Romance of Innocent Sexuality*. Eugene, OR: Cascade, 2011.

Ricketts, Thomas. "Pictures, Logic, and the Limits of Sense in Wittgenstein's *Tractatus*." In *The Cambridge Companion to Wittgenstein*, edited by Hans Sluga and David Stern, 59–99. Cambridge: Cambridge University Press, 1996.

Rivera-Pagán, Luis N. "Karl Barth and the Origins of Liberation Theology." In *Karl Barth and Liberation Theology*, edited by Kaitlyn Dugan and Paul Dafydd Jones, 15–30. London: T. & T. Clark, 2022.

Robinson, Denis. "Sedes Sapientiae: Newman, Truth, and the Christian University." *Theological Education* 40 (2005) 89–99.

Rowe, C. Kavin. "Do You Understand What You Are Reading? A Formation of Scriptural Imagination." *Divinity* 12 (2013) 4–9. https://divinity.duke.edu/sites/default/files/divinity-magazine/DukeDivMag_Spring13.3_pages.pdf.

Runyon, Theodore. *The New Creation: John Wesley's Theology Today*. Nashville: Abingdon, 1998.

Russell, Bertrand. "The Philosophical Implications of Mathematical Logic." In *Essays in Analysis*, edited by Douglas Lackey, 288–305. New York: George Braziller, 1963.

Sandoval, Chela. *The Methodology of the Oppressed*. Minneapolis: University of Minnesota Press, 2000.

Schmitt, Carl. *The Concept of the Political*. Translated by George Schwab. Chicago: University of Chicago Press, 1996.

Shelton, R. Larry. "A Covenant Concept of Atonement." *Wesleyan Theological Journal* 19 (1984) 91–108.

———. "The Redemptive Grace of God in Christ." In *A Contemporary Wesleyan Theology: Biblical, Systematic, and Practical*, edited by Charles Carter et al., 1:473. Grand Rapids: Zondervan, 1983.

Sluga, Hans, and David G. Stern, eds. *The Cambridge Companion to Wittgenstein*. Cambridge: Cambridge University Press, 1996.

Smart, James D. *The Strange Silence of the Bible in the Church: A Study in Hermeneutics*. Philadelphia: Westminster, 1970.

Smith, Harmon. *Where Two or Three Are Gathered: Liturgy and the Moral Life*. Cleveland: Pilgrim, 1995.

Smith, Timothy L. *Revivalism and Social Reform: American Protestantism on the Eve of the Civil War*. Gloucester, MA: Peter Smith, 1976.

Spaulding, Hank. "Sanctifying Atonement: Womanist Theology, Wesleyan Ethics and the Future of Nazarene Atonement Theology." *Wesleyan Theological Journal* 50 (2015) 162–86.

Suchocki, Marjorie Hewitt. *The Fall to Violence: Original Sin in Relational Theology.* New York: Continuum, 1994.

Summerfield, Donna. "Fitting Versus Tracking: Wittgenstein on Representation." In *The Cambridge Companion to Wittgenstein*, edited by Hans Sluga and David Stern, 102–122. Cambridge: Cambridge University Press, 1996.

Steinmetz, David C. "Forgiveness Springs From Their Faith." *Raleigh News and Observer*, October 13, 2006.

Stiver, Dan. *The Philosophy of Religious Language: Sign, Symbol, and Story*. Cambridge: Blackwell, 1996.

Taylor, Charles. *Sources of the Self: The Making of the Modern Identity*. Cambridge, MA: Harvard University Press, 1989.

Taylor, John V. *The Go-Between God: The Holy Spirit and the Christian Mission*. London: SCM, 1972.

Taylor, Richard. *The Theological Formulation. Volume 3: Exploring Christian Holiness.* Kansas City, MO: Beacon Hill, 1985.

Terrell, JoAnne Marie. *Power in the Blood? The Cross in African American Experience.* The Bishop Henry McNeal Turner/Sojourner Truth Series in Black Religion 15. Maryknoll, NY: Orbis, 1998.

Thiessen, Elmer John. *In Defence of Religious Schools and Colleges.* Montreal and Kingston: McGill-Queen's University Press, 2001.

Thomas, Owen. "Theology and Experience." *Harvard Theological Review* 78 (1985) 179–201.

UMKC School of Law. "Lynchings: By State and Race, 1882–1968." *Famous Trials.* http://law2.umkc.edu/faculty/projects/ftrials/shipp/lynchingsstate.html. Statistics provided by the Archives at Tuskegee Institute.

von Balthasar, Hans Urs. *The Glory of the Lord: A Theological Aesthetic, Vol. I: Seeing the Form.* Translated by Erasmo Leiva-Merikakis and edited by Joseph Fessio SJ and John Riches. San Francisco: Ignatius, 1982.

———. *The Glory of the Lord: A Theological Aesthetic, Vol. II: Studies in Theological Style: Clerical Styles.* Translated by Andrew Louth et al. and edited by John Riches. San Francisco: Ignatius, 1982.

———. *The Glory of the Lord: A Theological Aesthetics, Vol. VII: Theology—The New Covenant.* Edited by John Riches. Translated by Brian McNeil. San Francisco: Ignatius, 2012.

———. "Liberation Theology in Light of Salvation History." Translated by Erasmo Leiva. In *Liberation Theology in Latin America*, edited by James V. Schall, 135–52. San Francisco: Ignatius, 1982.

———. *Mysterium Paschale: The Mystery of Easter.* Translated by Aidan Nichols, OP. San Francisco: Ignatius, 2005.

Wainwright, Geoffrey. *Doxology: The Praise of God in Worship, Doctrine, and Life.* New York: Oxford University Press, 1980.

Walker, Andrew, and Andrew Wright. "A Christian University Imagined: Recovering *Paideia* in a Broken World." In *Faith and the University*, edited by Richard Feist and Thomas L. Reynolds, 69–89. Ottawa: University of Ottawa Press, 2003.

Ward, Graham. "Bodies: The Displaced Body of Jesus." In *Radical Orthodoxy: A New Theology*, edited by John Milbank et al., 162–81. New York: Routledge, 1999.

———. *Cities of God*. London and New York: Routledge, 2000.

———. "The Displaced Body of Jesus Christ." In *Radical Orthodoxy: A New Theology*, edited by John Milbank et al., 163–81. London and New York: Routledge Press, 1999.

Watts, Isaac. "Psalm 20." In *The Psalms of David*, 38. Christian Classics Ethereal Library. https://www.ccel.org/ccel/watts/psalmshymns.Ps.47.html.

———. "Psalm 60." In *The Psalms of David*, 104. Christian Classics Ethereal Library. https://www.ccel.org/ccel/watts/psalmshymns.Ps.129.html.

———. "Psalm 67." In "From Experiential Educator to Nationalist Theologian: The Hymns of Isaac Watts," by John Hull. *Panorama: International Journal of Comparative Religious Education and Values* 14 (2002) 99.

———. "Psalm 67." In *The Psalms of David*, 115. Christian Classics Ethereal Library. https://www.ccel.org/ccel/watts/psalmshymns.Ps.143.html.

Weaver, J. Denny. *The Nonviolent Atonement*. 2nd ed. Grand Rapids: Eerdmans, 2011.

Wells, Samuel. *Transforming Fate Into Destiny: The Theological Ethics of Stanley Hauerwas*. Eugene, OR: Cascade, 1998.

Wesley, Charles. "Hymn IV." In *Hymns for the Nation* (1781), 8. Duke Center for Studies in the Wesleyan Tradition, Duke Divinity School. https://divinity.duke.edu/sites/divinity.duke.edu/files/documents/cswt/78_Hymns_for_the_Nation_%281781%29.pdf.

———. "Hymn V." In *Hymns for the Nation* (1781), 10. Duke Center for Studies in the Wesleyan Tradition, Duke Divinity School. https://divinity.duke.edu/sites/divinity.duke.edu/files/documents/cswt/78_Hymns_for_the_Nation_%281781%29.pdf.

———. "Psalm XX." In *MS Psalms*, 43. Duke Center for Studies in the Wesleyan Tradition, Duke Divinity School. https://divinity.duke.edu/sites/divinity.duke.edu/files/documents/cswt/81_MS_Psalms.pdf

"———. "Psalm 47." In *Collection of Hymns and Psalms*. 2nd ed. London: Strahan, 1743. Duke Center for Studies in the Wesleyan Tradition, Duke Divinity School. https://divinity.duke.edu/sites/divinity.duke.edu/files/documents/cswt/17_Psalms_%281743%29_mod.pdf.

———. "Psalm LX." In *MS Psalms*, 157. Duke Center for Studies in the Wesleyan Tradition, Duke Divinity School. https://divinity.duke.edu/sites/divinity.duke.edu/files/documents/cswt/81_MS_Psalms.pdf

Wesley, John. "Brief Thoughts on Christian Perfection." In *The Works of the Rev. John Wesley*, edited by Thomas Jackson, 11:466. London: Wesleyan Methodist Book Room, 1872.

———. "The Character of a Methodist." 1742. https://www.fumcfairfield.org/wp-content/uploads/2018/06/Character-of-a-Methodist.pdf.

———. "The Circumcision of the Heart." In *The Works of John Wesley*, edited by Albert C. Outler, 1:402–12. Nashville: Abingdon, 1984.

———. *Explanatory Notes Upon the New Testament*. Repr. Peabody, MA: Hendrickson, 2007.

———. "The General Spread of the Gospel." In *The Sermons of John Wesley*. 1872 ed. https://wesley.nnu.edu/john-wesley/the-sermons-of-john-wesley-1872-edition/sermon-63-the-general-spread-of-the-gospel/.

———. "God's Love to Fallen Man." In *The Works of John Wesley*, edited by Albert C. Outler, 2:423–38. Nashville: Abingdon, 1985.

———. "The Image of God." In *The Sermons of John Wesley: A Collection for the Christian Journey*, edited by Kenneth J. Collins and Jason E. Vickers, 1–9. Nashville: Abingdon, 2013.

———. *The Journal of John Wesley*. May 24, 1738. In *The Works of John Wesley*, 233–36. Kansas City, MO: Beacon Hill, 1979.

———. "Letter to John Smith." In *The Works of the Rev. John Wesley*, edited by Thomas Jackson, 12:72–82. London: Wesleyan Methodist Book Room, 1872.

———. "The Means of Grace." In *The Works of John Wesley*, edited by Albert C. Outler, 1:381–97. Nashville: Abingdon, 1984.

———. "The New Creation." In *The Works of John Wesley*, edited by Albert C. Outler, 2:500–509. Nashville: Abingdon, 1985.

———. "Of the Church." In *The Sermons of John Wesley*. 1872 ed. https://wesley.nnu.edu/john-wesley/the-sermons-of-john-wesley-1872-edition/sermon-74-of-the-church/.

———. "On the Education of Children." In *The Sermons of John Wesley*. 1872 ed. https://wesley.nnu.edu/john-wesley/the-sermons-of-john-wesley-1872-edition/sermon-95-on-the-education-of-children/.

———. "On God's Vineyard." In *The Works of John Wesley*, edited by Albert C. Outler, 6:246–256. Nashville: Abingdon, 1986.

———. "Sermon 139: On Love." In *The Sermons of John Wesley*, 1872 edition. https://wesley.nnu.edu/john-wesley/the-sermons-of-john-wesley-1872-edition/sermon-139-on-love/.

———. "On the Trinity." In *The Works of Wesley*, 6:205. Kansas City, MO: Beacon Hill Press of Kansas City, 1979.

———. "On Working Out Our Own Salvation." In *The Works of John Wesley*, edited by Albert C. Outler, 3:203–17. Nashville: Abingdon, 1986.

———. "On Zeal." In *The Sermons of John Wesley*. 1872 ed. https://wesley.nnu.edu/john-wesley/the-sermons-of-john-wesley-1872-edition/sermon-92-on-zeal/.

———. "Original Sin." In *The Works of John Wesley*, edited by Albert C. Outler, 2:181–99. Nashville: Abingdon, 1985.

———. "A Plain Account of Christian Perfection." In *Wesley's Works*, 11:366. Kansas City, MO: Beacon Hill, 1979.

———. "The Scripture Way of Salvation." In *The Works of John Wesley*, edited by Albert C. Outler, 2:371–80. Nashville: Abingdon, 1985.

———. "Sermon 53: On the Death of the Rev. Mr. George Whitefield." In *The Sermons of John Wesley*, 1872 edition. Wesley Center Online. https://wesley.nnu.edu/john-wesley/the-sermons-of-john-wesley-1872-edition/sermon-53-on-the-death-of-the-rev-mr-george-whitefield/.

———. "Upon Our Lord's Sermon on the Mount, Discourse One." In *The Sermons of John Wesley*. 1872 ed. https://wesley.nnu.edu/john-wesley/the-sermons-of-john-wesley-1872-edition/sermon-21-upon-our-lords-sermon-on-the-mount-discourse-one/.

———. "What Is Man?" In *The Sermons of John Wesley*. 1872 ed. https://wesley.nnu.edu/john-wesley/the-sermons-of-john-wesley-1872-edition/sermon-109-what-is-man/.

———. "Sermon 10: The Witness of the Spirit, Discourse One."In *The Sermons of John Wesley*, 1872 edition. https://wesley.nnu.edu/john-wesley/the-sermons-of-john-wesley-1872-edition/sermon-10-the-witness-of-the-spirit-discourse-one/.

———. *The Works of the Rev. John Wesley.* Edited by Thomas Jackson. 14 vols. London: Wesleyan Methodist Book Room, 1872.

Wesley, Samuel, Jr. "Upon Altering the Psalms, To Apply Them to a Christian State." In *Poems on Several Occasions*, 311–12. 2nd ed. London: Cambridge University Press, 1743.

Wiley, H. Orton. *Christian Theology*. 3 vols. Kansas City, MO: Beacon Hill, 1943.

Williams, Delores. "Black Women's Surrogacy Experience and the Christian Notion of Redemption." In *Cross Examinations: Readings on the Meaning of the Cross Today*, edited by Marit Trelstad, 19–32. Minneapolis: Fortress, 2006.

———. *Sisters in the Wilderness: The Challenge of Womanist God-Talk*. Maryknoll, NY: Orbis, 1993.

Williams, Rowan. "Balthasar and the Trinity." In *The Cambridge Companion to Hans Urs von Balthasar*, edited by Edward T. Oakes and David Moss, 37–50. New York: Cambridge University Press, 2004.

———. "The Body's Grace." In *Our Selves, Our Souls and Bodies: Sexuality and the Household of God*, edited by Charles Hefling, 58–68. Boston: Cowley, 1996.

———. *Faith in the Public Square*. London: Bloomsbury, 2012.

———. *Lost Icons: Reflections on Cultural Bereavement*. Edinburgh: T. & T. Clark, 2000.

———. *On Christian Theology*. Malden, MA: Blackwell, 2000.

———. *A Ray of Darkness*. Cambridge, MA: Cowley, 1995.

Wittgenstein, Ludwig. *The Blue and Brown Books*. New York: Harper and Row, 1969.

———. *Culture and Value*. Edited by G. H. von Wright. Translated by Peter Winch. Chicago: University of Chicago Press, 1980.

———. *Lectures and Conversations on Aesthetics, Psychology, and Religious Belief.* Edited by Cyril Barrett. Berkeley: University of California Press, 2007.

———. *Philosophical Grammar*. Edited by Rush Rhees and translated by Anthony Kenny. Berkeley: University of California Press, 1978.

———. *Philosophical Investigations*. 3rd ed. Translated by G. E. M. Anscombe. Englewood Cliffs, NJ: Prentice Hall, 1958.

———. *Tractatus Logico-Philosophicus*. Translated by D. F. Pears and B. F. McGuinness. London: Routledge, 1961.

Ziegler, Philip G. *Militant Grace: The Apocalyptic Turn and the Future of Christian Theology.* Grand Rapids: Baker Academic, 2018.

Index

www.ingramcontent.com/pod-product-compliance
Lightning Source LLC
LaVergne TN
LVHW091249110826
845146LV00002BA/696

9798385242016